How to Attack Debt, Build Savings, and
Change the World Through Generosity

How to
ATTACK Debt,
BUILD Savings,
and CHANGE
the World Through
GENEROSITY

A Catholic Guide to
Managing Your Money

Amanda and Jonathan Teixeira

Our Sunday Visitor
Huntington, Indiana

Our Sunday Visitor Publishing Division
Our Sunday Visitor, Inc.
200 Noll Plaza
Huntington, IN 46750
1-800-348-2440

ISBN: 978-1-68192-742-8 (Inventory No. T2614)
eISBN: 978-1-68192-743-5
LCCN: 2021941073

Cover and interior design: Lindsey Riesen
Interior art: Jonathan Teixeira

PRINTED IN THE UNITED STATES OF AMERICA

To our entire WalletWin community — thank you for inviting us to walk with you in creating financial peace.

—

And to Josephine, Charlotte, and Eleanor: It's the greatest honor and privilege of our lives to be your parents — even when we're wiping noses or getting puked on. We cherish every unicorn/LEGO/crayon/Narnia-infused minute of it.

Contents

Part IV: Grow Your Wealth

Part V: Live Financial Freedom

Introduction

Amanda

Have you ever looked back in shock on certain events in your life, realizing that God teed the whole thing up *long before* you realized he was even at work? I had that moment when someone asked about the first time I met my husband, Jonathan. We had known one another for many years before we started dating, so I'd never really reflected on our very first meeting. But when I recalled the memory, I laughed at how obvious God was being with my vocation in that moment.

It was June 2008, and I'd graduated from the University of Nebraska with a bachelor's in nursing a few weeks prior. However, I did not take a nursing position straight out of college — I wanted to work in campus ministry, and so accepted a job with FOCUS (the Fellowship of Catholic University Students). New staff training that summer was in North Carolina, and my introverted personality was completely overwhelmed with meeting hundreds of new people.

Working as a missionary with FOCUS meant we fundraised 100 percent of our income. You read that right: We relied completely on the generosity of others to earn a living. This terrified me (as it does many) and I was dreading the first infamous Mission Partner Development training — a.k.a., "learning how to ask people for money without feeling weird about it, in a culture that totally feels weird about it."

The evening was hot and muggy as I gathered my books, said a prayer, and headed across campus for my first official fundraising class. As I walked, I fought down nausea and could feel knots forming in my stomach (or was it just the bad dorm food?). To say I felt nervous would be an understatement.

In the months prior to this moment, several family members and friends tried to talk me out of this job. They were certain I would fail at fundraising and that nobody would support me. They even went on to say I was an embarrassment to the family for foregoing the traditional route of getting a secure and stable paying nursing job … that I was choosing to be a shameful beggar.

I knew this wasn't true, as many people support all sorts of non-profits and their staff members, but I started doubting myself. Was I capable of this? Could I come out of my introverted shell and be so bold as to ask someone to financially partner with me in this mission? Would I be able to raise enough to not only eat and keep a roof over my head, but pay my student loans back or save for my future? Questions and doubts swirled as I clenched my fists and began walking even faster to class.

Halfway to the intimidating concrete building in which class was being held, with my anxiety mounting, I decided that if I made sure to take fundraising class seriously, I'd be all right. That would mean taking copious notes every class, practicing pitches for hours, making sure I did every single assignment, and booking as many appointments as possible. There would be no joking around for me that summer. I was there to prove my doubtful family and friends (and myself) wrong.

As I got closer, I heard music behind me. I stopped in my tracks and turned around to see some guy with elbow-length hair and a laptop propped on his shoulder like a boombox. Out of the speakers, "For the Love of Money" by the O'Jays was blaring. You know how it goes, right? "Money money money money … money!"

My jaw dropped as this surfer dude, with his "boombox," danced, obliviously swaying past me and up to the building. *"I bet that guy fails at fundraising!"* was my next thought, as I shot judgy eyes in his direction. *"He's clearly not taking this seriously like I am. He's doomed financially."* I went inside, grabbed a seat as far from the jokester as I could, and got ready to work.

As I reflect on that moment, I can't help but smile. So much of my future was wrapped into that one encounter ... but I was clueless at the time.

Little did I know that four years later I would go on to marry the one and only Jonathan Teixeira — otherwise known as the surfer hair/jokester dude, who was actually a landlocked Pennsylvania boy. I also had no idea that finances would not be the wedge that drove us apart; but would instead be the single biggest unifying factor early in our marriage. Certainly, I wouldn't have believed that we'd go on to help tens of thousands of others create financial peace in their lives by starting WalletWin, our own company dedicated to teaching people what Mom and Dad didn't about money. But that's exactly what happened, and it's one heck of a story.

You'll hear more of how it all unfolded, and the lessons we learned along the way, in the chapters ahead. Through WalletWin we offer resources and tools for smart money management, and have built a welcoming community of like-minded folks working toward their goals and helping one another along the way. This book is designed to be both an introduction to the WalletWin Method of managing your finances, and also the perfect companion for when you are ready to take action.

Our aim in this book is to give you hope, encouragement, and a step-by-step plan to winning with money *without* losing your soul. You won't find a collection of one-off "life hacks" that will allow you to scrimp and save your way to riches so you can swim in a vault of money, Scrooge McDuck-style. Instead, this is your comprehensive guide to stewarding your finances with peace and wisdom. Unlike your typical stuffy financial book, your journey ahead in our book is full of humor, real-life examples, simple yet effective strategies, and complete transparency. (And no judgy eyes looking your way!)

What do we mean by *winning with money*, anyway? Winning with money isn't owning three yachts, making it rain at Michelin-starred restaurants, or taking exotic island vacations every month. Winning with money means *living with peace of mind.* How? By making a budget that will work for you, instead of the other way around. By un-inviting Visa and Sallie Mae to the party and freeing your income from endless debt payments. By embracing the freedom to say "yes" to where God leads, since your bank account isn't screaming "no" in his face. By realizing that money isn't bad or good, but rather a tool — a tool that can be a blessing not only in your own life, but in the entire world, when used the right way.

•••

🏴 *Jonathan*

Hi! Jonathan here. I remember the lead-up to that class a little differently. While it's probably true that I wasn't as serious of a fundraising student as Amanda, I was just as deliberate in how I came to class. Yes, I swayed my way to class, laptop "boombox" on shoulder, playing "For the Love of Money" as loud as my MacBook's tiny speakers could handle. But it wasn't to *make fun* of the situation, it was to *have fun* with it. I figured a few of my fellow missionaries might be nervous about the class (hearing Amanda's version, I was right!), and if I could help them smile and have a little fun, they might do better.

Which, come to think of it, describes part of what makes WalletWin WalletWin. We know that just thinking about money can make some folks anxious and upset. So we do our best to make learning about your finances and managing your money not just informative and helpful, but fun and entertaining.

We do all this because we believe that your personal finances are important. Money colors and impacts so many aspects of your life and relationships. That's the big deal: We want you to have your money in order, not for your money's sake, but for your own sake and that of the whole world. You were created for greatness, to have life and have it to the full, to be loved and to love others well. Without the shackles of money stress weighing you down, you can more easily become who you were created to be. Financial pressure kills creativity, destroys relationships, ruins lives, wreaks havoc on health, and chokes out generosity. We don't want that for you. We want you to thrive. We wrote this book to help you get intentional with money so you can be a blessing to yourself, family, friends, community, and the world.

Got a little deep there, didn't we? Money can be serious stuff, but don't worry, we'll keep it fun, informative, entertaining, inspiring, and practical as we go along. Buckle up, because here we go!

Part I

Getting
Started

CHAPTER 1

What to Expect from This Book

"I plead with you — never, ever give up on hope, never doubt, never tire, and never become discouraged. Be not afraid."
— Pope St. John Paul II[1]

🏴 *Amanda*

Nobody grows up hoping they'll land themselves deeply in debt, living paycheck to paycheck, unable to afford even small unexpected expenses and emergencies. Yet, regardless of income, that's exactly where the majority of folks end up.

Total household debt in the US, including mortgages, auto loans, credit cards, and student debt, climbed to $14.35 trillion in the third quarter of 2020 — that's over $43,000 of debt for every single American, and eclipses the previous peak at the height of the great recession in 2008 by $1.62 trillion. Nearly 80 percent of Americans are stuck living paycheck to paycheck, and 40 percent of households couldn't afford a $400 unexpected expense without turning toward debt.

Those bleak statistics are the result of the last seventy years of shifting financial habits, economics, marketing, and the ever-growing availability of debt. If you find yourself in this majority, don't despair! Hope is on the way in the pages ahead.

An appropriate question is, "How did we get here?"

A better question is, "How can you change it?"

The American love affair with debt didn't happen overnight. It's been an evolving situation that dates back to the late 1800s. The ability to offer consumers delayed payment on purchases was a convenience, but because lenders weren't able to charge much interest to make the transaction profitable, it wasn't a common practice. Of course, there were shady extortionists who would privately lend for high interest rates, but these practices were illegal at the time.

As the 1900s dawned and World War I broke out, laws began relaxing around lending. During the Great Depression, lending laws relaxed even further. As the economy recovered and eventually boomed after World War II, consumer demand for debt was way up. The 1950s saw the rise of the first credit card, Diner's Club. And the mentality of "buy now, pay later" became marketed, normalized, and deeply ingrained into our culture over the last seventy years.

Many like to think money is head knowledge: It's simply math. But if you're doing the math, it's obvious that the average American is not winning with money — they aren't living with financial peace of mind — because their income is being drained by debt obligations: student loans, credit cards, auto loans, medical debt, mortgages, and more. Turns out, managing money is only 20 percent knowledge. The other 80 percent is behavior — knowing what to do with that knowledge.

If you want to win with your money, don't worry about your ability to do math. As long as you can add and subtract (or better yet, use a calculator!) you're good to go. What you really need to dive into and study is human psychology and knowledge of yourself. Why do we do what we do? How do habits form? Can we change and shift our learned behaviors? Where does motivation come from? How does our brain chemistry shape and reinforce our behaviors? What personal strengths, weaknesses, priorities, and values are we bringing to the table? These are the questions that matter most.

In this book, we'll break down the numbers behind smart and strategic financial decisions. More importantly though, we'll break down the human psychology behind your money. When you understand your relationship with money and how to create smart money habits, that's when you unlock the door to financial peace.

Before we dive in, let's walk through what you can expect from the journey ahead. This isn't a typical personal finance book, so it's important we break down what this book is, and more importantly, what it isn't.

This book *isn't* dull.

Most people hear the word "financial literacy" and think an afternoon of watching paint dry sounds more entertaining. We get it — many books in our subject area are dry and dull, so we're not offended by your hesitation. We do want to challenge it, though.

This book *is* fun.

We're not your run-of-the-mill finance experts. Jonathan and I *enjoy* having fun with our money, and we enjoy teaching you how to make money fun. We want your brain to light up when you think about budgeting, giving, or investing — and so we've put a lot of effort into making this book (and all the work we do) an adventure.

This book *isn't* going to ask you to give up everything you love.

One reason so many people push back on creating a plan for their money is because they assume it means the end of all joy and happiness. They think creating a budget, getting out of debt, and building savings may as well be synonymous for becoming a hermit and living a so-called life of sheer boredom and ruthless penny-pinching. We will invite you to alter your mindset and behaviors with money in the pages ahead, but we won't ask you to say goodbye to everything you enjoy or tell you that the only time you should see the inside of a restaurant is if you're working there.

This book *is* going to help you clarify what you love most.

In fact, what we're going to do is help you discern your deepest desires and craft a plan to make those dreams a reality. We'll help you protect and prioritize the things you value, even as you make rapid progress toward your financial goals. We'll teach you a special set of skills we've mastered over the years, of finding creative ways to live a fun and joyful life even if trimming your spending is needed to nail your next goal.

This book *isn't* complex.

If you're "not a numbers person" and generally don't like math, fear not. This book isn't an intellectual treatise on economic theory. It's dedicated to step-by-step milestones that take you from where you are — whether that's knee-deep in debt or starting to invest — to the end goal of living financial freedom and radical generosity. If you are willing to follow the plan, you can't mess it up.

This book *is* going to challenge you.

What we teach in this book is simple and straightforward, but it's not easy. Acknowledging money myths you've believed, or the destructive financial habits that you've unknowingly embraced, is hard work. We've been around the financial block and made plenty of mistakes; but instead of letting those define or hold us back, we learned from them. We chose hope that our future could be different, and we want to share that hope with you. While the pages ahead aren't rocket science or brain surgery, be prepared to be challenged deeply in your beliefs, habits, and emotions surrounding money.

This book *isn't* a Bible study about money.

While there's plenty of Scripture verses on the pages ahead, this book is by no means an in depth biblical analysis of money or a Bible study about personal finances. While we've also included excerpts from the *Catechism of the Catholic Church*, stories from the lives of the saints, Scripture, and quotes from papal encyclicals, this book is not written exclusively for Catholics. It's for anyone who wants to learn how to wisely handle money, and create financial peace in their life using a proven plan that works. Money touches every aspect of our lives — physical, emotional, behavioral, intellectual, *and* spiritual. We can't have a conversation about money in a holistic sense without including spiritual elements.

This book *is* written from a Catholic worldview.

We are practicing Catholics. That means we believe everything the Catholic Church has affirmed as truth, and to the best of our ability, with God's grace, we choose to live in alignment with that.

Because that's who we are at our very core, we can't write about money without our fundamental worldview shaping our experience, perspective, or recommendations. No matter what faith background you come from, we hope our program will offer a new perspective on your relationship with money, and smart strategies to live by.

And one last thing.

This book *isn't* going to teach you to get your financial ducks in a row *before* inviting you to be generous. We often get asked when people should incorporate giving into their finances. We teach that from Day 1 of being intentional with your money you should prioritize giving. Living generously is like building muscle. If you want to bench press 250 lb. but have never worked out, you can't just mosey on into the weight room, throw the weights on the bar, and expect to be pumping iron moments later. My father tells a hilarious story about a time he was in his high school weight room and trying to lift weights. To look stronger than he was, he loaded the bar with a massive amount of weight that was too heavy for him — which he only realized after he went to do a barbell clean. Call it cat-like reflexes or dumb luck, but he was able to hoist the bar away from his body (where it certainly would've crushed him) and onto a bench, which snapped in half on contact.

If you've never worked out before, the key to benching 250 lb. is starting with no or very minimal weights and repetition. As you build muscle, you're able to add more weight to the bar, and as you consistently do your reps with ever-increasing weight, you'll be benching 250 lb. in no time.

Point being — if you don't give when you have a little, you won't give when you have much. Giving is a muscle. If you build wealth your whole life yet your giving muscles are weak and atrophied, you won't be capable of responsibly handling that money generously. You're my dad trying to clean an amount of weight you have no business attempting — it won't be pretty, and there's a good chance you could harm yourself or others in the process. Build the giving muscle from the get-go and you'll be healthy and ready as your wealth builds over time.

Now that we've laid the framework for where we've been, where we're going, and what this book is and isn't, it's time to dive into understanding money. Remember when we shared about money being more behavior than math? Well, that's exactly where we're heading next.

CHAPTER 2

What *Is* Money, Anyway?

"The good Lord does not do things by halves; he always
gives what we need. Let us then carry on bravely."
— St. Zélie Martin

> *Jonathan*

This is a book not only about money, but how we interact with it and use it in our lives. Before we dive into practical tips and strategies — don't worry, there will be plenty of those! — we have to ask the question: What is money?

Some say security, others power, and still others influence or freedom.

But what do you say money is?

Security, peace, influence, freedom, power, prestige, opportunity, the root of all evil — money can help to bring about these things in your life, but money isn't these things in and of itself.

A popular multi-level marketing company's recruitment page tries to convince prospective sellers that the money they make selling the company's products will enable them to "live the life of your dreams"[1] and "own your life!"[2] Sounds like this MLM is saying that money is freedom and power.[3] In an interview in *The New*

York Times Magazine, Paul McCartney talked about money as security.[4] Speaking of music, a trip around the radio dial will tell you that money is more essential than love ("Money, That's What I Want," Barrett Strong), powerful and corrupting ("Money Changes Everything," Cyndi Lauper), solves every problem ("Money Money Money," ABBA), only causes more problems ("Mo' Money Mo' Problems," Notorious B.I.G.), drives people to do all sorts of terrible things ("For the Love of Money," O'Jays), isn't worth thinking about — because it's corrupting, perhaps? ("Money on My Mind," Sam Smith), or an illusion that only perpetuates inequality and division ("Four American Dollars," U.S. Girls).

We have any number of competing ideas of what money is bouncing around in our heads and hearts, jockeying for position and influence. Which one — or combination thereof — will rise to the top and be what you say money is?

While it's vitally important to know what you think about money, it's even more important to know what money actually is, and make sure your understanding of it is in alignment with the truth.

What *Is* Money?

More than anything, money is **a tool**. We use it as **a way to assign value to things** — prices are a great example of this. That baseball card may be a few cents worth of cardboard and ink, but because that ink has put a picture of my favorite player on that cardboard, it's now more valuable to me, and I'm willing to pay more money for it. Have the right person — my favorite player — scribble on it with a fraction of a cent's worth of permanent marker, and I'm willing to pay even more.

We use money as a **more efficient way of trading** than bartering. If I'm a carpenter and want some steak, I just need to sell a table for an amount of money and then go to the store and buy a steak. Without money, I'd need to find a restaurant or farmer who not only needed a table, but also had steak (or a cow) they were looking to trade, or come up with a series of trades to arrive at my steak dinner.

We use money as a **medium to express our priorities**. There are any number of ways I can use the money in my bank account. I could go to the movies five nights a week. I *do* love movies. I could order out buffalo wings every night. I *do* love me some chicken wings. But more than those things, I value time with my family and providing my children a good education. So instead of eating wings and watching movies every night, I get wings or go to the movies every now and again, while more regularly spending money on activities with my family and putting money into my kids' college funds. And of course, the causes, charities, and apostolates I choose to support express my priorities for what good I'd like to see done in the world.

So, Is Money Good or Bad?

There seems to be a lot of conflicting evidence — just look around in the world! And if we're coming at this personally influenced by Christianity, doesn't the Bible say things like "For the love of money is the root of all evil?" that "Man cannot serve God and mammon," or that it's "harder for a rich man to enter heaven than for a camel to pass through the eye of a needle?" Have you seen how small the eye of a needle is? And what about all those saints who gave their riches away? They're holy! Doesn't that mean money is bad? But what about the money I give every Sunday at church or to other charities? Does that mean money is good? When you really start thinking about it, it can be hard to know what to think!

Let's put these big-picture questions to the test.

Money Is Bad?

This line of thinking includes beliefs like "Money is evil," "Money corrupts," "Less money is always better," and "Poor people are holier than rich people."

Thoughts like these often find their root in a person's dissatisfaction with their financial situation. Perhaps we don't have as much money as we'd like, and it's easier (and makes us feel better) to believe myths that tell us that it's good we don't have more money. Some people wear extreme frugality as a badge of honor or have made "getting by" an art form.

I understand that thinking. In fact, I believed those money myths for a long time. I thought that anybody who had a lot of money must be a greedy jerk who didn't care about anyone except himself and Ben Franklin. I thought that money either made you bad, or you had to be bad to get a lot of it.

I didn't have a lot of money, and the money I did have, I managed poorly. Believing those myths helped me feel better about my less-than-desirable financial situation. *"If having a lot of money makes you bad, I don't want it anyway! Or if I have to be bad in order to get money, then I'd rather remain good and go without!"* were my thoughts.

In the Catholic Church, we have the gift of the lives of the saints to illuminate how those who've gone before us have followed God. Many of them gave up riches to follow him. St. Francis of Assisi even left his family's lucrative business to follow Jesus and eventually start the Franciscan Order.

And he's a saint because he followed Jesus entirely, doing whatever was asked of him. Walking away from the family business was one of those things. But it was saying yes to Jesus that made him a saint, *not* saying no to the business.

While many saints (and consecrated men and women even today!) make a vow of poverty, God can use any circumstance to make us holy, wealth included. To show just that, I can think of no better examples than the Drexel and Martin families.

The Drexels

Francis Anthony Drexel was a banker in Philadelphia in the nineteenth century, and quite a successful one too. He and his brother were business partners in Drexel, Morgan, and Co. That's right, their business partner was J. P. Morgan.

At the time of his death in 1885, Drexel's estate was worth about $15 million. That's $15 million in 1885. Adjusted for inflation, that's roughly $400 million in 2020. All that money must have corrupted his heart and made him a selfish jerk, right? The Drexels were corrupt, hoarded all their money, and stayed in a bubble of only super-rich friends, right?

Not so much.

The Drexels were incredibly generous. The family gave food,

clothing, medicine, and other assistance three times a week to the needy who came to their door. They spent nearly half a million dollars a year (in today's dollars) doing this. They also gave generously to multiple charities and religious orders.

Upon Francis's death in 1885, after giving 10 percent away to various charities and religious communities, the estate was split up among Francis's three daughters.

Following their parents' example, each girl used her fortune to help those in need; however, one Drexel sister and her work are more well-known than the others. St. Katharine Drexel used her inheritance to establish the Sisters of the Blessed Sacrament and start 145 missions, 50 schools for Black Americans, and 12 schools for Native Americans. She and the Sisters also started Xavier University of Louisiana, the only Catholic HBCU (Historically Black College or University).

None of this would have happened if Francis Drexel had run away from money, squandered his wealth, or ignored the call placed on his heart to give generously. It is because of the Drexel fortune, not despite it, that good was able to be done in the world.

The Martins

Louis and Zélie Martin lived in France in the nineteenth century. Both Louis and Zélie seriously discerned religious life, but ultimately neither entered. They later met, got married, and started a family. Louis was a watchmaker and jeweler, and Zélie was a highly-skilled lacemaker. So highly skilled, in fact, that her lace business was so successful that Louis sold his business to go work for his wife!

If their business was that successful, they must have had to have done some shady things, right? Were they cold-hearted? Did they make money their number-one aim?

No way.

Of their nine children, five survived infancy. And of those five, *all five became nuns*, including their youngest, Marie Françoise-Thérèse, Sister Thérèse of the Child Jesus and of the Holy Face — better known as St. Thérèse of Lisieux, affectionately called the Little Flower, and a Doctor of the Church.

And in 2015, Louie and Zélie became the first married couple to be canonized together.

The Martins did not run away from money. They ran two businesses — one so successful they sold the other to focus more time on it. It's also plain to see they didn't put all their attention and focus on money. They taught their children, by their example, about the most important things of both this and the next life. Yes, it's harder for a rich man to enter heaven than for a camel to pass through the eye of a needle. But as the Martins show us, that camel must have made it through, and perhaps it was through one of Zélie's lace-making needles.

What About the Bible?

We did promise this wasn't going to be a Bible study about money — and it isn't — but we'd be remiss if we didn't take a few minutes to discuss the Lord's advice on the topic. Let's take a quick second to look at what Scripture says about money, one verse at a time:

> *"For the love of money is the root of all evils; it is through this craving that some have wandered away from the faith and pierced their hearts with many pangs." (1 Timothy 6:10)*

We wholeheartedly agree with what Paul writes here. The love of money does indeed pierce hearts with many pangs. We are created to, in the words of Venerable Fulton J. Sheen, "love people and use things, rather than to love things and use people." When our priorities and motives get mixed up, our actions inevitably follow.

Be sure to note that Paul says it is "the *love of* money" that is the root of all evil (emphasis mine). Too often, people mishear or mis-remember this verse as saying "Money is the root of all evil." Money isn't good or evil. It just is — more on that in a bit. But putting money in a primary place in our hearts? Yeah, that's bad.

A few verses later, Paul also says, "As for the rich in this world, charge them not to be haughty, nor to set their hopes on uncertain riches but on God who richly furnishes us with everything to enjoy. They are to do good, to be rich in good deeds, liberal and generous, thus laying up for themselves a good foundation for the future, so that they may take hold of the life which is life indeed" (1 Tm 6:17–19).

Paul doesn't say, "as for the rich in this world, they should empty their bank accounts immediately." Having money (even a lot of it) isn't a sin in itself, but it can be a temptation. Paul offers them direction on remaining humble, placing their trust in God, and making generosity the aim of their lives. A healthy attitude and prudent use of riches can be a blessing to many, but it takes work.

The love of money is the problem being called out in this verse, not money itself:

> *"No one can serve two masters; for either he will hate the one and love the other, or he will be devoted to the one and despise the other. You cannot serve God and mammon." (Matthew 6:24; see also Luke 16:13)*

"Mammon" means money or riches, especially with an evil influence or inspiring a sense of greed. The Gospels, quoting Jesus himself, are in the same vein as Paul — you must have your priorities in order, and if you put money first, you're going to get wrecked.

This is a good warning for everyone, but should be taken especially seriously by those who believe in God and try to live accordingly. This is a clear-as-day warning from the mouth of God that your life's ultimate motivation should be the ultimate good found in him alone and that riches offer a uniquely tempting alternative. Beware.

Now, this isn't to mean that we should totally disregard money just because we shouldn't put it first. In fact, our finances should serve our higher goals. In the Parable of the Talents (see Mt 25:14–30), Jesus uses the example of good money management as an example of faithful service.

Make sure your priorities are in order. Don't put money first.

> *"It is easier for a camel to go through the eye of a needle than for a rich man to enter the kingdom of God." (Matthew 19:24)*

Jesus' disciples were shocked[5] and asked (in the next verse) "Who then can be saved?" Jesus gives us the key, and the real meaning of this message: "With men this is impossible, but with God all things are possible."

Jesus is talking about a rich man because he had just invited a rich young man to come follow him, but he refused, because he was told to "go, sell what you possess and give to the poor," and he couldn't, after which "he went away sorrowful; for he had great possessions" (Mt 19:21–22).

This is a perfect capstone to our previous discussions. This young man was earnestly striving to serve God, but had put money first in his heart. He couldn't decide which master to serve, and, at least in this decisive moment in his life, allowed the love of money to guide him.

Even modest riches can be a stumbling block in our hearts to being who we are truly meant to be. God knows this, has compassion on us, and will give us the grace to do what is impossible on our own: Make it to heaven.

Money Is ... Good?

Now, you might be saying, "All right, Jonathan, you've convinced me that money isn't bad. So, it's good, right?"

Not necessarily. We've seen that money is not evil, and cleared up some of the more common biblical misconceptions that lead folks to think money is bad. Lots of good can come from money — the food pantry in town uses money to buy food and give it away to those who need it. Our parish paid the company and workers who built our beautiful church building with money. I like getting birthday presents — even cards with cash from Grandma! I can go to work and earn a salary and then use that money to provide for my family's needs.

But all that doesn't mean money is inherently good. In fact, St. Ignatius of Loyola, in his *Spiritual Exercises*, shares that one of the devil's first strategies is to tempt us with a longing for riches.[6] If money is good, it must follow that more money is better.

It's tempting to think that financial freedom is the same thing as extreme — or even moderate — wealth; or that you need great wealth in order to have and enjoy financial freedom. This is simply not true.

We'll talk about it more later in this book, but financial freedom comes from using our money wisely to provide for our needs and those of others. The amount of money we have certainly factors into things, but it is not the determining factor. We can use what we have wisely and experience financial peace no matter how much (or little) money we have to our name.

In fact, if we're using money poorly, more money can be a very bad thing for us. More money comes with more responsibility to use it well — and more temptation to use it foolishly or even sinfully.

Abigail Disney spoke with *The New York Magazine* about the effect of great wealth on her parents, Patricia Disney and Roy E. Disney (longtime Disney exec, son of Roy O. Disney who cofounded Disney with his brother, Walt). Her comments on her family's private jet (a Boeing 737) are especially interesting:

> All of the sudden [*sic*], we went from being comfortable, upper-middle-class people to suddenly my dad had a private jet. That's when I feel that my dad really lost his way in life. … If I were queen of the world, I would pass a law against private jets, because they enable you to get around a certain reality. You don't have to go through an airport terminal, you don't have to interact, you don't have to be patient, you don't have to be uncomfortable. These are the things that remind us we're human. …
>
> It's not a small thing when you don't have to be patient or be around other people. It creates this notion that you're a little bit better than they are. … So there are people walking around with substantial wealth who think that they have it because they're better. It's fundamental to remember that you're just a member of the human race, like everybody else, and there's nothing about your money that makes you better than anyone else. If you don't know that and you have money, it's the road to hell, no matter how

much stuff you have around you. …

[My parents] liked the shortcuts that wealth gave them. It's very hard to say no to things like that. But what ends up happening is you end up being surrounded by people who don't tell [you] "no," ever. And as my father's drinking problem grew, he was surrounded by people who wouldn't say, "You have a terrible drinking problem. You need to go get some help."[7]

More money was *not* better for Abigail's family; in fact, it sure sounds worse. More money enabled her family to isolate themselves from others, avoiding even small sufferings, and they paid a price. So, if less isn't better, but more isn't better, what's the balance? We're back to *how* money is used.

Instead of spending that money to live an incredibly lavish life, Abigail decided it could be used to help others. In fact, in the same interview, she mentions that if she had given away all her money in her 20s as she was tempted to do, instead of managing it wisely like she did, she couldn't have given away nearly as much as she has.

In the hands of a good steward, more money can be good — think of the Parable of the Talents in the Bible (see Mt 25:14–30). The servant who proved himself to be a wise manager was given more money to manage well. However, in the hands of a poor steward, more money can lead to more problems. And of course, if we're using money for something bad, like fueling a gambling, drug, sex, or other addiction, more money is likely *very* bad for us.

We're often tempted to think that more money, even just a little bit, could solve all our problems. True, having a little more money can make many things easier and provide opportunities — if we use it wisely, and have healthy boundaries in place.

Having an extra $700 a month in my budget could allow me to buy healthier food and spend less time going to four different stores to snag deals, freeing me up to spend more time with my family. Or it could be used to free me from debt, invest for retirement, or pay for a family vacation that creates lifelong memories of time well spent together.

On the flip side, I could blow it on a variety of frivolous purchases and lead myself further into overspending due to lifestyle creep, all the while making no progress toward any real financial goal, and wind up thinking, "*If only I had a little more money!*"

Money Is Neutral

"All right Jonathan, I get it! Money is neither good nor bad, and in that case, I'll just not bother. Who cares about money? I guess it just doesn't really matter, huh?"

The truth is money is neither good nor bad. It just is. It's *amoral*, meaning it has no moral value in and of itself. Just like a knife — I could use a knife to slice apples and bake an apple pie for my family, or I could use it to stab and murder someone. One of these is in line not only with the proper understanding of a knife, but also with how God wants you to use knives. (Hint: It's the one that's full of cinnamon and delicious with ice cream.)

Money has no inherent moral value, so the morality of each monetary act comes down not only to how you use it, but also *why* you use it.

I could make that apple pie because it's my friend's birthday, they really like my pies, and I want to make them happy. Or I might make that pie because it's my friend's birthday, they really like my pies, and that is the perfect excuse to show off my baking skills and get loads of compliments at the party, even though I know another friend is making cupcakes for dessert.

To get a little more technical, the morality of an act is made up of three parts: the act, the intentions, and the circumstances.

The three components of any moral act apply to managing finances, too.

1. The act in and of itself must be good or morally neutral (putting money into emergency savings, for example).
2. The intentions must be good. (I want to make sure my family isn't harmed if unexpected expenses pop up.)
3. And the concrete circumstances of the act must be good. (I obtained the money ethically and, if applica-

ble, received my spouse's whole-hearted agreement on this spending decision.)

In order for an act to be moral, each of the three parts must pass the test. If one part is immoral, then the whole act is immoral. Rains on the whole "ends justify the means" parade, huh?

Money can be used for good. For instance, if I decide to buy a homeless person a meal; and my intention is to love that person in response to their inherent dignity; and it's cold out, they were hungry, and the money I spent wasn't needed for anything necessary for my family — that's a good act. The act itself, the intentions, and the circumstances are all good.

Money can also be used for evil. For instance, hiring a hit man to murder someone. In this case, the act itself is evil no matter the intentions or circumstances. The fact that money can be used for either good or evil acts lets us know that money, in and of itself, has nothing to do with the moral outcome of an action. It's all about our actions, intentions, and circumstances.

Money is neither good nor bad. It's totally neutral. But does that mean we should ignore it?

Is Money Even Important?

You can probably guess our answer to this question, based on the fact that we started a business teaching people about money and wrote a book on the topic. But it's not *our* answer that matters — which is yes, by the way.

Just because something is neutral, that doesn't mean it's inconsequential. Our understanding and practices around money influence can shape so much of the rest of our lives that we need to make sure we understand and approach our finances in a healthy way.

Depending on the study, financial problems and differences are cited as a contributing factor in as many as half of divorces.[8] Financial matters are the most likely cause of stress, and people who are financially stressed are more likely to miss work and get sick.[9]

When we pay attention to our money, we are not only able to put it to work for our own fulfillment and our family's, but through generous giving we can also help others reach theirs. If we're intentional with our finances and giving, think of all the meals we could provide the hungry, how many wells we could build for the thirsty, how many children we could send to school, how much (insert impact of your favorite cause/charity/corporal work of mercy here) we could have in the world.

Simply put, our money has too much potential to do good in the world, and too much potential to harm our lives, to ignore. If we ignore our finances, we risk ending up with either bland mediocrity and frustration, or financial hardship and extreme stress. Our only path toward transforming the world through generosity is to first transform our personal finances, which only comes by prudent management.

And I'm not the only Jo(h)n who thinks so. There's a section of Scripture I've always found fascinating; John the Baptist is preaching of the coming Messiah in the third chapter of Luke and gathering crowds. His message is stern: "The Lord is coming, and he ain't happy with what he sees. You better shape up, or he will ship you out — to hell." (I'm paraphrasing.)

His message gets through to the crowd, and they ask him, "What then should we do?" He tells them: "He who has two coats, let him share with him who has none; and he who has food, let him do likewise" (Lk 3:10–11).

The tax collectors — even those guys! — get in on it. They ask John what they should do. He tells them: "Collect no more than is appointed you" (Lk 3:13). Then the soldiers (he's got everybody out there) ask John what *they* should do. John tells them: "Rob no one by violence or by false accusation, and be content with your wages" (Lk 3:14).

He tells them a few other things, which the Scriptures only record as "with many other exhortations, he preached good news to the people" (Lk 3:18).

Let's review:

John the Baptist's preaching about the coming of the Messiah is so compelling that people are coming from all over to hear him. John's first message is "It's about to get real. You need to change the way you're living or you're on the highway to hell."

They stick with him, responding, "Okay, what do we need to do?"

And this is what he tells them:

1. If you have extra clothes or food, share with the person who has none.
2. Stop ripping people off to make yourselves rich.
3. Stop intimidating people into giving you money. Be content with the amount of money you make.

The three things John tells people that Luke bothers to write down are all about money. No "stop yelling at your kids," no "stop lusting," not even a "make sure you're keeping the Sabbath!"

We don't know what was included in the "many other exhortations" he followed those up with as he "proclaimed the good news," but what *do* we know? John's opening instructions were about money.

Why money?

Because relationships.

Money is connected to everything and influences so very much of our lives. Have you felt that in your own experience? You drop your phone, and when you pick it up you see a cracked screen and a $200 bill to fix it. Now you're short with your spouse and kids. Or you find a stray $20 bill in the pocket of a jacket the first time you put it on in the fall, and you get a bounce in your step and are more agreeable than usual.

Not only can money indirectly influence relationships, but because it is so closely involved in providing for the well-being of ourselves and our family, money directly affects relationships, too. A debt owed to your parents makes family get-togethers a little more awkward. Your opinion of a friend changes after you find out how much they spent on *that thing*.

Let's go back to John the Baptist for a second. The three things he told people to do, in order to prepare for the coming of the Messiah, were all about both money *and* relationships. Be generous and share. Stop ripping each other off. Stop letting greed drive your interactions with each other, and be happy with what you have. It's all money, and it's all relationships.

Money, for better or worse, touches all our relationships: with God, our friends, our family, our work, even ourselves. Your personal financial situation can color your entire outlook on life and influence how you interact with everyone else. So yeah, money is important.

Using money wisely isn't just about getting a good return on your investments or making sure not to waste what you've been given. It's not about the dollars and cents at all. It's primarily about understanding money correctly, and then *managing* it prudently. And as you do that, you'll find its influence on your relationships is a positive one.

Can I Speak with Your Manager?

As discussed in this chapter, getting our personal finances together matters. *A lot.* While money is inherently neutral, it's entrusted to each of us, by God, to be managed for him. What exactly does it mean to be a manager? Whether it's of a big corporation or a tiny start-up, managers are responsible for supervising, motivating, inspiring, leading, serving, correcting, and encouraging the staff under their leadership. Much of a business' success or failure can often boil down to the health of its management. Translating this to money, God is the King of the Universe. All the money (and every resource, including the very air in our lungs) belongs to him. Any money given to us is to be managed for him — meaning for our good and the good of others. But how do we know how to practically manage the dollars and cents?

The good news is: It's not hard to do. You just need to follow a plan that works, like the WalletWin Method. Let's head over to the financial kitchen and talk through the recipe.

CHAPTER 3

Recipe for Success

Introducing the WalletWin Method

*"For which of you, desiring to build a tower, does not first
sit down and count the cost, whether he has enough to
complete it? Otherwise, when he has laid a foundation, and
is not able to finish, all who see it begin to mock him, saying,
'This man began to build, and was not able to finish.'"*
— Luke 14:28–30

 Jonathan

While I had a little more cooking experience (and plenty of experience watching *Good Eats*) under my belt than Amanda, we both needed some help in the kitchen when we got married.

When we wanted to cook something, we turned to the internet to find a recipe. Early in our marriage, those searches led us to Allrecipes. And true to its name, it seemed to have all the recipes for everything — cookies, bread, salad dressing, meatballs, frosting, it's all there! We started searching through the virtual stacks of recipes and trying them out. Eventually we upgraded to a paid version of their app. We were all in on Allrecipes.

But the more we used their recipes, the more frustrated we got.

Sometimes the recipes didn't quite work out for us. Some had steps that were confusing, or even missing altogether. And a lot of the comments on the recipes were full of substitutions and modifications, even on highly rated recipes. We never knew if we were going to get a 5-star soon-to-be family favorite, or a 1-star bowl of gruel destined to be forgotten leftovers in the back of the fridge. We just couldn't trust Allrecipes.

We started a search for a new source of guidance in the kitchen.

Cookies, Anyone?

One choice for our new culinary guide was *The New York Times* (NYT). The food section has a great reputation in the food world, and I had used one of their recipes before.

This may seem like a basic requirement of being considered a member of the species *homo sapiens*, but I love cookies, and a great chocolate chip cookie is nearly impossible to beat. That's why I was always looking for a new chocolate chip cookie recipe.

I grew up making the recipe on the back of the bag of chocolate chips. It's a good cookie, and I can't tell you how many of them I've eaten over the years. But I figured there was something more waiting for me.

In college, I stumbled across a recipe for chocolate chip cookies from *The New York Times*. From the source alone, I figured these would be pretty good. And they were. They also took a *ton* of work. The recipe calls for cake flour, bread flour, two types of salt, and specifies the cacao content of the chocolate disks (no chips here). After making the dough, it needs to sit in the fridge for twenty-four to thirty-six hours. (No tips on how to not devour all the dough in that timeframe, though.) And when it comes time to put the cookies in the oven, the recipe instructs the baker to "[make] sure to turn horizontally any chocolate pieces that are poking up; it will make for a more attractive cookie."

Don't get me wrong, the NYT recipe makes a pretty good cookie. But it requires special ingredients and more time and effort than should be invested in a cookie I'm planning to stuff in my face the moment they come out of the oven. The NYT recipes might make good food, but those cookies were just too much work.

But then we came across our now-beloved America's Test Kitchen (ATK). Every recipe worked. Every recipe was delicious. And ATK gave us not only the recipe, but also background on why the recipe was written the way it was, why it worked, and what didn't.

What sets ATK apart is that they take a recipe, then try dozens of variations. What if we subbed butter for oil? What if we decreased the butter by a quarter cup? What if we baked it at a lower temp for longer? This recipe works in a gas oven, but what about an electric oven? Each recipe is tested and tweaked until a fool-proof, gold standard recipe is found.

When I'm cooking an ATK recipe, I don't have to wonder what substitutions might be needed or which modifications I should have made. It's already been tested. I know it works.

Let's talk about the ATK recipe for their so-called Perfect Chocolate Chip Cookie.

It uses one type of flour: all-purpose flour — you know, the kind everyone has on hand — and chocolate chips, not discs. And it doesn't require an overnight rest in the fridge. Yet it's a solid step (or five) up from the standard back-of-the-bag recipe.

Through their testing, ATK found a few small tweaks that result in oversized results. For example, instead of just melting the butter, they instruct the baker to go one small step further and brown it. The browned butter, combined with *dark* brown sugar (vs. the often-used light brown sugar) provides a much deeper and more satisfying flavor without much more work.

The "Recipes" in This Book

I've talked about recipes and cookies not because I love cooking and baking (I do) but to help you better understand our WalletWin method.

The WalletWin Method and the money advice in this book isn't back-of-the-bag stuff: straightforward, but leaves you wanting more. It's not Allrecipes: Sounds good, but when you try to follow it in real life you have to make tons of adjustments, and you never quite know if you're gonna achieve a good result. And it's not *The New*

York Times Food section either: You don't need the financial equivalent of two types of specialty flour and chocolate pieces you can only buy at boutique cooking stores.

Think of WalletWin as the financial America's Test Kitchen: Everything we tell you about has been tested to find you the best results using simple yet efficient strategies. Now, we might tell you to do a few things differently. You might need to brown some butter. You might need to swap out the light brown sugar for some dark. If you want different — and better — results than you've gotten in the past, you need to change your recipe a bit.

We'll build up your financial fundamentals. We'll show you which tweaks produce oversized results and are worth your time and effort. We'll show you what pitfalls to avoid. And we'll share it all with you inside.

Grab a cookie, a tall glass of milk, and let's get started.

Our Recipe: The WalletWin Method

Amanda

We meet many people trying to do *all the things* financially because they "should," because someone in a Facebook group mentioned it, because they feel guilty, or because they honestly don't know exactly what to do but doing something feels better than doing nothing.

Enter stage left, The WalletWin Method.

It consists of **Four Financial Phases** and **Twelve Money Milestones** that establish a strong foundation, create massive momentum, grow your wealth, and provide you with freedom to live generously. This method is the backbone of everything we personally do with our money and what we teach others.

The Financial Phases help you identify what season of your financial journey you're in, and the Money Milestones tell you which best next step you should be working on at any given moment. If you're ever unsure where you are in your journey, or what you should be doing, just work though the phases and milestones, checking them off as you go, until you arrive at the one you haven't completed yet. You might find yourself, at various points, backtracking to an earlier Milestone — and that's okay. Slowly or quickly, you'll surely be making progress.

While we'll unpack the individual **Money Milestones** chapter by chapter, I want to provide a quick overview of the **Four Financial Phases** before we dive in.

Financial Phase 1: Establish Your Financial Foundation

Think about building a house. Before the construction team can start building, there's a whole lot of steps they have to take first: file for permits, clear the land, dig a *huge* hole, and finally pour a foundation. *Then* they can build the house. Without the foundation, the house would fall down on top of itself. If you skip the **Establish Your Financial Foundation** phase, as most people unknowingly do, your financial plan will collapse.

This Financial Phase helps you unpack your past and current relationship with money. And if you're engaged or married, this phase gets you both on the same financial page. You'll dive deep into cultivating a healthy Money Mindset, replacing lies about money with the truth. And on the other side, you'll come out with a budget you love, insurance to protect yourself, a Starter Rainy Day Fund, and freedom from the dreaded paycheck-to-paycheck cycle.

Financial Phase 2: Gain Momentum With Your Money

After the foundation has been laid, it's time to take all those early quick wins and become a force to be reckoned with. This is the turning point, as you establish smart money habits. On the other side of this Financial Phase, you no longer simply *hope* you can win with money, you've shown yourself that you can.

Here you'll use proven methods to quickly eliminate all of your debt and experience the security of a fully stocked Rainy Day Fund. You'll follow homebuying strategies to ensure homeownership is the American Dream instead of the all-too-common nightmare. These Money Milestones will move you from financial stress to financial peace.

Financial Phase 3: Grow Your Wealth

This Financial Phase is made up of Money Milestones you set up and let run until their job is done. There's a line from an old infomercial, "Set it and forget it!" While that might work for cooking a rotisserie chicken, it applies to this phase of your financial life too!

During other Financial Phases, you work through their Money Milestones individually and in order, step-by-step. Phase 3 is unique because the Money Milestones within can happen simultaneously.

You're making sure you'll be able to retire, set up education savings so you can stop the generation-defining student loan debt cycle, and pay your mortgage off early so you can unleash the full power of your income without payments. In this phase, you become a person who *makes* interest to serve your future instead of *paying* interest to serve your banker's future.

Watching your savings earn money for your future is a peaceful place to be. This phase is exciting because you're taking advantage of the wonder that is compound interest as you set up retirement and education investments. When you pay off your mortgage early, the sky's the limit now because you get to call all the shots with your money.

Financial Phase 4: Live Financial Freedom

This is when you lean into living radical generosity. You've been working to get to this point, and now you're here. Living generously and blessing others becomes the name of the game. While generosity has been a priority up to this point, your life and wallet can now center around the very thing you were created for: giving of yourself to others and receiving them in return. This is generosity.

Help a struggling single parent pay the rent, leave a $1,000 tip for a slice of pie, take your entire extended family to Disney World, fully stock your local food pantry, make that big gift for your parish renovation, buy that cabin in the mountains you've been dreaming of and give your family a place to make memories for generations, build a well in the developing world and change the lives of an entire village, or support missionaries around the world in work you can't personally go do. It's time to bless others as much as you can. This is the most fun you'll ever have with your money.

• • •

There you have it: the WalletWin Method from a bird's-eye view, our tested and proven recipe for financial success, the plan that will give you peace of mind, help you control your finances, live with freedom, and retire with dignity while leaving a generous legacy in your family and our world. You'll see these Money Milestones again throughout this book as we move through them chapter by chapter. Don't worry if you don't understand how it all fits together, or the order in which we've laid them out. For now, seeing the big picture is all you need. We'll dissect the whats and whys in the pages to come.

The next chapter is all about your Money Mindset. We'll start there because, often, the biggest factors working against most of us arc our own attitudes and beliefs about money (our Money Mindset) and our financial habits. The bad news is that those can be pretty ingrained in our minds and hearts. The good news is that we've seen people time and time again make the decision to improve their Money Mindset and transform their financial habits. You can do the same.

Part II

Establish Your Financial Foundation

FINANCIAL PHASE 1

CHAPTER 4

Money Mindset

"For where your treasure is, there will your heart be also."
— Matthew 6:21

Establish Your
Financial Foundation

🚩 *Amanda*

One Saturday, early in our marriage, Jonathan and I went out to finish buying items we needed for our apartment, using gift cards we received as wedding gifts. In a span of close to six hours, we hit up Bed Bath and Beyond, Target, and Walmart. It felt like we were on Supermarket Sweep, putting all these shiny new kitchen gadgets, pillows, and appliances into our cart without having to spend our own money! It was awesome!

To cap it all off, we stopped at the supermarket and got our groceries for the week.

In true Amanda style, we hadn't stopped to eat lunch. I was a woman on a mission and couldn't rest until the goal was achieved. We closed the car doors, and I remember turning to Jonathan to ask him where he wanted to eat. He looked back at me with a puzzled face. "Home?" he suggested. Wrong answer. We'd just shopped till we nearly dropped, and now that the spree was complete, I was *hangry*. But instead of insisting to go somewhere, I let Jonathan drive us home where I proceeded to give him the silent treatment for the next several hours.

That evening, after I'd given Jonathan the cold shoulder for hours (Elsa had nothing on me!) he tentatively approached me and asked what was going on. The truth was, I didn't really know … so we talked it out. Over the next ten minutes we both realized that growing up we had massively different "Saturday errand running" experiences. In my family, if you're out and about running errands for hours on end, the reward at the end is eating out as a family, enjoying the rest and convenience. But when Jonathan was a kid, they'd usually go home and eat, especially if his family had a trunk full of groceries.

These differences in our experiences as kids were influencing our **Money Mindsets** as adults.

Our Money Mindsets surrounding restaurants couldn't have been more different. One wasn't better than the other, they were just different. But until we recognized what was going on and put it into words, we couldn't uncover what was underneath the surface. As we crafted our financial game plan to begin budgeting and dump debt, part of that was deciding *together* that we wanted to pay off debt as quickly as possible while still finding free or low-cost ways to enjoy ourselves. That meant, for a time, I had to shift my Money Mindset around those Saturday afternoon errand running sessions, and find a new tradition to reward our hard work and have quality time together.

Money Is ...

📣 *Jonathan*

Fill in the blank: Money is _____ .

I asked this question in a Facebook post and got a wide variety of answers: freedom, the cause of many evils, essential, lacking, stressful, security, imaginary, overrated, a gift given to give to others, and so on. Each of these answers (and yours) provide a window into a person's attitude about money, and a guess at a small piece of his or her personal history.

Give yourself a minute to consider what else is at play in your answer, then finish this sentence:

I believe money is _____ because _____.

Perhaps you've had specific experiences in your life: having a card declined at the grocery store because of insufficient funds or being over your credit limit and the embarrassment that can bring; receiving an inheritance and being able to quickly move past obstacles you've been struggling with for years; or how good it felt to give, even in a simple way, like buying the coffee of the car behind you in the drive-thru.

It's easy for us to think our own personal views on money are the one right, true, standard, neutral, normal definition of money. But the person who grew up never having enough is going to interact with money very differently from someone who never had to think about money.

A few important things to keep in mind about your Money Mindset:

1. Your Money Mindset is not only influenced by your past, but also influences how you act now and in the future.
2. Your Money Mindset is unique to you, shaped by your personality and your experiences.
3. Parts of your Money Mindset are probably healthy and good. Others may need some reshaping. Others are neutral and just are what they are.
4. Taking the time to understand your Money Mindset is

essential for beginning the journey of personal finances. You need to know where you're coming from before you can start moving forward.

In this chapter you'll learn how to discover your Money Mindset and decode what that little voice inside your head is saying about money.

Keep Your Fork, There's Cake!

If you're married, it's vital that you and your spouse not only understand your own Money Mindsets, but each other's as well. Remember: You each have your own unique, personal definition of money.

When you're finished reading this paragraph, I want you to close your eyes and think about cake: Imagine what it looks like, smells like, tastes like, and so on. When you've got a pretty good picture of cake, open your eyes and keep reading.

…

Anybody else drooling?

Now, I want you to say out loud, write down, draw, or think about that cake. What type of cake was it? What shape was it? Was it the whole cake or just a slice? Was there ice cream on the side?

For me, I think of yellow cake with chocolate frosting in a 9-by-11-inch cake pan. The cake is from a box, and the frosting is homemade. Why is this my mental picture of cake? Because that's what cake was in my house growing up. That's what I ate every birthday.

There's a good chance your cake was different. Perhaps you grew up with layer cakes, so you pictured that. Or you do a lot of baking, so you thought of the last cake you made. Or you thought of that cake you had on vacation that was one of the best things you've ever tasted.

Let's imagine you and your spouse are bringing a cake to a friend's birthday party. Your spouse was at the grocery store yesterday and grabbed ingredients while they were out, and you're planning to make the cake this afternoon.

You grease and flour two round cake pans and start to gather ingredients. There's no baking soda or baking powder in the pantry.

I thought she went to the store! You check the fridge for the butter. Not there. *Are you kidding me?! And why did she buy so many eggs?!* There's no cocoa powder in the pantry to make your famous chocolate frosting. *Has she lost her mind? We have a party to go to and we're bringing the cake, what's going on here?!*

You call your spouse on the phone and she can tell you're on edge as you ask where everything for the cake is as soon as it connects. "The eggs, cream, and strawberries are in the fridge. We had enough flour, sugar, and salt, and those plus the cream of tartar should be in the pantry."

You did wonder about those berries in the fridge earlier.

"Strawberries? What are you talking about?"

"I thought they'd be nice on the cake with some whipped cream."

"WHA-A-AT?"

Turns out you were planning to make a nice homemade yellow layer cake with chocolate frosting, but your spouse bought ingredients for angel food cake with whipped cream and berries.

Either of you, working alone to make this cake, would have successfully executed your idea of cake and brought it to the party. Working together, your two understandings of cake — both valid — have collided, and caused an argument.

This argument could have been avoided if the two of you talked about what you were thinking of when it came to that cake, and made a plan on how you'd work together to realize your shared idea of that cake.

If you don't first understand your own Money Mindset, and secondly, discuss it with your spouse, you're going to find yourselves frustrated, resentful, and having arguments about more than cake. While your Money Mindset may have a lot of overlap with your spouse's, it's important to be aware of the differences and how they influence both of your expectations.

The best way forward is for both of you to go through this chapter and better understand your Money Mindsets, then set some time aside to talk about what you've come to understand about yourselves, perhaps over a nice cup of coffee or a glass of wine. Once you understand where each of you is coming from, you can make a plan to meet your family's goal as a team.

Pass the Popcorn

Let's talk about your money story up to this point. One easy and fun way to go about this is to imagine your life with money as a movie. Here are a few examples:

- **Titanic** — You're taking on water and trying to find a lifeboat, since it's only a matter of time until the ship sinks.
- **The Exorcist** — Talking money makes your head spin round and round until you throw up.
- **Richie Rich** — You've got so much money that you have a McDonald's in your house, a roller coaster in your backyard, and a giant carving of your face on the mountainside nearby.
- **Finding Nemo** — You're on a winding, never-ending journey where you don't even know the final destination, let alone if you'll reach it.
- **The Pursuit of Happyness** — You worked your tail off year after year after year and eventually saw massive success as your hard work paid off.
- **Jaws** — You've got creditors circling you and sooner or later you'll have to confront them. (*Smile, you son of a lender!*)
- **Inside Out** — One day your financial progress makes you joyful. Other days you're angry, sad, fearful, maybe even disgusted with past financial mistakes you've made.

What's *your* Money Movie? Stop and think about it for a minute or two. You'll probably be able to come up with one that fits the broad strokes of your story and your attitude toward them.

A deeper question, however, is what has written, or at least influenced, the script up to this point? What has been the source material for your personal Money Movie? This film is inspired by a true story, but what *is* that story? And what if you want to edit the script and change the ending?

The only chance of making a sequel better than the original is to understand what influenced you in the first place, what makes up that true story of your life. The events are the events; there's not too much we can do to change those (other than borrowing Doc Brown's DeLorean). What you *can* do is understand what makes up your Money Mindset and move forward with full knowledge (and maybe an adjustment or two).

Your Money Mindset is heavily influenced by the following:

- Family history
- Personal history
- Generational tendencies
- Financial personality

Let's take a look at each one.

We Are Family

Our early years are the most formative. We pick up a *lot* from our families as we grow — the words and phrases we use, our holiday traditions, and even our attitude toward money.

While some things may be passed on explicitly from one generation to the next, like my undying (and until 2016, unrequited) love for the Chicago Cubs. Others — most likely including attitudes toward money — can be passed on without even trying or noticing.

You might need to dig deep to discover them, but there's a good chance some of your attitudes toward money are linked to the way money was handled (or mishandled) in your family.

First off, what was the overall financial situation in your family? Was your family scraping by to make ends meet? Did you often go without? Maybe your family was poor but acted like they were wealthy through racking up debt, or perhaps your family was wealthy but acted like they were poor, constantly pinching pennies and never enjoying money. Or did you get everything you wanted?

One interesting question to ask yourself, however, is if you remember any particular events — even small ones — that had a financial component to them. How did you feel then, and do you see any connection to your attitudes now? If you remember something from your childhood, *and* that money was a part of it, *and* how the episode made you feel back then, there's a good chance it could still be influencing you now.

One example that comes to mind for me is getting clothes in junior high.

It's an awkward and uncertain time for most of us, and that was definitely true for me. (How did I ever think a center part and gelled bangs were a good look?!) As a growing teenage boy, one of my hobbies was outgrowing my clothes and needing new ones. There were also certain brands of clothing I wanted or particular stores I wanted to shop at.

For whatever reason, I always worked myself up for weeks before asking my parents if I could have some money to buy some clothes. And this wasn't a frequent occurrence by any means. I wasn't asking for new clothes every month or looking to totally revamp my entire wardrobe, just a couple of shirts or a pair of pants, or some new shoes when mine were getting worn or small.

I would want to ask for some clothes, and I would stress myself out about it. It sometimes literally took weeks for me to ask my parents. And without fail the answer was, "We'll look at our finances and see what we can do." And I think every single time, I was able to get some clothes.

And here's the thing: I don't remember if I was ever told how much we had to spend. If anything, maybe it was in the number of things, like two shirts and a pair of pants, something like that. I never knew the full situation of how what I wanted fit into the broader financial situation of my family. I'd find some things I liked, then present them to my parents, who would approve the purchase or veto some of the items.

Flash forward a little bit to when a junior high club lacrosse team was trying to get started. One of my friends was really into it and invited me to the week of free lacrosse clinics after school to learn the game. I attended, thought it was pretty fun, and was definitely interested in joining the team. And then they talked about equipment costs. Shoes, pads, helmet, stick. It would be a couple hundred bucks. I immediately counted myself out and never even asked my parents. I resigned myself to school sports like track, where you buy a pair of shoes and everything else is provided.

I felt like my family didn't have enough money for me to play lacrosse. I felt like I didn't have any way to earn the money needed to play lacrosse. There just wasn't enough money, and I couldn't do what I wanted because of that, and I had better get used to not doing anything because there will never be enough money to do it.

When I think back on it now, I should have asked my parents. And if I did, we probably would have figured it out. Remember: I didn't have a clear picture of my family's financial situation. Now, my dad was a teacher and my mom didn't work much outside the home. We certainly weren't rolling in dough, but I believe now that if I really wanted to play lacrosse, it would have been possible. But I didn't even ask, didn't give my folks the chance to say yes or get creative to find a way to say yes.

I've seen this (and likely countless other interactions and events that influenced what I described above) influence my Money Mindset much later in my life in two ways:

1. My default idea is that there's *probably not enough money*. Things (especially those I want or want to do) are "expensive," and there's not enough for them. So don't even ask. Once I identified this part of my Money Mindset and where it might be coming from, I could consciously correct it. Yes, some things are going to be too expensive *right now*. But I shouldn't automatically write things I want off. I should ask — even just ask myself — if it's possible.

2. When/if there are things I want or want to do that are seemingly too expensive, I have learned that it's possible to get creative and find a way to say yes.

A great example of this is when a surprise opportunity came up to grow our family through adoption for the third time in four years.

Amanda was away at a business conference, and I was hanging out with our two daughters, visiting my parents in Pennsylvania.

Amanda's conference was in Canada, so we didn't talk on the phone much. We didn't have international calling on our cell phone plan, so we chatted when she had Wi-Fi (which wasn't often). So when my phone rang in the middle of the day, I knew something must be up.

I answered the phone, and she said, "Jonathan, I just heard from the adoption agency, and we're being asked to adopt again."

This was completely unexpected and out of the blue. We were not actively looking to adopt again at that time and weren't even home study approved. So, once I got through the surprise of it all, my mind did its trick.

I knew our first two adoptions were expensive, and this time we hadn't saved anything up and were on an even shorter timeline. My initial, knee-jerk, no-thinking reaction was: *It's too expensive. We don't have enough money. We can't do it.*

Thankfully, before I even had a chance to say anything out loud, Amanda followed up "We're being asked to adopt again" with "and I've been talking all morning with other business owners *way* more experienced than us, and we've come up with a plan to earn the money for the adoption expenses."

At that moment I was able to identify that my initial reaction was coming from parts of my Money Mindset that weren't based in truth. If something is important enough, it's worth it to get creative and work hard to make it possible. That's exactly what we did. And two months later we welcomed home our third daughter, who's an absolute joy: Eleanor Mae.

Personal History

As much as Dr. Otto Von Scratchandsniff may want you to believe, everything about you wasn't determined in your childhood. As you've gone through life, your experiences have continued to shape your outlook, including your Money Mindset.

Things to think about in your personal history are your WalletWins and WalletWinces. When is a time that you did really well with money? Maybe when you landed a new job or got a raise? Perhaps you built up a lot of savings or had an opportunity to be generous.

When are some times that you could have done better? Maybe you got sucked into trading apps and lost money, or you went on aimless trips to Target and came back home with a few bags full of things you never really needed or didn't have the money for at the time. Maybe you've racked up some debt.

Have you done anything dumb and had to pay for it? I sure have!

One day I went to work and my usual spot in the parking garage was taken, so I parked in a different stall. Now, the thing about this garage to take note of in this story is that it was on the basement level of the building, so it had a number of pillars that held up the rest of the building. Some of the parking spots had pillars right on the corner of the space.

This day, I had parked in one of those spots.

At the end of the day, I pulled out of the spot just like I did every other day: Put the car in reverse, twist around to look out the back window, pull out a little bit, then turn the wheel to start angling out of the parking space — *crunch*. I ran my driver's side door into the pillar, smashing it in, and giving it a good scrape.

After saying a few choice words, I pulled forward, backed out (more carefully this time), and drove home. I had to pay to get that dent and scrape fixed, and it was all because of me not being careful.

Now, I could let this seep into how I see myself and my Money Mindset and start believing things like *I screw things up because I'm not careful*. Or *I make dumb mistakes that cost me money*. Or I could just see it as an accident and move on.

We've *all* done dumb things and paid for them later. It's more helpful to look back on them with a smile, knowing we'll do better next time, than ruminating on them till kingdom come.

All these WalletWins and WalletWinces come together to influence and shape your Money Mindset. If you'd like some help taking a look at your past, head over to WalletWin.com/mindset and download a copy of our personal history inventory.

Talkin' 'Bout My Generation

We've covered the ways *how* we've grown up can affect our Money Mindset, but *when* we grew up can also leave a lasting mark on who we are and how we relate to money.

You may be familiar with the idea of generational cohorts, or more likely, their labels: Baby Boomers, Gen-Xers, Millennials, Generation Z or iGen. Grouping people by generation helps researchers identify trends among age groups across a variety of disciplines. The generation we're a part of can have an impact on our financial outlook and behaviors.

Baby Boomers (born 1946–1964)

This generation is also referred to as the "Me Generation." Many of the advancements in technology and society during their lives have allowed for an expectation that things will just continue to get better with time. Cultural shifts in the 1960s and 1970s led many of this generation to throw off more traditional expectations and find their own path forward, developing a more individualistic mentality.

You may see that many members of this generation fell into a "keeping up with the Joneses" mentality as suburban life grew during their lifetimes. Product development has followed this large population group as they've grown older, with the development and marketing of the self-help industry and age-defying makeup. Baby Boomers are also the last generation to have widespread participation in a job market that provided many jobs with pensions, which influenced their saving and investment priorities.

Gen-X (born 1965–1980)

This generation grew up during the 1980s. Many were the first to experience both parents working. Wall Street experienced a bull market (share prices going up) during most of the '80s, driving more interest and activity in the stock market, and a "greed is good" attitude in some of the culture.

In addition to both parents working, members of this generation may have experienced their families going through separation or divorce, as divorce rates were higher during this generation's formative years than during the previous or preceding generations. Gen-Xers also saw an increase in both parents working versus earlier generations.[1] These changing family dynamics may have had an influence on finances, or on how money and spending intertwine with Gen-X relationships.

Millennials (born 1981–1996)

This generation is sometimes called the "Echo Boomers," because most are children of Baby Boomers. They are also a generational cohort with a large population. Born in 1985 and 1986, both Amanda and I are definitely Millennials.

Members of this generation were the first to embrace commerce with a cause — brands like Tom's shoes or Warby Parker glasses built their businesses with a buy one, give one model where a pair of shoes (or glasses) were given to those in need with each purchase made.

You'll also see us perhaps buying things we don't need, as advances in manufacturing technology — especially in the realm of personal technology — rapidly increased, bringing to market products like smartphones, smartwatches, even smart refrigerators and robot vacuums. A lot of this buying "power" was realized through consumer credit, as credit cards and other forms of lending have become quite normalized for this generation. While more well-off than the next generation, Millennials are likely to have a hefty bit of student loans, as well.

Gen-Z (born 1997–early 2010s)

This generation is just beginning to enter the job market, but they are already having a huge impact in the world. They don't remember a time before the internet, personal computers, or cell phones. Gen-Zers are making a splash with their digital savviness and entrepreneurialism. They're extremely influential in their households because they know how to access information quickly — whether product reviews, reliability studies, or the latest gig economy opportunities or ways to earn a living online.

Gen-Z is also the most educated generation, with more of them going to college. Unfortunately, this means they are graduating with more student loan debt than any other generation before them. This has led younger members of this generation to question the necessity of college altogether and instead specialize in valuable skills that don't come with a ball and chain. Many members of this generation grew up in the aftermath of the financial crisis of 2008, an experience that may have shaped their earliest impressions of money.

Take a look at your generation, or, if you were born near the edges, the generations you may have some overlap with. Some of your financial behaviors and attitudes may likely be influenced by when you grew up, and it's important for you to be aware of any particular triggers or attractions you may have as part of your Money Mindset.

What's Your Financial Personality?

We know there are as many personality types and quizzes out there as there are people, but we aren't talking about how being an INFJ (or Green Parachute, or choleric-sanguine for that matter) influences your finances. If you're into a particular personality system, you can probably see how your personality type in that system can apply to your approach to money. And if you're into that, certainly go for it.

Whether you're going to run things through another system or not, we want you to think about how you relate to money in two ways. One of them is a pretty common way to look at things, and the other might be new to you.

The first will be to know if you are a Spender or a Saver. These are the two most common impulses we can have when money comes into our possession. I grew up being told that money was "burning a hole in my pocket" because I'd want to ride my bike to the convenience store or get a ride to the mall to buy something, even if I had just gotten the money earlier that day. I got an allowance growing up, and I rarely had any left by the time my next allowance was paid out. I like things. I like buying things. Hi, my name is Jonathan, and I'm a Spender.

🚩 *Amanda*

On the flip side, I'm a natural Saver. No story proves this point (or baffles Jonathan more) than the day I moved to college. After a long day of hauling boxes and furniture to my dorm room and helping me get set up, my dad gave me a hug and slipped me $100 in twenties. Four months later, when I returned home for Christmas break, I still had $60 left — meaning I'd only spent $40 that entire semester. If I'm not mistaken, it was to buy a few sorority t-shirts, not to buy pizzas like Jonathan would've done. I mean, all my food and shelter needs were covered; what else was there to spend money on? Hi, my name is Amanda, and I'm a Saver.

🚩 *Jonathan*

The most important thing to remember here is that when it comes to being a Spender or a Saver, one is not better than the other. This is *particularly* important when it comes to being in a relationship with someone of the other type. Spenders may think Savers are boring. Savers may think Spenders are impulse-driven and never think of the future. Neither is quite true.

The truth of the matter is that a healthy relationship with money involves both spending *and* saving. We need to save enough to have enough when we need it, but also spend some to take care of our needs, give to others, and have fun making memories along the way.

What's important is having a good *balance* of Saver and Spender mentalities, both in your own personality, but also in a relationship.

As soon as I said "Saver" and "Spender," some of you immediately self-identified as one or the other. Some of you may be on the fence, trying to figure out which camp you fall in. Don't worry, we have a quiz that can help!

But let's talk about the other component of your Financial Personality. This aspect describes your attitude toward the details of handling your money. Simply put, when money talk comes up, do you Geek Out or Tune Out? Do you love the details, or would you love for someone else to take care of them?

This might follow your attention to detail or need for information or context in other areas of your life, but it might not. At first glance, it might seem that Spenders are going to Tune Out and Savers are going to Geek Out, and while that can happen, it doesn't always. For example, in most things I have a much stronger attention to detail than Amanda. However, when it comes to finances, her desire for context kicks in, and she's all about the details, especially when it comes to planning. When it comes to money, we *both* actually Geek Out.

This works out great in our relationship: Amanda enjoys getting into the numbers, making the first drafts of our budgets, and I go through them, looking at the details. She can see the big picture of a project and easily set an overall budget, and I can see the details of how to divvy up that budget to get the project done. We have very complementary Financial Personalities. But any combination of Spender/Saver and Geek Out/Tune Out can establish healthy communication and ultimately, financial peace. It all comes down to self-knowledge and using that to get on the same financial page.

The WalletWin Financial Personality Test will help you identify where you fall on both the Saver/Spender and Geek Out/Tune Out spectra. Head on over to WalletWin.com/quiz.

The Voice Inside Your Head

Our family history, personal past, generational tendencies, and Financial Personality come together to influence our Money Mindset, which then fuels the thoughts and attitudes we have about money. Essentially, it forms the voice we hear in our head when money comes up — and that voice can say things that are good and true and encouraging, as well as things that aren't. While your Money Mindset is unique to you, there *are* some common thoughts and beliefs about money that we've seen come up that are just plain not helpful. We're going to hold these up to the light and reveal the truth.

"I'm not good with money and never will be."

This is certainly one we see a lot. And why not? When something's been hard in the past, or we've never done it before, it's tempting to just throw our hands up and say that things are the way they are and they're not gonna change, so why try.

We're tempted to think this because it provides a reason for why things are the way they are, *and* that it's not our fault — in fact, because we're supposedly "not good with money," there's no possible way things could be different! So no need to feel bad, beat ourselves up, or expect anything different.

The problem with this line of thinking is that it's based entirely on a lie. Our thought is incomplete. Maybe you have made some mistakes. Maybe you feel that it's close to the truth to say you're not good with money. But the real truth is that you're not good with money — yet. Or you weren't wise with your money at the time when you made X decision.

This line of thinking bases itself on the lie that we are forever locked into an existence that can never change, a life that is determined by your past (mostly your past mistakes) and leaves absolutely no room for growth or improvement. And that's crazy!

You've learned so many things! You've learned to cook, to do whatever it is you do at work, to read, to write, to walk even! And speaking of, let's think about a baby learning to walk.

They don't know what they're doing, and how could they — they've never done it before. But they try. And they fall down. A lot. And we expect them to. When each of our kids learned to walk, they did it one step — really, one stumble — at a time. When they took two steps and then fell on their butts, what did we do? We went crazy celebrating the two steps! Because they were *learning* how to walk. And as time went on, they took more steps and had fewer stumbles. And now they not only walk and run, but jump off the couch and climb the shelves in the pantry to steal chocolate chips.

So you haven't learned to be awesome with your money yet. You've fallen down a time or two. Big whoop. You didn't know what to do. Maybe (probably) no one taught you what to do, and perhaps you weren't even trying to learn. Well, *now's* the time to start learning. You might stumble a bit as you start, but that's totally expected. And the important thing is you are taking steps. You'll be jumping off the couch and stealing chocolate chips in no time.

So let's change that lie. If you're tempted to think, *I'm not good with money and never will be*, every time that thought comes up, re-place it with, *I'm not awesome with money yet, but I can learn how to handle money well and do it the rest of my life.*

"I'm not _____ enough."

Fill in the blank with your "favorite" way to get down on yourself: I'm not smart enough. I'm not good enough. I'm not disciplined enough. I'm not rich enough. I'm not diligent enough. I'm not from the right background. I'm not enough, period.

Thoughts like these are extensions of the lie we already talked about. We're tempted to lock ourselves into a life that has no hope of movement or growth, but we know we can grow.

You are enough.

You have what it takes to use money well. A little short on the practical experience? That's why you're reading this book!

You haven't failed to handle your money well in the past because you are fundamentally flawed in your character — you just haven't learned how yet. You got this. We'll help you.

Let's change that thinking from *I'm not _____ enough* to *I can do this.*

"I can't get my spouse on board."

 Amanda

This belief is a toughie. If I'm being honest, this was a big fear of mine at the start of our marriage. During our engagement, after freaking out about Jonathan's credit card debt (you'll hear more about that later) I asked him to read some personal finance books. This was my attempt to outsource "fixing him," and not so shockingly, it didn't work. Not only did he blow off reading the books, he felt like I was nagging him, which wasn't exactly how I wanted to kick off newlywed bliss.

I had to back into the conversation differently. Instead of blaming, shaming, and manipulating him into change, I created space and time for us to dream together. We had a blast sharing our hopes for the future! After creating clarity around what (and more importantly, *why*) we wanted our married life to look like, we naturally turned to the practicals, toward making it happen. Since money touches everything, our conversation went in that direction.

It was then that we decided *together* that if we wanted our goals and dreams to happen, we needed to make financial shifts. It was easy for both of us to change when we had this crystal clear and motivating future in our mind's eye. If you've tried to coerce your spouse into changing their financial habits without first sitting down to dream together, that's what I'd recommend doing first. Let your individual and shared dreams for the future do the heavy lifting for you.

"I don't make enough money."

It's not about how much you make, it's about what you do with it. You'd be surprised at how many six-figure earners are barely making ends meet because their bank account is like a bucket with holes in it. Sure, a lot of money goes in, but it's flowing out faster than you can blink due to out-of-control spending and debt payments. On the flip side, you'd be surprised at how many low- or middle-income earners rise to millionaire status because they sealed up all the holes so their bucket doesn't leak at all. Not a lot of money goes into that bucket, but every dollar has a job and it works hard for their dreams.

Financial freedom has little to do with how much money we earn, but everything to do with how we handle it. It's up to you whether or not you'll let your limiting beliefs around what your income is capable of dictate your success. But if you're willing to learn new strategies, change your habits, and think outside the box, you can win with money no matter what your income level is.

"This might happen for other people, but I won't be able to achieve financial freedom."

🏴 *Jonathan*

Maybe you've overcome the thoughts above, or they weren't an issue for you. You know you can learn how to take care of your finances. You also know you're enough to transform this area of your life. But perhaps in the back of your mind, you think the big wins and the jaw-dropping results are for everyone else but you. That you will be the one person or family that this method just won't work for. That you might make slow progress but it won't actually lead to long-term financial freedom.

I'm not saying that everyone everywhere has the same amount and quality of opportunities in life. I'm not saying that it's not harder for some people to have success than it is for others. What I am saying is it's not impossible for *you*. Despite flaws in the system, fluctuations in the economy, or your individual circumstances, you *can* carve a path to financial peace.

The truth is you can do this. We know because the WalletWin Method of handling your money worked for us and we've seen it work for others in a wide variety of circumstances time and again.

Maybe you think there's some aspect of your current situation that is just *too* out there, *too* far gone, *too* dramatic, *too* different from everyone else that what worked for them just won't work for you.

That's exactly why we've created a step-by-step plan for you to follow, a plan that generates results both in the short-term and long-term. The WalletWin plan *works*. We've seen it work over and over again for single people, married people, big families, small families. It works because it breaks it down to doing the right thing at the right time.

When we put our energy into the right action at the right time, we make progress. And when we keep doing that, we make continual progress. And continual progress leads to us winning with our money.

Maybe your story won't be as dramatic as someone else's, but it will always be worthy of celebration. We define success as having peace of mind regarding your finances, living with the freedom to say "yes" to God's will in your life, and being able to retire while leaving a generous legacy in your family and our world. No matter your starting point, you can achieve that in your lifetime.

Understanding your Financial Personality and Money Mindset sets the stage as you begin the more practical steps of transforming your finances. Don't skip this important foundational work — take the personality quiz and download the Money Mindset worksheets at WalletWin.com/book.

When you're ready to continue, we'll see you in the next chapter, where we're chatting about the "B word."

Success Story
Ashley and Josh Doehring

Managing money and creating a budget was never taught to me while growing up, but here I was, engaged and ready to take on the role of the money manager for our household. My first task was to budget our expenses, plus find a way to pay for our wedding. Our budget was under $10,000, easy peasy. I started searching around YouTube to find anyone that could teach me how to properly budget. I found a lot of videos: "How to do a zero-based budget," "envelope system," and so on, but never found a direct way to manage our money. I made it work for the time being. After I successfully budgeted our wedding, it was now time to budget for a child, and I was able to plan accordingly, for the most part.

Then, two months after having our first child, I was called into my manager's office to find out that I was now laid off. Sadly, that was when I turned to credit cards to help with our piling bills. As much as I regret the choices that I made, looking back on that time made me want to look at ways to get out of debt, and *quickly*. I used other programs but never felt that we were getting much traction with tackling our debt.

That was when I found WalletWin, which was exactly what my husband Josh and I needed. Other programs felt extremely impractical, and we desperately needed to find a program that would fit into real life. Amanda and Jon made budgeting more practical. We have since been able to pay off $35,000 in debt in less than a year. This is the biggest accomplishment we have made in the past five years. What is even more exciting is that Amanda and Jon have taught us how to live prudently even after losing one income. In the face of what would normally scare me, the lessons and tools I have been taught from WalletWin have prepared me to face any money challenges in the future.

CHAPTER 5

Live with a Budget

"Know well the condition of your flocks,
and give attention to your herds."
Proverbs 27:23

Establish Your
Financial Foundation

🐦 *Amanda*

You're strolling Target on a Saturday afternoon and as you casually peruse the Hearth & Hand section by Chip and Jo, you spot the most beautiful accent chair and side table. Together, these would look totally Pinterest-worthy when paired near your bedroom window with those new curtains you got last week. You imagine the coffees sipped, deep thoughts journaled, and dreams conjured up in that spot. Accent-chair-and-table you is peaceful, calm, and intellectual.

They're all but purchased when you turn the tag over and internally wince — $199.99 and $99.99 respectively. With tax, we're talking over $300 for the set. You stand in the aisle, mentally debating. You tally up all the reasons you deserve this, while batting away any thoughts of reason telling you to look around or wait on the purchase. Finally, you pull your phone out and log in to your bank. You glance down and see $974.28 available. A smile crosses your face as you load the chair and table into the cart. Whew! You have enough money to afford them. Or so you think ... until you get home and remember that paying the pile of bills might have been a better use of those 300 bucks.

We call this *bank balance budgeting* and it's how most people budget, even though it's not actually budgeting at all.

In this chapter, we're diving deep into budgeting — what it is, what it's not, how to get started, and how to craft a habit that sets your finances free. By the end, you'll be ready to wave goodbye to bank balance "budgeting" that never worked anyway, and welcome in a budget that unlocks the path to your dreams.

What Are Groceries?

After having a blowout money fight on our honeymoon (*that* story is coming in chapter 9!), we knew something had to change. After reading books, listening to podcasts, scoping out blogs, and talking with financial mentors, we knew where we had to start: the budget.

At first glance, budgeting seems easy. Look at the money you have. Make a plan for it. Boom, you have a budget. But when you actually start budgeting, it can get tricky faster than you can say, "Bob's your uncle."

It's not hard for questions to overwhelm us into inaction. Software or pen and paper? Do we both budget together or does one of us create it and then present to the other? What percentage of our income should we be saving? How do we track spending? What happens when I overspend? How do I make sure my budget and my bank balance say the same thing? What if we forget to look at our budget for a few weeks?

You get the idea.

On January 1, 2012, we enthusiastically dove headlong into our first budget. A few days into our brand-new budget, we ran into our first problem: groceries. You see, we'd budgeted $60 for the entire month for the two of us. Well, one trip to the grocery store is all it took, and we'd spent the whole month's fund in one fell swoop. Oops. I blame the fact that in college I'd lived in a sorority and didn't have to cook. In my first job out of college as a missionary, all my meals were provided at the Newman Center cafeteria. I'd never *actually* bought groceries or planned meals.

But here we were, newlyweds, and I wanted to make a few home-cooked meals per week instead of us perpetually eating in a dining hall cafeteria with college students. Don't get me wrong, I liked the cafeteria. But being married twenty-somethings grabbin' a slice and having Fruity Pebbles for dessert was getting weird. So we had to re-arrange the budget. We call it "gettin' fudgy with the budgey."

A few days after the grocery store budget debacle, we needed an oil change. And guess what? We forgot to budget for it. After that came some household items we needed. The final nail in the coffin that month was toiletries we needed that I hadn't even considered budgeting for. Our shiny, intact budget was now lifeless and in shambles. We'd robbed Peter to pay Paul and then had to rob Paul to pay Andrew … all month long.

Despite that discouraging first month, we decided to keep going, to try again and not give up. We've been around the block enough to know that learning a new skill involves a learning curve. Budgeting isn't hard. But *new* things are hard, simply because they're new. Our brains like comfort and try to convince us to abandon ship when things feel hard or if perceived failure is on the horizon. It's a learned self-preservation technique to save face, but it keeps us stuck.

Think about kids learning how to ride a bicycle without training wheels — at some point, they inevitably end up in a bush or with a scraped knee. But does that prevent them from learning? Nope! They just keep getting up, trying again, and getting stronger every time. They don't let limiting beliefs hold them back from learning how to ride a bike. As adults, we must be aware of this learned sabotage that threatens to stall our growth and keep us from becoming who we were created to be.

So we continued on.

That second month of budgeting was still rough, but less so. The third month was even better. By the time we got to month six of budgeting, we were pros. We knew how much we needed to budget in the various categories like groceries, car maintenance, or toiletries. Crafting the budget, using it to inform our spending, tracking our expenses, and reconciling our bank account were now firmly established habits. They were as easy as breathing — we didn't have to think about them anymore. They just were. And the peace, freedom, and control we gained from these habits far surpassed the stress, pressure, and fear we had when we weren't budgeting.

Think Eating Plan, Not Juice-Cleanse

Jonathan

Just like a diet, budgeting can get a bad rap. That's right, Jonathan's back with another food analogy!

When most people think of dieting, they think of saying no to everything they love — cookies, pizza, pasta, dessert — in order to get healthy or lose weight.

Same goes with budgeting. You think you have to say no to everything you love — restaurants, vacations, new clothes, food that doesn't involve a microwave or have "instant" in the name — in order to clean up piles of debt or other financial disasters.

Turns out that's not actual dieting, or budgeting either.

Budgeting is intentionally assigning a role to our money so we can reach our goals. People who are successful, whether in physical or financial health, and those who want to be successful, are intentional about their choices.

Just as specific health goals are only achieved with a sensible, maintainable, targeted eating plan, your financial goals will become reality only with a targeted spending plan; that is, a budget.

What a Budget *Isn't*

Before we jump into what a budget is and how to use one, let's make sure we know what a budget *isn't*.

A budget is not restrictive by nature.

Using a budget doesn't mean spending as little money as possible. It doesn't mean never seeing the inside of a Target or the bottom of a Starbucks cup for as long as you live. Perhaps your current financial goal calls for you to reduce spending so you can save or pay off debt faster. Your budget will reflect that goal and shape your spending to make sure you achieve the goal. Any cutting back is driven by the goal, not by the mere act of budgeting.

A budget does not mean we are in scarcity mode.

When we start paying attention to our money and tracking our spending, money can suddenly feel in short supply, and the bank account seems to be draining faster than ever! And because money is so scarce, we must obsessively keep track of the details, lest it vanish forever. But that's not what we're doing with budgeting: We're paying attention to our spending not because there's so little money to go around, but because we want to make sure the right amount goes to the right place.

A budget is not a whip to penalize us.

We don't start using a budget to make up for past mistakes or because we've "been bad" with money in the past. We also don't use one to punish a spouse or divvy out an allowance as if they were a child. It doesn't matter what you (or your spouse) have done or not done in the past. We use a budget because we have a plan we're executing now in the present, not only for today but also for our future.

A budget is not only for poor people.

A budget is for *anyone* looking to be intentional with their money. Budgeting is fundamental to good money management and impacts your finances no matter how much — or little — you have. It's a great starting point for many, but it's an essential habit for all. The only way to meet your goals — whether that means getting out of a mountain of debt or buying another investment property — is by being intentional with your money. Budgeting is not only the "secret" to beginning a financial turnaround, but is also the "secret" to keeping it going and growing.

What a Budget *Is*

We're clear on what a budget isn't. So what *is* a budget then? Simply put, a budget is permission to spend your money on your current goals, values, and priorities so you can reach your best next financial goal. Practically speaking, a budget is a tool to plan your spending, saving, and giving.

The power of a budget is the power it gives *you*. With a completed budget in hand, you're no longer worrying if you'll have enough money left at the end of the month to pay the bills or meet your savings goal. You don't have to feel ashamed when you go shopping and buy something that wasn't essential. You can stop and grab a latte, free of that "Did I just spend my rent money?" aftertaste.

A budget frees you up to spend. You've planned it all out already. You know how much you're going to spend on groceries. You know how much you're going to spend on utilities. And that there's enough money to spend on both. You can walk out of Target knowing the money for that accent chair came from the household goods category and didn't wreck your grocery budget for next week.

Living *with* a Budget, Not *on* a Budget

One little word can make a huge difference when it comes to your outlook on budgeting. Living *on* a budget puts the control in the hands of the "budget" and sets you up to be disappointed, resentful, and ultimately unsuccessful in reaching your goals. It comes out in phrases like, "Sorry, I can't go to that concert, I'm on a budget," or, "Oh, I'm on a budget, I can't." When you say and think things like that, you focus on the negative, restrictive aspects of your budget. You only see the small "no"s without the larger "yes." And with an attitude like that, you won't be budgeting (or moving toward your goals) for long. Seeing your budget as an overly restrictive burden standing between you and life will only lead you to abandon it, and that's a shame — because a proper understanding of budgeting unlocks the potential of your income to work for you and get you to your goals.

Now let's think about living *with* a budget. When you live *with* a budget, it means you are living your life and using a budget to help you realize your goals. Budgeting is something you do because you know it's going to help you win with money. You plan your spending. When you're invited to go to that concert, you can say "I haven't budgeted for that but let me see if I can adjust my plan to see if it fits!" Whether you end up saying yes or no to the concert, you're communicating to yourself and others, "I plan my spending so I can protect and achieve my goals. Let me see if I can flexibly shift things around without harming those."

Living with a budget doesn't mean you say no to everything you love all the time. Budgeting means saying *no* to some things you like so you can say *yes* to the things you really love.

How to Budget

 Amanda

We've cleared up what budgeting is and isn't. We know that budgeting is a plan for using your money to achieve your goals, financial and otherwise. Now, let's set about the practical process for budgeting your money. We'll break it down in nine steps.

Budget Frequency

We recommend budgeting on a monthly basis. This means you'll create twelve budgets per year and they'll coincide with the natural rhythm of life — birthdays, holidays, anniversaries, and seasonal activities/celebrations. Monthly budgeting keeps the process simple and straightforward, which is good because when things feel difficult or unclear, our brains like to abandon ship.

When just getting started, you might need to budget paycheck to paycheck, which is fine. But shifting out of the paycheck to paycheck cycle and into a monthly budget cycle is an early priority, since it simplifies the process and gives you a wider view of your financial situation. In fact, it's so essential we've made it the fifth Money Milestone. (But more on that later, let's keep focusing on Money Milestone 2, Budgeting.)

Step 0: Prepare Yourself

This sounds like a serious step, and it is — you seriously need to have fun when you're budgeting. Making a budget *is* something to celebrate! You are one month closer to paying off debt, taking that trip to France, making your last mortgage payment, or buying those shoes you've been saving for!

Budgeting is a good thing, so make it feel like one with a BUD-GET PARTY! Bring your favorite treats and beverages along, whether that's scones and tea, cheese and wine, or pizza and beer. Get creative and make it special, especially when you're first starting out.

Play a pump-up jam to set the tone before you dive in to get your blood flowing and up the excitement level around budgeting. Biased opinion, but we think every song from Jock Jams is worth considering.[1] Cultivating an atmosphere and environment that is welcoming, inspiring, and fun will make you (and possibly a reluctant spouse) want to show up to the party.

Step 1: Choose Your Method

You're ready to budget — now let's figure out the tool you'll use to create your budget.

You can do this in a variety of ways: ye olde pen and paper, spreadsheets like Excel, or using budgeting software. It really boils down to knowing yourself, and while we'll make some recommendations based on our experience, the best budget is the one you'll use.

When Jonathan and I got started budgeting, we wanted to remove all obstacles, so we kept it simple with pen and paper. I'm one of those types that get insanely overwhelmed by technology and it takes me a while to learn new systems and trust them. So this was the best fit for us from the get-go.

About a year into budgeting, as we got the hang of it, I grew tired of doing math on paper and didn't enjoy handling cash anymore. I wanted a virtual budget and to use my debit card for purchases. Jonathan proceeded to dive headlong into the world of Google Sheets. He created the spreadsheet of all spreadsheets. It was thorough, thoughtfully designed, color-coded, and had tons of columns. But I hated it. Absolutely loathed the thing! It felt cold, sterile, ugly, and semi-inaccessible since I had to clunkily operate it on my phone via the browser. I tried so hard to use and like it, I really did. But six weeks into this spreadsheet, I had to kill the whole operation.

Enter stage left: the world of budgeting software and apps. There are many options out there if you decide to go the software route. Ultimately, budgeting software is what we've found works best for us and our students.

That said, you'll find no shortage of software to use and they're not all created equal. While many people like to start their search for apps beginning with those that are free, I'll share why we recommend you skip the free resources out there and head straight to the paid services.

In the world of free budgeting software, the big ones you'll find are Mint and Personal Capital. While they are easy to use, we recommend avoiding them entirely. It didn't take us long to realize these platforms were free because they were giant advertisements for a variety of financial products and services, many being credit or debt offers. They also sell user data and information to companies, and that's something we avoid if we can. If you can pay a small fee and not be marketed to non-stop via your budgeting software, that's absolutely worth it.

As you move into the world of paid budgeting tools you'll find software like YNAB (You Need A Budget), MVelopes, EveryDollar, and Quicken's Simplifi. We've tried them all and can safely say that YNAB is hands-down the best for a variety of reasons.

YNAB, EveryDollar, and MVelopes are all zero-based budgeting apps that have the ability to sync with your bank accounts. However, YNAB won't let you budget money you don't have in your bank account. If you try, you'll see a negative number in red at the top of your budget … reminding you that you've budgeted beyond what's actually in the bank. This feature makes it easy to scale the budget back to reflect reality. This is hugely important, because life happens. Sometimes that second or third paycheck you were hoping would come that month … doesn't. Or it's lower than you anticipated. You'll never be left spending money you don't have in hand using this app, which ultimately protects you.

YNAB also stands far above the others with its financial education resources, ability to track your net worth, track goals, and produce reports with charts and graphs so you can visualize your money trends. You can have more than one budget set up with them as well, so if you're a business owner or you have a side hustle you want to budget for separately (I recommend you do!) you can seamlessly move between your various budgets. Quicken Simplifi stands toe to toe with YNAB regarding robust features, but the cost is practically the same and YNAB is more user-friendly, placing them at the top of our recommendation list.

Head over to WalletWin.com/howtoYNAB to check out our videos that make getting started with YNAB a snap. We recommend a few different services on our site. WalletWin has entered into a business relationship with some of these services to provide a small commission if you should decide to become a customer of theirs. We only seek out affiliate relationships with companies and products we use and respect. We recommend products and services because we think they are great, not because they pay us (and many don't).

Whew! Now that we've dropped the deets on all the different methods you can use to create your budget, it's time for you to pick one to try. If it works for you and you use it, great, keep going! If not, try another method and keep moving forward until you find an option that works with your personality and needs.

Step 2: Create Your Budget Categories

Now that you've chosen a budgeting tool, here's how to set up your budget.

First, you're going to define the various categories you plan to spread your money between. Think charitable giving, electricity, groceries, gasoline, toiletries, clothing, household items, date night, childcare, etc. Notice that we encourage "giving" as a budget category from your budget's inception. We'll talk more about tithing, giving, and generosity later on, but what you need to know now is that giving should always be part of your budget no matter your income level or the Money Milestone you're currently on.

If you need help coming up with the major categories you spend your money on every month, simply go through the last ninety days of bank statements. You'll notice patterns and expenses you need to include in your budget. If you're new to budgeting, one of your categories should be "Forgotten Expenses" because you will forget things, and this category will cover your hiney until you can adjust your categories for the future.

One common question we get from folks as they begin budgeting is this: Is my grocery budget the catch-all for not only food but shampoo, toilet paper, razors, dog bones, and laundry detergent?

While I'm all for simplicity and not having unnecessary budget categories I would NOT recommend your grocery budget being a catch-all for everything you might buy at the supermarket. The reason being, it's important early on to become familiar with how much you're spending and where. If you're battling chronic overspending and impulse purchases, it's critical you know where your money is going. What do you do at the grocery store, then? Check out in one transaction (because who has time to do several different ones?) and when you open up YNAB, it allows you to "split" the transaction when you track it. You can split the transaction yourself if you're using paper and pen, of course. Easy peasy.

Download an example budget — complete with categories — as part of our budget tool pack at WalletWin.com/budgetsheet.

Step 3: Assess Your current Needs and Goals

By this point, you know that a budget is a plan to meet your current financial goals. So, this step is to, of course, identify those goals and assess your needs!

Each budget you create will be colored by your current financial goal, usually determined by your spot in the Financial Phases and Money Milestones. For example, your restaurant category will look different when you're working to get out of debt, versus when you're completely debt-free and have a Full Rainy Day Fund.

Each budget will also be influenced by your current financial needs based on the month. School is starting and you need to go to the store and purchase the list of school supplies from your kids' teachers? Those school supplies need to fit into the budget this month. It's April and you're hosting Easter brunch? Upping the grocery budget will come in handy for the extra food you'll need to buy.

Once you have a handle on your goals and current needs, you can move on to the next step.

To assist you in making sure your budget has everything you might need in that given month, **download a copy of our monthly BudgetJoggers at WalletWin.com/budgetjoggers.**

Step 4: Count Your Money

In order to make a plan for how to use your money, you need to know how much money you have to use. This is every bit of income you have for the month. Ideally, you'll have all the money you need for the month at the beginning of the month. But it can take some time to get there — more on that in Chapter 8, Live a Month Ahead.

If you aren't coming into the month with all the money you'll have to spend, but will instead be using your paychecks as you get them, do your best to estimate what those paychecks will be so you have an accurate as possible picture of the month ahead. If your paychecks are the same amount each time, this is easy. For those with irregular incomes, look back over past paychecks and make your best guess. When in doubt, estimate a bit lower. It's always easier to increase your budget than to trim it.

And when I said all your income earlier, I meant all your income. If you make some money from a side hustle, it goes in the budget. You get a birthday check from Grandma (Thanks, Grandma! Love you!) it goes in the budget. Find a forgotten $10 bill in your jacket pocket from last year? Guess where it goes. That's right! The budget!

Now you have your total amount of money available to spend.

Step 5: Plan Your Spending

At WalletWin, we teach zero-based budgeting. That's a fancy way of saying that every dollar you receive gets a job inside your budget. No money is left blowing in the wind doing nothing. All your buckaroos are lined up, tasks assigned, hard at work for your goals.

Once you have written out your categories, it's time to take the money you have available and spread it out amongst your priorities. Jonathan and I have only ever had irregular income — we've actually never had the same amount of income from any given month to the next. This is why we approach planning your spending from a prioritized angle. You need to first fund your top priorities before moving on to lesser important categories.

Let's say it's the first of the month and you have $5,500 to assign amongst your categories. Start with expenses like your mortgage or rent and move into utilities, food, and transportation. Once these basic necessities are covered, you can begin assigning your money to paying down debt, buying clothes, going to the movies, or keeping that Spotify subscription.

Prioritized budgeting makes sure your needs are taken care of above all. After covering all your needs and assigning your money among the categories you'd like to fund, if there is any money left, its job is to help you accelerate progress toward your next money milestone. Going back to the $5,500 available for the month — after taking care of needs and a few wants, there might be an extra $1,000 available. If you're working on paying off debt, boom, you get to lay into some debt with a big punch. If you're saving for a new-to-you vehicle or a Full Rainy Day Fund, you're that much closer.

You might be asking yourself, "But how do I know what I should budget in each category? Are there certain recommended percentages?" Some personal finance folks like to use percentages, but we don't. The reason being is that your priorities shift and change on any given month, and certainly from one Financial Phase to another. Your income also can fluctuate, and that alone can make percentages irrelevant.

For example, let's say you used a recommended 10 percent for food-related expenses with a $5,500/mo. income. That's $550. If you only have two people in your household, you could utilize meal planning to lower that amount without sacrificing your health or tastebuds. If your income grows and all of a sudden you're bringing home $9,000/mo. that doesn't mean you have to now start budgeting

$900/mo. for food.

You might gravitate toward percentages because you feel lost and you're looking for something to let you know if you're "doing it right" or not. A percentage just won't be able to provide that guidance. It's too generic. That's why we teach prioritized budgeting and moving from one financial phase to the next. As you grow in freedom, you will be able to pick and choose where you want to allocate your money based on your goals and dreams.

Step 6: Spend According to Your Budget

Many people complete these first five steps of budgeting and then here, on step six, they fall off the wagon. Their budget blows up — and then they give up. We want to provide you with simple strategies to make sure you move from creating a budget on paper (or in an app) to letting that budget inform your spending.

A Tale of Two Costco Trips

Our trick has always been this — once I pull up somewhere, let's use Costco for example, I open YNAB on my phone to peek at the budget. I can quickly see I've got $300 left in groceries, $40 left in household goods, $100 for kiddos, and $20 left in toiletries. Now I head into the store with mental financial bumper guards on. As I cruise Costco, coasting in and out of their strategically-crafted aisles that promote impulse buys, I feel empowered to make choices because I know what I have available and what our needs for the rest of the month will likely be.

Let's say I head down the toy aisle and see *Frozen* Lego kits from last season on closeout for $19.97. I happen to have three daughters, all equally obsessed with both *Frozen* and Lego, so this is a no-brainer birthday gift for at least one of them. I already know in my bones that I've got $100 set aside in kiddo-related expenses, so into the cart it goes with ease and confidence. Now I'm cruising through the refrigerated area of the store and sampling a brand-new food. It's cheese … but not any ordinary cheese. It's merlot-soaked cheese that would make a perfect addition on my lazy-dinner charcuterie platter. I already reviewed that I have $300 in groceries left, so into the cart it goes without batting an eyelash. Last up, as I head toward checkout, I notice they've got their Kirkland Signature Moisturizing Shampoo and Conditioner on sale (which, according to the internet rumor mill, is Pureology in a store-brand bottle). I've been waiting for it to go on sale and while it's tight, I know I have $20 in toiletries! Boom, baby!

One of the worst feelings I've ever had (and I'm sure you've experienced too) is standing in an aisle deliberating a purchase and being completely in the dark as to whether I can afford it or if it will wreck my bank account.

Let's imagine what might've happened had I *not* looked at the budget (or not budgeted at all) before heading into Costco:

As I pass the toy aisle and see the *Frozen* Lego sets on sale, I instantly tense up. They're the perfect birthday gift … but haven't I bought the girls a bunch of stuff lately? Didn't I buy something even a couple of weeks ago? Why can't I remember anything anymore? It's such a good deal, but Jonathan will kill me if I spend more money on the kids. I pass the gift, resentful of Jonathan and how he's always "breathing down my neck" about buying things for the kids I think they need. Now I hit the merlot cheese. Oh man, it's good. It's really good. I decide to buy it — and a few wines to go with it because subconsciously suppressing the Lego sets caused a knee-jerk reaction to spend more. Now I see the shampoo and conditioner on sale. Again, I have been waiting for these to go on sale but I struggle with buying self-care items. Buying for others? Easy. But for myself? Hard. I end up feeling bad I bought so much wine … and my cart is full of food … this is easily a $275 Costco run … can we handle that? We don't get paid until next Friday. Ugh, I better not get them. I'll buy some super cheap Suave at Walmart instead. I put all my items on the belt and moments later the total pops up. $459.74! What? I swear there are only a dozen items in my cart! Oh well. I guess I'll put it on the credit card to buy some time before having to pay it. Fifteen minutes later my husband calls because he got a text that there was a credit card charge to Costco. He's not happy. Ugh.

Very different Costco runs, huh?

Using the budget to quickly inform yourself before spending money is the difference-maker between spending in peace and with confidence, and spending with a sense of unease and worry. A budget can help you make decisions easily because you're working with actual information and not estimations of what you think your bank account has left.

It can also help you avoid purchases you know will break or bust your budget, or require you to make the necessary adjustments if you decide to shift the budget mid-month. For example, let's go back to Costco. Let's say while I was passing the electronics section, I noticed a Ring Security System for $50 off regular pricing … but it's still $179.99 plus tax. Well, I'd peeked at my budget before I came in and I know there was $40 budgeted for household goods. This is way more than that, plus I still need to buy toilet paper and laundry detergent. It's easy to pass up and move on from.

However, if a Ring Security System *was* a priority for us and we'd been waiting on a sale for it, as adults, we can go back to the budgey and get a little fudgy. There's a pretty good chance we can shift the other numbers around and find the available funds for the purchase. After looking around, I notice that we came in under budget on a few utilities, and we hadn't used up our entertainment funds for the month. I can reallocate the money left in those budget categories to make this purchase instead.

Either way, I used the budget to stay informed, and that ultimately led to peaceful and confident spending.

Making it Work, Together

Now, one caveat to add here is for married couples. It's not uncommon for two spouses to finally be on the same financial page, wanting to reach their money goals — but failing to reach them because one or both spouses aren't actually using the budget to inform their spending.

Pick budget software? Fine. Enter my income? Sure. Allocate the money amongst the various categories? No prob. But when the rubber meets the road and it's time to align spending habits *with* the budget? It can be hard for some personalities. While there isn't a panacea (there can be different root causes — ADHD, resentment, depression, addiction, or plain old forgetfulness to name a few), I encourage these couples to go back to *why* they want financial peace.

Anytime you can connect your new financial habits with why you're on this journey in the first place is a good thing. Let your dreams do the heavy lifting if possible. If that's not enough, then it's worth diving deeper into what's causing the budget breakdown and identifying the exact unique challenge that's in the way. When you know what you're up against, you can create a unique plan of action to counteract it and be on your way to budgeting like a boss. Got a forgetful spouse? Stick a Post-It note in their car reminding them to review the budget before spending — or set an alarm on their phone every day as a gentle reminder to enter in any purchase they've made. Something more serious at play, like mental health challenges or addiction? Therapy might be necessary to get the right tools in play to establish the habit of budgeting.

Step 7: Track Your Spending

After making a purchase, it's time to track it. Back when we used paper and pen, our rule was that in the checkout line, immediately after paying for our items, we pulled out the budget and updated it right then and there. Sometimes if it had to wait, it was in the car in the parking lot. But we never waited longer than that, because I didn't want to face a waning memory and an avalanche of receipts.

Now that we have YNAB, this part is very simple. Since our bank account is synced up with YNAB, every time we make a purchase, the app auto-imports the transaction into my budget and tracks it for me. The only expenses I manually import these days are when I spend cash, since there's no record of it with our bank.

Depending on your bank, it might take a little while for transactions to show up and sync with YNAB or other apps. That's why it can still be a good idea to enter your spending as it happens, and use the syncing feature to double-check things later.

Keeping your budget up to date by tracking your spending in a timely manner is very important. Let's say you had $50 left in gasoline for the month. You're at a gas station after work and decide to fill up your tank for $37 but you decide not to track it in your budget. Now your spouse is off work and he too decides to stop for gas in his vehicle on the way home. He still sees $50 available in gasoline, so he fills up for $42. Together, you're now nearly thirty dollars over budget in gasoline and will have to rob Peter to pay Shell to make it right. If that happens once, no big deal. But if it becomes the norm, it's going to make budgeting a major pain *and* cause conflict in your household.

This is one more reason we recommend software like YNAB: to make sure this aspect of budgeting is seamless and easy. **Grab our free YNAB tutorials at WalletWin.com/howtoYNAB.**

Step 8: Reconciling Your Budget

Last and certainly not least, it's time to reconcile your budget. That's just a fancy way of saying you need to make sure your budget match-es your bank balance. For those of you older than 30, just remember back to being a teen and learning how to reconcile your check-book with your bank account. Same concept but *way* easier thanks to budgeting software. Reconciling is the process where you see that the $73 you spent at Target last week is accounted for both in your budget and in your bank account. If it's missing in either place, fur-ther investigation is needed.

We recommend reconciling your spending with your budget at least once per week. It should take you less than five minutes. YNAB makes this process extremely simple since it's connected with our bank account. All I need to do is login and let it sync. Once it pulls in the various expenses I simply make sure they're allocated cor-rectly (e.g., my $37 Shell gasoline expense is properly assigned to the gasoline category and not to groceries). Once all imported expenses are assigned to the right category, I "clear" the transaction so I know it's been correctly entered and doesn't need to be looked at again. If you aren't using YNAB and choose to go the paper and pen route (it's what we did for the first few months we were budgeting), you sit down with your paper budget, receipts, and your bank account pulled up. Review each receipt and check it against your budget and bank account. When you see each transaction is accounted for in both, you're reconciled.

Reconciling is an important step to ensure your budget and bank balance are always in good relationship with one another and showing you the correct information.

Step 9: Wash, Rinse, Repeat

    0. Prepare Yourself
    1. Choose Your Method
    2. Create Your Budget Categories
    3. Assess Your Current Needs and Goals
    4. Count Your Money
    5. Plan Your Spending
    6. Spend According to Your Budget
    7. Track Your Spending
    8. Reconcile Your Budget
    9. Wash, Rinse, Repeat

The beauty of budgeting is that it is an ever-evolving tool that will stay with you, helping you organize your money and ensure you nail your life's goals and dreams since inside the budget is where you get to prioritize them with real numbers. Every month you budget is a month that will bring you closer to your goals.

Many people think of a budget as something they create once and then it's done. But when have you ever had the same month twice? Never! This is why we teach monthly budgeting based on the unique circumstances that the month ahead brings. Christmas is always in December. Road trips are usually in July. Pumpkin spice brews reign supreme in October. But birthdays? Growth spurts? Anniversaries? You and your family have unique aspects that will inevitably shift and change what the budget looks like each month.

Lastly, the budget will shift as you move forward in the Money Milestones and through the Financial Phases. Early on, you'll prioritize emergency savings and debt payoff. Farther down, you'll be saving a down payment or investing. These too will impact how your budget evolves and changes.

While you likely won't create the same budget twice, you and your budget will begin to move in tandem until the process is as easy and routine as brushing your teeth.

Budgeting is a foundational financial habit, and we want to make sure you get started on the right foot. **Download our free budget tool kit — complete with budget forms, BudgetJoggers, a tutorial on how to get started with YNAB, and a sample budget party for married couples — at WalletWin.com/budget.**

Success Story
Karissa O'Hearn

"**N**o one has ever been through this. Not like me." This is the lie that the devil whispers whenever we are reaching for success. For me, this is what I thought when I started reading about Amanda and Jonathan's debt-crushing journey. I was without hope. I thought it was my circumstances that would forever keep me in debt. I was Mario in King Koopa's castle with only one life left. (I've never been too good at video games.)

All was well in my world when my husband and I got married. Yes there was the reality of combining our debt, but if I squinted then I didn't have to see that. We were happy, we spent money on frivolous things. We were starting a family. Life was sweet. Well ... a little sour, but mostly sweet.

Within the first five years of our marriage, my husband left. I found myself a single mom of our three kids. I was working full-time and living on my own. I had my own rent, regular bills, day-care bills, and children to take care of. Guess what else? I was keeping my debt in my blind spot. Amanda was an old college friend, so when I saw that she and Jonathan were launching WalletWin, I was scared, but knew I had to try it.

Because of my circumstances, I thought that Amanda would look at my situation and be like, "Oooh girl, I don't think we can help — good luck." I am glad she didn't. For the first time I was facing something I had been avoiding for five years, and that was over $65,000 of debt. Yes! You read that correctly. I was terrified. When WalletWin challenged me to start facing my monster, that was the first time I truly understood what interest was and how my debt was snowballing, but backwards. It was multiplying every day. It's been a journey, but after putting a halt on all my "sorta needs" and focusing on my budget, I started kicking the debt monster in the face. I am Mario facing King Koopa, and I finally kicked that debt monster in the face for the last time. Don't listen to the lie; your circumstances don't define your ability to face your financial strife — at least they don't define mine!

CHAPTER 6

Insure Yourself

"A prudent man sees danger and hides himself;
but the simple go on, and suffer for it."
— Proverbs 22:3

1 Money Mindset   2 Live with a Budget   3 **Insure Yourself**

Establish Your
Financial Foundation

🚩 *Jonathan*

Now we're going to cover an area of personal finance that is a bit different from the rest. In the WalletWin plan, whether in this book or elsewhere, we work our tails off to help you understand how to use money wisely. A bedrock part of using money wisely is getting a good deal, getting your money's worth.

If you follow our advice in this chapter, and everything goes according to plan, you will be wasting piles and piles of money over your lifetime. If things go the way they're "supposed to," you'll be just as well off flushing your money down the toilet and spending more of it to hire a plumber to unclog the pipes.

But in your life, everything will not go according to plan. Things will not always go the way they're supposed to. And when that happens, sometimes there are great financial consequences. If you're not prepared, those financial consequences can have a worse and longer-lasting impact than the event that started the ball rolling (maybe through your living room window) in the first place.

I'm speaking, of course, of insurance. Insurance is the one area in all of life and finances where you want a terrible return on investment. It's the thing you hope you never have to use, but thank heaven above that you have it when you need it.

Simply put, you pay a regular (monthly, annual, etc.) amount, called a premium, to an insurance company, in exchange for guaranteed compensation when particular losses, damages, illnesses, and so on, occur.

In other words, you pay an insurance company in order to shift certain risks from you to them.

It's like having a life raft on a sinking ship — while that raft can't stop the disaster or accident, it can shield you from being drowned in the financial fallout.

Why You Need Insurance

One way to explain the need for insurance is that it arises from the potential for personal economic ruin. If event X happens and it would totally wreck your finances, you would be wise to have insurance against it.

Another way to explain is that insurance helps you cover certain unexpected expenses that you'd otherwise have no way of covering.

You're working hard toward financial freedom for you and your family, and so naturally you want to be sure that everyone and everything is protected. Accidents and disasters can and do happen, and if you aren't adequately insured, you could end up with a massive financial hangover at the worst possible moment. When life's already got you down, being uninsured is giving life permission to kick you while you're on the floor.

A Policy for Everything

Some folks have taken out insurance policies for, shall we say, unique risks. Silent film star Ben Turpin was famous for his crossed eyes, and it's said he took out an insurance policy against his eyes uncrossing, for fear that it would end his career.[1] Pittsburgh Steelers safety, Troy Polamalu, was famous not only for his on-field abilities but also for his super long curly hair. He landed an endorsement deal with shampoo brand Head and Shoulders, and as a result, his hair got insured for a cool million bucks.[2]

While these insurance policies may sound silly, and perhaps were taken out to generate more publicity than protect against loss, they *do* fulfill the role of insurance. Pay a little money now as an insurance premium, so in case of something bad happening later (Ben's eyes uncrossing, Troy's hair falling out) we can get paid to cover the expected loss of income.

There are insurance policies for almost everything: livestock, bed bugs, even cold feet (in case you get left at the altar and still need to pay for the wedding). Insurance companies are businesses, too, and are ready to offer insurance policies priced so they'll make money. And that's their right. They're taking on the risk, so they should get some reward.

If an insurance company isn't making any money — if they're paying out more in claims than they're bringing in via premiums — they'll go out of business and won't be around to pay your claim when you need it. To ensure profitability, insurance companies have actuaries on staff, continuously eying the statistical risk of insurable events, which in turn inform the price of policies.

The task for us as consumers when it comes to buying insurance is to determine which events we really need coverage for, and buy the appropriate policies. While in the end we want every dollar we pay for insurance to be "wasted," we also want to make sure we're not throwing our money away on something we would never need or use.

There are a *lot* of types of insurance out there. Some of them are essential, and you need them. Others are garbage and you need to stay away from them. We will be thorough and get technical, but stay with us. Future you will thank today you for covering your/their rear with the proper insurance. Ready to learn? Here we go!

Insurance Dos

These types of insurance are the most helpful and essential. They're the policies that will keep your financial plan moving forward even when the worst happens.

Health Insurance

Gone are the days of visiting the town doc for some stitches and paying your bill with a chicken and a jar of jelly. For a myriad of reasons, healthcare costs aren't as simple as *Dr. Quinn, Medicine Woman* made them appear to be. In fact, they're out of control. A routine visit to the doctor can cost hundreds of dollars, a visit to the emergency room thousands, and a stay in the hospital can easily be six figures.

Health insurance is essential because one accident could rack up a bill large enough to wreck all your work and completely derail your financial progress, no matter where you are in your journey. For example, our second daughter found herself in the NICU for a month after birth. The hospital bill was well over $100,000, which would have been a major hardship for our family if we didn't have insurance.

Health sharing ministries are more common now than ever. These ministries are not insurance (there's no guarantee of coverage), and typically have more exceptions and limits on coverage than insurance policies, but for some families can be a great way to shift the risk of unexpected medical expenses if they cannot afford traditional insurance premiums and deductibles. If you are considering these, get the highest level of coverage offered, even if cheaper options are available.

You might have a feel for how often you and your family visit a doctor or specialist in a year, but you can never see expensive emergencies coming. You need a way to shift that ultra-expensive risk away from your family, and the right health coverage is the way to do it.

Auto Insurance

Auto insurance is a great idea not only because it's required by law, but because it's very unlikely you'll be able to cover all the costs associated with a wreck. State minimum coverages are simply not enough — if you end up in a serious accident, you'll find out the hard way just how minimum the coverage is.

There are three types of coverage your auto insurance policy should include:

1. **Liability** coverage kicks in to pay for the damages and injuries to other vehicles/property/people involved, if you are in an accident that is determined to be your fault.
2. **Comprehensive** coverage takes care of your car when it's damaged due to non-collision events, like weather, vandalism, or theft. It's not very expensive, and can really save you money and headaches if/when you need it.
3. **Collision** coverage kicks in to cover your car when, you guessed it, you're in a collision. In an accident that's deemed your fault, liability covers the *other people* in an accident, while collision insures *you*. It can also help cover your end of things if you're not at fault in case the other party is un- or under-insured.

Renters'/Homeowners'

Renters' insurance covers all your stuff inside the apartment (or condo, or rental house). Everything to do with the structure, HVAC system, and so on will be covered by the landlord's insurance policies on the building.

The main benefit of renters' insurance is that first one: personal property coverage. Imagine if there was a fire or your place was hit by a burglar. You'd need to replace your stuff — all of it in the fire, and probably the expensive stuff in the robbery. Renters' insurance is an easy — and cheap! — way to add a layer of protection between you and life's unexpected emergencies. Your policy may also include some liability coverage for accidents happening in your home, and coverage of some living expenses if your home becomes uninhabitable due to a covered event. And did I mention it was cheap? The typical policy costs about $15 a month. Definitely a no-brainer. Get it.

Now, if you're a homeowner, then Homeowners' Insurance (creative name, isn't it?) is for you. This covers both the house and what's in it. Take the example of a fire again. In an apartment, your renters' insurance covers the replacement of your stuff while your landlord's policy on the building covers the repairs to the building. When you own your home, your homeowner's policy does both. Like a good renters' policy, it typically also provides a certain level of personal liability protection as well.

While homeowners' insurance isn't required by law, if you have a mortgage, it's nearly guaranteed that your lender will require you to have it. Homeowners' insurance is pretty affordable: The typical policy comes in around $100/month.

Disability

Life insurance is a great tool that protects your family if you pass away unexpectedly, by replacing your role as financial provider (more on life insurance shortly). But death isn't the only way financially providing for your family can be compromised. Injury, illness, or disability can impact your ability to work, and with it, your ability to provide for your loved ones.

Disability insurance replaces a portion of your income when you're unable to work. There are two forms of disability insurance, short-term and long-term. Both replace your income, but there are a few differences, and we only recommend one of them.

Obviously, from their names, they cover you for different amounts of time. While each policy is different, typical short-term coverage will replace a portion of your income, typically 60–70 percent of your salary) for three to six months, while long-term coverage will replace 40–70 percent for years.

A short-term disability can certainly impact your life. However, a number of employers include short-term disability insurance in their compensation plans, and even if you don't have coverage through work, your Full Rainy Day Fund (we'll talk about that soon) should be able to cover you in the event of a short-term decrease in your earnings. Because of this, most people don't need to go out and buy short-term disability insurance.

Now, a long-term disability is different. If you were to get in a car crash tomorrow and be unable to work for a year while in rehabilitation, neither your Starter Rainy Day Fund nor your Full Rainy Day Fund would cut it, and your family would be left out in the cold. That's why we recommend long-term disability coverage. Policies can last anywhere from a few years all the way up to retirement age, depending on the policy.

ID Theft

This wouldn't have been on the list fifteen to twenty years ago. But with corporate hacks getting more and more common these days, the question of your personal info getting compromised is sadly more a question of when, not if. The resulting identity theft can not only wreck your credit and cost you money, it can also suck up your time trying to deal with it.

We recommend getting ID theft protection that will not only keep you proactively alerted but also help you clean up the mess. You may have ID theft protection included as part of your homeowner or auto policy, so check that first before seeking out a separate policy.

Long-Term Care

More than half of people 65 and older will need long-term care sometime in their lives — things like nursing homes and assisted living facilities, adult daycare, in-home care, and even home modifications and upgrades to make living at home possible.

Other types of insurance like health or disability don't cover long-term care needs, so you'll need specialized insurance to cover it. And with how much long-term care costs — a shared room in a nursing home is more than $89,000 a year and an in-home aide is over $51,000 a year — you'll likely want or need insurance to be able to handle the costs and get the care you need.

Long-term care insurance is a perfect example of getting the right insurance at the right time to shift risk away from you and your family. As you can probably guess, the likelihood of needing long-term care increases as you get older. Buy insurance when the risk is low, and the premium will be low. Buy insurance when the risk is high, and the insurance company will charge you a high premium since it's very likely you'll be using the insurance.

Now, if you buy a long-term care policy when you're young, you'll lock in a low rate, but you'll be paying it for a looong time before ever needing to use it. However, if you wait until you're seventy-five and are more likely than not to need care, your premiums will be sky-high. You need to time it right when it's early enough to get a good rate, but close enough to the window when you may need care to make paying the premium worth it. For most folks, that's going to be around your sixtieth birthday.

Umbrella Insurance

It's nice to have some coverage in place when a storm wind blows and turns your umbrella inside out, breaking it in the process, especially if it's one of those nice, big (and expensive) golf umbrellas.

No, umbrella insurance isn't really insurance for umbrellas (sorry umbrella fans!). It's a type of insurance policy that goes on top of your other policies, like an umbrella covers you in a storm. And like a real umbrella, you're always thankful to have it when a big storm comes.

You can consider umbrella insurance to be personal liability insurance that goes above and beyond your other policies, like homeowners' and auto. If an accident occurs on the road or at your house and someone is injured, you can be found liable for those injuries and be sued for medical bills and damages. Damages brought by a lawsuit are likely going to be greater than the liability insurance in your existing policies, so an umbrella policy kicks in at that point to take care of things.

Not everyone needs an umbrella policy, but you should consider it if you find yourself in situations where, if something bad happened, it could get costly — coaching youth sports, hosting guests in your home or property, owning rental properties, running a business, having a dog or other potentially dangerous pet.

You'll also be more likely to find an umbrella policy helpful if you have a net worth of over $500,000. Most policies start at $1,000,000 of coverage for a few hundred bucks a year. That's a good place to start, but don't forget to grow the size of your umbrella as your net worth climbs so it's big enough to cover everything.

Term Life

I saved the most important for last!

A more accurate name for life insurance might be death insurance, but that might make it a harder sell. The idea with life insurance is that the insurer pays out a monetary benefit to designated beneficiaries when the insured person dies. Life insurance is an essential tool for protecting your family.

There are a *lot* of different types of life insurance out there, and only one of them is worth your time and money. The rest are junk — and we'll get to those, but before we do, we need to talk about when and why you need life insurance.

Who needs life insurance? You do, if people are depending on you for their well-being and you not being around anymore would make things financially difficult. Simply put, if you have dependents, you need life insurance. If you don't have dependents, then you don't really need this type of insurance. While your loved ones would be devastated should they lose you, nobody would be left in financial ruin.

One of your roles as a parent is to provide for your family. You go to work and bring home the bacon. If you die, the bacon isn't going to bring itself home. You need to replace that part of how you provide for your family. Your life insurance benefit will provide your family with a replacement for your income. That's the goal of life insurance, to replace your money-making role in your family.

Imagine the (all-too-common) alternative: You pass unexpectedly, leaving your spouse and a handful of kids not only mourning your death but stressed and worried about how the mortgage will be paid, where grocery money's coming from, how they'll pay for college tuition. This is especially hard on a family when the surviving spouse is a stay-at-home parent. Now the whole family routine will be upended because he or she will need to leave the home and start earning an income. And all this has to begin right away after your passing, leaving precious little time for your family to process their grief.

In order to replace your income, your insurance policy should be ten to fifteen times your annual income. That amount will give your family a nice, big cushion to help them for *years* after you're gone. Invested well and spent responsibly, that amount should give your family a long runway to get things going again without you.

And life insurance isn't just for someone working outside the home. Let's imagine the above scenario but switched. Your stay-at-home spouse passes away, and now you're on your own trying to figure out how to take care of a handful of children — some of whom aren't even in school yet — take care of the housework, *and* manage to keep on top of your work. You're going to need to figure out childcare, schooling (especially if you were homeschooling!), running the household, and getting up to speed on all that as fast as possible. You'll likely need to turn to outside sources of help to cover everything your spouse was doing without pay! Where will you find the money to cover it all?

Remember the criterion for needing life insurance: Other people depend on you for their well-being and will be left in a tough spot (primarily financially) if you die. If you're a stay-at-home spouse, you need a life insurance policy. Your policy needs to be ten to fifteen times the amount needed to replace the financial value of everything you do for the family. How much will it cost for childcare, schooling, help cleaning the house, and the rest? Depending on your family's situation and the cost of living in your area, something in the $500,000–$750,000 is probably appropriate.

How long do you need life insurance?

Think about the job we're asking life insurance to do: replace your financial provider role for those who depend on you in the event of your untimely death (while they're still depending on you).

Most of the time, that means your kids, while they're still in your house. You'll need your life insurance to cover them for the first 18–22 years of their life. Once they're out of the house and on their own, they're not depending on you to provide for them financially. Also, if the kids have flown the coop, your spouse is most likely available to find a job and go to work if he or she wasn't already working. Keep in mind that as you progress through the Financial Phases and Money Milestones, you'll start building up wealth, making it possible to provide for your family even without life insurance.

All that is to say you don't need life insurance to last forever. You only need it to last as long as it's needed. Most folks need life insurance until their kids are out of the house. Depending on their ages and how much longer you may be growing your family, term life insurance with a 15–30-year term will do just fine.

Term life insurance is a life insurance policy that's good for a certain term. If you die during that time period, it pays out. If you live longer, it expires and you've lost some money (money you'll be happy to lose!) For instance, when we got married in our late twenties and got serious about our finances, we got life insurance with a 30-year term. We chose that length because we figured we may be having kids for the next decade and would need to be covered until they were 20-ish. If your family's done growing or your kids are older, a shorter policy may be a better fit for you.

Don't worry about term life insurance running out and not being covered. By that point, you'll either not have anyone vitally depending on you financially, or you'll have enough savings and investments to essentially "insure" yourself, or both.

Now, there *is* another type of life insurance that doesn't have an end date. However, those policies are garbage and are at the top of the list of insurance you don't need.

Insurance Don'ts

We've covered the insurance you need, but there are policies for *everything* out there. And while you probably won't be tempted to insure your hair like Head and Shoulders' policy on Troy Polamalu's locks, there are a number of terrible types of insurance that get peddled regularly. These are the insurance policies you just don't need. They are for situations you won't face enough to make it worth it, or for situations that are better served by other insurance solutions — or they're total trash. Hold your nose, here we go!

Whole Life Insurance

Life insurance is essential for most people (we covered it above), but that doesn't mean all life insurance is good insurance. The only life insurance policy you should ever get is a term life policy. The rest are junk, and that includes whole life.

The cornucopia of whole life insurance is full of different varieties, each with its own unique take on junky and expensive. An insurance agent may try to sell you things like whole life, universal life, permanent life, traditional whole life, variable universal life, and so on. If it's not *term life insurance*, don't buy it, no matter who's selling it.

Remember what we said about life insurance — you need it to take care of your loved ones and provide for them financially, in the event of your death while they are dependent upon you. If your kids have grown up and moved out, you don't need to provide for them anymore, and your spouse could easily return to work if they haven't already. And if you're retired or approaching retirement, your retirement savings will be in place to take care of your surviving spouse.

Your financial responsibility upon death is to make sure those who depend on you will be taken care of. That's the role of life insurance. Not to secure them a windfall; not to leave a huge inheritance. To take care of them. And that only really applies to a particular window of your life. Once that window passes, you don't need it. It exists only for a time — a term — and term insurance is the right (and essential) tool for doing it.

But boy do those insurance agents work hard selling whole life policies. Why is that? It starts with an "M" and it rhymes with honey. That's right — money! It makes them a lot of money. Whole life policies are more expensive than term policies. Those higher premiums and longer terms make the insurance companies more money, and it's not a stretch of the imagination to think they might reward their salesmen for selling more lucrative types of policies. In fact, insurance agents can make thousands in commissions selling a whole life policy, versus just a few hundred selling a term policy.

These policies are more expensive for a few reasons. For one, you're insuring yourself (if you keep up with the premium payments) for the rest of your life. Every whole life insurance policy that's held until death will pay out. If the insurance company is paying out more than they're taking in, they won't be around for long.

Of course, policies that lapse or are canceled before death contribute to the company's profits, but those statistics are hard to pin down. Curiously (or not!), life insurance companies aren't keen on sharing that information.

But what about "cash value"?

Another big reason these policies are more expensive is that they build so-called cash value inside the plan. Here's what the salesman will tell you: "Your whole life policy will not only cover you your whole life and give money to your loved ones when you die, but will build cash value during your lifetime!"

Now, who doesn't love cash? But here's the problem: That "cash value" isn't cash. The insurance company is charging you a higher premium than they need to, and is taking that money and investing it on your behalf. You're mixing insurance and saving/investments. It's like going to a barber for a haircut *and* a cake. Go to the barber for a haircut. Go to the baker for the cake.

Not only are you mixing insurance and saving/investing, but it's a bad investment! Because of fees and how the policy is structured, that "cash value" doesn't build up to anything meaningful for *years*. And here's the worst part, and why I've been putting "cash value" in quotes. It's not cash and it's not that valuable.

What can you do with your "cash value"? Take it out and spend it? Only as a loan that needs to be paid back. With interest. That's right, you're paying interest to the life insurance company for the privilege of taking out a loan of what's supposedly your own money.

But at least your loved ones will get the death benefit and the cash value when you die. It'll be like an extra boost to the policy, right? Nope! The only entity that gets the cash value when you die is the insurance company.

With a whole life policy, you pay for an insurance death benefit and a savings/investment account. But you can't have both. If you die, the insurance company keeps the cash value, and the only way to really get the cash value (that's not a loan!) is to cancel the policy, which means you don't have life insurance anymore.

So here's the deal with whole life: You're taking out a life insurance policy that's expensive, because it's designed to cover you longer than you need. On top of that, you pay even more to fund some terrible investments that build fake "cash value" that isn't cash nor is it of any real value to you. And if you end up paying these sky-high premiums *your whole life*, all that extra money you paid to build "cash value" is essentially buried in the ground with your body because nobody gets it but the insurance company. And the insurance agent will tell you it's a good idea because he'll make a *significantly higher* commission on it.

As financial expert and former CNBC host Suze Orman says, "Buy term, invest the difference!" We agree wholeheartedly. You're better off getting a term life policy for the time in your life you need it, and investing separately.

Children's Life Insurance

A quick quiz to see if you've been paying attention. (Yes, flipping back a few pages is allowed if needed.)

Q: When does someone need life insurance?

A: When the financial well-being of others depends on them.

Whose financial well-being depends on your child going to work and bringing home a paycheck? Nobody's — unless your kid is a wildly successful child actor. And even in that case, you could go to work yourself and take care of things.

Maybe you've seen the commercials designed to stir up fear in the hearts of new parents, and tell them they can "protect their children" and "give them a head start for pennies a day." Don't fall for it. It doesn't protect them from anything, and the only thing you're giving them a head start on is a junky, overpriced "investment."

When it comes to children, the only concrete financial impact upon their death is the cost of their funeral and burial. They have no outstanding debts. They don't have an income that needs to be replaced. While the emotional impact of losing a child is unrivaled, the financial impact is relatively minor and can be covered by your Full Rainy Day Fund. If you don't have that in place yet, you can add a rider[3] to your own term-life policy that covers all your kids for next to nothing each year.

Accidental Life Insurance

Whether people depend on you for their financial well-being does not change depending on how you die. If you die in an accident, your loved ones are not in any more need of financial stability. Your normal term life policy will take care of them, no matter how you die. You might get Accidental Life thrown in as a benefit at work, and that's fine, but you do not need to go out and get a policy for it.

Mortgage Life Insurance

This insurance policy will pay your mortgage if you die. The rates are high and usually fluctuate; the payout is restricted to paying your mortgage, instead of helping your beneficiaries as they see fit; and if you needed any more warning, it's usually sold using shady practices like sending new homeowners letters in the mail that look like vitally important official notices, designed to trick them into signing up. Steer clear of this one.

Extended Warranties

When you think about it, buying an extended warranty on a product (like a TV) is essentially an insurance policy. You're looking to shift the risk of repairing the item from you to the insurance company. The fact of the matter is that if your new TV/computer/electronic device is going to break because of a bad part, it'll probably break during the normal warranty. The low price of these extended warranties should clue you in to how infrequently the company has to pay out on them. Save yourself some money and skip the extended warranty.

Supplemental Health Insurance

Your regular health insurance should cover you just fine, and as far as lost wages or things like that go, your Rainy Day Fund (we'll talk about that next) is there to protect you. Remember: The point of insurance is to guard against financial costs that would be too much to bear without it. Your Rainy Day Fund is one of your forms of self-insurance against life. That, combined with normal health insurance, should be all you need.

Credit Card Insurance

Credit card insurance will pay your credit card payments if something happens — injury, disability, job loss, and so forth — and you can't. Typically, it will only pay the *minimum* payment, leaving you with plenty of debt when you come out on the other side. Other insurance policies like disability insurance and life insurance, not to mention your Rainy Day Fund, are there to take care of your bills during hard times. Really, the target market for credit card insurance is people who use their many credit cards a lot. But you're not going to be taking on new debt, and you'll be getting out of debt soon (that's Money Milestone number 6) if you're not already debt-free. Credit card insurance is a junky product and you just don't need it.

Pet Insurance

Let's say it together — you insure yourself against the catastrophic events that you would be unable to recover from financially. Your pet getting sick, injured, or needing grooming isn't one of those. Most pet insurance policies are riddled with fine print detailing limitations and exclusions that prevent them from being very useful: they don't cover cancer, breed-specific issues may be excluded, often there are maximum coverage amounts, and you have to pay the bill up front and then take on the insurance company yourself. If you own a pet, just save what you would've paid in pet insurance premiums every month, and pay out-of-pocket for whatever comes up. You'll save boatloads of money over your pet's lifetime.

Insurance — the *right* insurance — is an invaluable tool as you steward your finances and provide for your loved ones. Getting the right mix of insurance policies in place can provide peace, protection, and stability for you and your family even in the worst of times, and it can be affordable, too.

The Blessing Box

 Amanda

Insurance isn't the only way you can protect yourself in a time of loss or crisis. Where insurance protects your financial plan, your Blessing Box provides peace of mind for you and your loved ones in the event of an accident, illness, injury, or death. What in the world is a Blessing Box? Simply put, your Blessing Box is where you keep all relevant information for your life so others aren't burdened with hunting it down at the worst possible moment.

We already dove deep into the world of insurance, but policy information is only part of the box's contents — don't worry, we'll cover exactly what needs to be included shortly. The Blessing Box might not be the gift anyone really looks forward to giving or receiving, but it's truly an act of love for your family and friends in times of emergency or death. Grave sickness or the death of a loved one is hard, emotional, and trying. Having every bit of information your loved ones could possibly need to sort through easily in a Blessing Box is ultimately your gift to them. It provides them the space to process and grieve instead of throwing them into a chaotic frenzy searching for bank accounts, wills, insurance policies, and logins.

A few tips as you create your Blessing Box:

1. Your loved ones need to know where it's at and how to open it should they need to.
2. It should be well organized where your family could open it and literally find what they need in under a minute. Remember, they are likely grieving and stressed. The easier you make things, the better.
3. We recommend it all be contained inside a fire and waterproof lock box to keep it safe in case of a fire or flood.

You can get these in many sizes, shapes, and prices at almost any big box store or online.

OK, we know what a Blessing Box is and why you need one — let's talk about what it should contain:

1. **Introductory letter.** This is simply a letter introducing and showing your loved ones around your box. Provide the basic table of contents of what they'll find within.
2. **Financial accounts.** This is *any* type of account you have open with your name on it. Savings, checking, student loans, credit cards, investments, etc. This should include account names, approximate balances, and account numbers.
3. **Insurance policies**. Any insurance policy you have should be included. This includes type of insurance, who the policy is for, policy number, who the insurer is, and their contact information.
4. **Important documents.** Birth certificates, passports, car titles, house deeds, social security cards, and so forth.
5. **Letters to family and friends.** This is a chance to put a little bit of your own personal voice into the Blessing Box. You know your loved ones will be accessing this in the event of critical illness or death, so what final words would you want to leave? This box heavily leans toward your financial legacy, but what other legacies do you wish to impart to them? How do you want them to remember you?
6. **Trust, will, and estate plan.** Your Blessing Box should contain your will and any trust/estate plans as well as information for your Power of Attorney, Advance Healthcare Directive, a HIPAA release form, and attorney contact information.
7. **Funeral instructions**. We've already mentioned that the death of a loved one is hard and incredibly emo-

tional. Having to make all the logistical and hurried decisions that come with wake and funeral planning can drain your loved ones. List out all details and specifications for your funeral plans so your family can fulfill your wishes without having to deal with the stress of planning it all out. Married couples need one for each spouse.

8. **Monthly budget.** You need a copy of a typical monthly budget so your loved ones will know how to operate your household once you are gone. This will help them be aware of what bills and payments are due throughout the month so they can again focus on other things.

9. **Tax returns.** Many times you will have these in electronic files but in case you end up getting audited or end up having to amend a past return, your loved ones have the information ready and available to access. Include your accountant's contact information or login/ password for any tax software you've been using to file.

10. **Passwords.** It's hard for any of us to keep up with our own passwords, so imagine having to sift through the aftermath of a loved one passing on and leaving behind dozens of accounts that aren't accessible because no one knew the passwords. On a sheet of paper you need to list out all your login credentials with user IDs, passwords, pins, and lock combinations. If that sounds completely overwhelming, you can always provide the login details for a password manager such as BitWarden or LastPass.

11. **Important phone numbers**. The next-door neighbor, your doctor, your employer, babysitters you use, the pediatrician your kids see, the vet you take your dog to — you get the picture. Any relevant phone number and contact information needs to be provided. This is where you should also include the passcode to open your phone, in case they need to access your contacts list or any other relevant apps/data.

Whew! That's a whole lot of information you need to gather. But don't worry — this isn't something you need to create overnight. Nor is it something that needs to be Pinterest-worthy. Creating your Blessing Box will take time but it's time well spent as it provides you and your loved ones peace of mind in case of emergencies or death. Your Blessing Box rounds out the insurance chapter, as it protects what truly matters most.

Circling back to insurance, we're always evaluating insurance brokers and companies to help WalletWinners find the best policies at the best prices. **Use our free insurance policy checkup tool and find our latest recommendations at WalletWin.com/insurance.**

We also have a free printable checklist of what your Blessing Box needs and a few samples of physical boxes we recommend using. **Head on over to WalletWin.com/blessingbox to grab those when you're ready.**

Now that we've gotten insurance dos and don'ts out of the way, let's move on to establishing your Starter Rainy Day Fund.

CHAPTER 7

Starter Rainy Day Fund

"Precious treasure remains in a wise man's dwelling,
but a foolish man devours it."
— Proverbs 21:20

① Money Mindset ② Live with a Budget ③ Insure Yourself ④ **Starter Rainy Day Fund**

Establish Your
Financial Foundation

Amanda

Three months before our wedding, we were gearing up for a cross-country drive to move Jonathan from New York City to Champaign, Illinois. We made a pit stop at Jonathan's parents' house in Pennsylvania for a few days, and while there took the car into a mechanic for a quick look-see. Hours later we got a call reporting that the car had major mechanical problems that needed fixing before we could continue our drive — one being that the motor mount was damaged. The mechanic was sure that if we drove to Illinois as planned, the engine was going to leap out from under the hood and doom us to certain death.

We were scared for our lives, and our bank account. The repairs were estimated to cost around a thousand bucks, but we didn't have that much money between the two of us. After panicking, we called my dad who's been an auto mechanic for over thirty years. He agreed these were serious issues, but recommended a second opinion. We took the car to another nearby shop he vetted, told them about our travel plans, and asked for their recommendation.

A day later they called and said outside of a noisy belt and needing new brakes, they saw nothing wrong with the vehicle and we were fine to travel. When we went to pick the car up and pay for the belt and brakes, they told us there was no charge since we worked in ministry and were about to get married. We were blown away with gratitude. That second opinion allowed us to not only meet a generous mechanic and travel with confidence, but it also saved our bank account.

What Would You Do?

The situation could've ended very differently, all because we had literally no emergency savings and were stuck living paycheck to paycheck. As mentioned earlier, according to the Federal Reserve, 40 percent of American households can't afford a $400 emergency without leaning on debt, and 78 percent of households are living paycheck to paycheck. Based on the numbers, we were normal. But if being normal meant teetering on the edge of financial disaster and extreme stress, we wanted to be different, even though it would be a few months until we could articulate that desire.

What would you do if a couple of tires blew out tomorrow? Or your kid broke their leg and you hadn't met your deductible yet? Maybe you lose your job or experience a reduction in hours — all while needing to buy groceries, pay the mortgage or rent, and put gas in your car. If you're like most people, you slap the unexpected expenses on a credit card, cross your fingers, and hope for the best. I know that's what we would have done without knowing better.

But what if it didn't have to be that way? What if you could face an emergency and be financially prepared? Be merely inconvenienced instead of facing financial ruin? Well, you're in luck because that's exactly what we're discussing in this chapter.

The Problem with Change

Doesn't it seem uncanny that right when we're about to make a positive change in our lives, some seemingly random incident pops up and derails all our efforts before we've begun? Whether you're starting a new exercise routine and then you throw your back out mowing the lawn, or you're trying to establish a morning routine but suddenly all your children begin waking at 5:00 a.m. — when we're in those baby stages of transformation, we're vulnerable. It only takes the slightest disruption to completely unravel our hopeful aspirations and dreams of change. The same goes for transforming our finances.

This phenomenon, which you probably know as Murphy's Law, says that whatever can go wrong in any given situation will go wrong. While this way of thinking might seem pessimistic, considering what could go wrong actually sets you up for more success as you anticipate and create backup plans for potential problems. These redundancies help you maintain your hard-earned progress when things go sideways.

Emergencies will happen. Appendicitis, baseballs through windows, phones dropped in toilets, Taylor Swift finally hosting a concert in your area (joking on that last one … sorta), you get the picture. Emergencies aren't something you can control. They just happen. Being mentally and financially prepared for them is critical for crafting a strong money plan.

At the beginning of your personal financial transformation, motivation levels are high but competence is low. However, you don't know what you don't know quite yet, so you feel on top of the world and you're ready to become debt-free and begin building wealth ASAP. Psychologists call this the Dunning-Kruger Effect and it happens every time we learn new skills, habits, or begin a new venture.

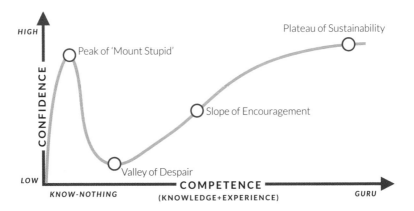

As you're getting started, you're excited to get different results and achieve your money goals. In order to protect your momentum, it's essential at this early and exposed stage to establish a Starter Rainy Day Fund. As you gain experience and inevitably come face to face with an emergency, these funds will save you as you sink into the valley of despair. Their mere existence will be the difference between the next emergency being a pothole in the road or the Grand Canyon.

What's a Starter Rainy Day Fund?

It's like an insurance policy for your financial transformation. When you don't have emergency savings, you're a sitting duck for unexpected expenses. Having a Starter Rainy Day Fund is like slipping an invisibility cloak over your bank account — because when you establish these funds, suddenly emergencies either disappear completely (thanks Murphy) or are easily taken care of and you can keep working your plan.

In the personal finance world, you'll often receive conflicting advice on what an initial emergency fund should look like. Some teach that all you need is $1,000 total as you get out of debt, as this amount covers most small possible emergencies while also lighting a fire under your tush to blaze out of debt and grow your savings on the other side. But this can leave you vulnerable to some of the larger emergencies that can occur, like a medical deductible.

Some will teach that you need six to twelve months of income saved, but this is a tall hurdle to ask people to clear early on. Again, 40 percent of households have less than $400 saved for emergencies. Saving a year's income doesn't provide early momentum, and ultimately backfires over the long haul as many are inclined to give up before reaching such a huge goal.

Weighing the numbers, and what we've observed in not only our lives but the lives of our WalletWinners, we recommend an initial Starter Rainy Day Fund of $1,000 that's easily available when needed. However, we've developed a way to craft a custom-tailored cushion that not only augments your Starter Rainy Day Fund, but also makes budgeting easier along the way. More on that in a later chapter. Here, we're focusing on the $1,000 Starter Rainy Day Fund.

Save It Quickly and Keep It Accessible

The first step is to save your $1,000 *quickly* and to place it in a separate bank account that is liquid but isn't linked to your everyday checking account. In financial speak, "liquid" means that it's easy to access — it flows quickly and easily, like liquid. For example, your everyday checking account is liquid, as you can interact with that money easily in real time. On the other hand, the money in a retirement account or in real estate is much more difficult to access, making those non-liquid assets. A high-yield checking, savings, or money market account, with debit card availability and without any fees, is the ideal home for your Starter Rainy Day Fund. Where might you find these mythical unicorns of the banking world? They can be hard to find and they're constantly changing, but we've got you covered. **If you visit WalletWin.com/banking we'll make sure to keep an updated list of the best options out there.**

We emphasize quickly because the faster you accomplish this step, the closer you are to getting your first big win. An early win makes your brain very happy, and so it wants to keep going after the next task to get another quick win. This is how smart money habits are built.

You can find these savings through a few different channels. You might look at your own budget and realize if you streamlined it for a month or two, you'd have $1,000 cash right there. Maybe you already have it available in your account, but never officially set it aside for this purpose. Or you might need to save this $1,000 through a more active approach: selling items you no longer need or use, picking up extra shifts at work, or trying your hand at various side hustles. The key here is going all in on saving this initial one grand and setting it aside, so you can swiftly move on to building financial momentum and completing more Money Milestones.

Now that we've established the *what* of a Starter Rainy Day Fund, let's play a little game — Name That Emergency! Try your hand at identifying which situations are emergencies and which are non-emergencies, but be careful — there are some tricky ones!

Emergency or Non-Emergency?

Mark each situation as an Emergency or Not an Emergency:

☐ ☐ Last minute invitation to go tubing with friends

☐ ☐ A screamin' good deal on roundtrip flights to Paris (you've ALWAYS wanted to visit)

☐ ☐ Impulse a Vitamix at Costco because "this deal only happens once a year"

☐ ☐ Black Friday TV deal

☐ ☐ Christmas presents for your children

☐ ☐ Family vacation

☐ ☐ Your 8-year old dog gets cancer and treatment costs $10K

☐ ☐ A down payment on a home

☐ ☐ Surgery to repair a broken arm

☐ ☐ Hot water heater died

☐ ☐ Flights to your grandfather's funeral

☐ ☐ Your vehicle's fuel pump went bad

☐ ☐ You overspent in a number of your budget categories but still want a fancy date night

☐ ☐ The baby stood on your laptop screen and then poured a LaCroix on the keys

☐ ☐ The toddler ate, broke, or used all of your makeup and you've got a business meeting

☐ ☐ You've lost your job but need to buy groceries

Answer Key

EMERGENCIES

Surgery to repair a broken arm

Hot water heater died

Flights to your grandfather's funeral

Your vehicle's fuel pump went bad

You've lost your job but need to buy groceries

NOT EMERGENCIES

Last minute invitation to go tubing with friends

A screamin' good deal on roundtrip flights to Paris
(you've ALWAYS wanted to visit)

Impulse a Vitamix at Costco because
"this deal only happens once a year"

Black Friday TV deal

Christmas presents for your children

Family vacation

A down payment on a home

You overspent in a number of your budget categories
but still want a fancy date night

GRAY AREA / PERSONAL DISCERNMENT

Your 8-year old dog gets cancer and treatment costs $10K

The baby stood on your laptop screen
and then poured a LaCroix on the keys

The toddler ate, broke, or used all of your makeup
and you've got a business meeting

It's important to get clear about what constitutes an emergency as you get started on your journey, lest you be tempted to rob your Starter Rainy Day Fund for something that wasn't an emergency after all. When stress rears its ugly head, one of the easiest go-to dopamine hits your brain will seek out is to spend money. When your brain is craving an impulse purchase, that is the time you do *not* want to be waffling on what's an emergency or not an emergency. It's kind of like going grocery shopping while hungry — you tend to not make great decisions under those circumstances. Same goes here.

Now some expenses, like surgery to repair a broken bone or buying flights to an immediate family member's funeral, are obviously unexpected events outside of your control. You can't plan for those types of expenses and thus, they fall under the actual emergency category.

On the other hand, a Black Friday TV deal is clearly not a need. It's a want, and it wouldn't ever qualify as an emergency. Nor would flights to Paris, or impulse-buying your way through Costco. Again, think, "If I had lost my job last week, would I still spend money on this?" If the answer is "no," it's not an emergency.

But what about those gray areas? It's relatively easy to answer most "Is this a need or a want?" questions. But there will inevitably be some gray areas that come up. In these situations it's important to remain flexible and open-minded about how to best approach the situation. Emergency or emergency-like situations pump up adrenaline production and put us into fight or flight mode. This is why we've personally created some rules in our household to safeguard ourselves in these gray times.

When $#*! Hits the fan

When our toddler stood on my laptop at the height of COVID quarantining in May 2020 and broke the screen beyond repair, the temptation in my cavewoman brain was, "*Must go buy computer at Apple Store immediately*!!" But we stayed calm and were committed to allowing space to come up with creative solutions. Within a few hours we discovered that I could plug the laptop into an external monitor and it still had perfect functionality. Whew! It looked like we didn't need to raid emergency savings after all — we could just take the next couple of months to save up for a new or new-to-me laptop. Sure, it was less convenient to have to work only in one spot in the house where the monitor was plugged in. But it was doable and actually a blessing in the end, since I could be more present to my family members in other parts of the house without my computer around to distract me.

However, when our toddler poured a full and opened LaCroix onto the laptop one week later (she was in that curious/destructive 18-month-old phase and being cooped up inside was NOT helping), it was gone. We attempted to dry the keypad using various means over the following day, but too much water had soaked too deeply into the computer and it wouldn't even turn on anymore.

The gray area shifted from an emergency we had initially avoided through creative solutions to an emergency with no viable alternative options. WalletWin is run entirely online, and I absolutely need a laptop in order to work, so the laptop had to be replaced. How we chose to replace it was another gray area, as we tried to delicately balance using the least amount of our emergency savings while fully taking care of the emergency. We looked into purchasing used, refurbished, or new laptops at various places and weighed the pros and cons alongside our technological needs at that moment and in the future. From that space, we were able to make the best choice for our family.

Point being, you want to be clear at the start of your journey on what constitutes an emergency. If you're married, this is essential for staying on the same team when these unexpected expenses pop up. You can't predict everything that will come your way. In those situations, it's important to have solid and objective questions to ask yourself, so you can make prudential decisions; questions like:

- "Is this a need or a want?"
- "If I lost my income, is this a purchase I would make?"
- "Is there a creative workaround or a way to minimize this expense?

- "Can I find a way to cash-flow this to avoid touching my emergency fund?"

Your Starter Rainy Day fund is one of the first concrete wins you'll have on your financial freedom journey. It's one of the most satisfying milestones to complete because once you're on the other side, you breathe easier at night. Not as easily as when you eventually become debt-free and have your Full Rainy Day Fund; but easier, as you've bought yourself time and options should an emergency rear its ugly head. You're no longer at the mercy of circumstance. Woohoo!

But wait, what happens if you need to *use* your Starter Rainy Day Fund? Knock on wood it doesn't happen; but if it does, you simply use it to cover what you need to. Then your priority goes to refilling it, before you move on to your next Money Milestone.

Once you've saved that $1,000, celebrate quickly and then move on, because there are big Wallet Wins waiting for you just around the corner.

CHAPTER 8

Get a Month Ahead

"A little sleep, a little slumber,
a little folding of the hands to rest,
and poverty will come upon you like a vagabond,
and want like an armed man."
— Proverbs 6:10–11

① Money Mindset ② Live with a Budget ③ Insure Yourself ④ Starter Rainy Day Fund ⑤ **Get a Month Ahead**

■ Establish Your
Financial Foundation

☛ *Jonathan*

Like the vast majority of Americans, when Amanda I started get-ting serious about our finances, we were living paycheck-to-pay-check. Money came in; money went out. When those two lined up, it was nice, but they weren't always in sync.

That made budgeting harder than it needed to be. On top of trying to figure out how much we'd get paid that month, and planning that spending across our categories, we also had to figure out when which bills would get paid. We had to determine which bills paycheck #1 would cover, and which would have to wait until paycheck #2. This added extra layers of stress and complexity to cultivating our new habit of budgeting.

One day while working through all the details, I sighed, "This would all be so much easier if we had all the money we needed for the month at the beginning of the month!" Oh well, we got paid twice a month and needed the money from the coming paycheck to cover bills.

But the idea of budgeting once a month stuck with me. If we had all that money we needed at the start of the month, we could just budget that money and be done with it. But our employer paid us twice a month, so there was no way to switch to monthly paydays — *or was there*?

In this chapter, we'll cover the benefits of switching from living paycheck to paycheck to having a month of money ready for a month of expenses (before the month even begins) and share the exact process we used to make to make the switch.

One Swing Ahead of the Sword

If you're one of the majority of Americans living paycheck-to-paycheck, you know the added stress of not only making sure you have enough to cover your bills, but making sure you have enough at the *right time.*

The money comes in, and the money goes out. This cycle can impact your finances in a few ways:

- Living paycheck-to-paycheck means you don't have a lot of flexibility with your money. You need money in your account because #bills. If you were feeling spontaneous and went on a shopping spree on payday, but didn't have any money available when the electric bill came a-knockin', the consequences would be dire.
- Similarly, if you're operating with little or no wiggle

room with your finances, it's a lot harder, if not impossible, to use your money to save for the future or to take advantage of money-saving opportunities. If all the money that comes in is already spoken for, it's nearly impossible to stock the deep freezer with ground beef when it's on sale, even if you could do it at half price. You simply don't have the money available to make it happen. If you spend it on thirty pounds of beef, you won't have money to pay the cell phone bill or the babysitter next week.

- Living paycheck-to-paycheck is stressful! You're Aladdin, always one step ahead of the next bill, one jump ahead of the next expense around the corner. If anything happens to jeopardize your income, everything is thrown into disarray. There's no flexibility, no margin of error, no runway to get back on your feet.
- And of course, you spend more time trying to figure out when things must be paid instead of simply paying them, because the bills and the paychecks don't always line up. And if you're budgeting your money as it comes in, you'll spend more time budgeting, because you'll constantly be adjusting and re-adjusting throughout the month instead of setting a budget and working it throughout the month.

It may seem that this paycheck-to-paycheck cycle is the only way. Maybe you've never known another way, or your paychecks are different every time, so you're always either guessing what will be there and adjusting along the way, or budgeting each payday so you know your numbers are accurate. You've accepted this painful cycle, even if it is causing you to go gray early. But it doesn't have to be like this.

Imagine: When it comes time to make your budget for the month, you know exactly how much money you have available to spend. When a bill comes, you have the money to pay it. You don't have to worry about timing. You enter each month with a whole month's worth of money ready to meet a month's worth of expenses.

If your income is irregular (as ours has been our entire marriage) this system allows you to eliminate the question of "How much do we have this month?" and can help you bring some predictability into your budgeting and spending.

The goal is that when the first of the month rolls around, you have 100 percent of the money you'll spend that month already in your bank account, waiting to be budgeted and spent. That transition alone eliminates so much stress.

And, if all this didn't sound good enough, you'll not only be getting off the paycheck-to-paycheck cycle, but you'll simultaneously be making that padding between you and emergencies a little thicker.

So, how the heck does it work? How do you make the transition?

Essentially, you'll build up a pool of money in your bank account (an app like YNAB makes this super easy) to get a month ahead. That might sound weird, but let's take a look at how it works.

Now, it might take you a little while to fill the pool the first time, but after that, it fills itself automatically every month. First, we'll look at that initial fill up, then we'll see how this system sustains itself for the long haul, and finally examine how this budget-smoothing pool of money also helps protect against emergencies.

Fill 'Er Up!

Out of each paycheck, you'll put some money aside into a budget category for this purpose. Each time you get paid, you build up the

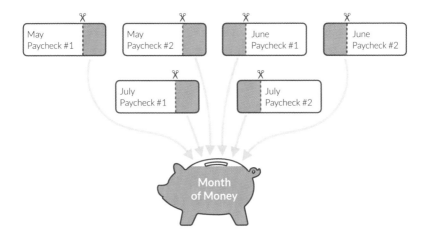

money inside your Month of Money piggy bank. If you're at this Money Milestone, *this* is your current financial goal, so put as much into this fund as you can to reach your goal quickly.

Paycheck by paycheck, your Month of Money will grow until it becomes the size of (you guessed it) one month of money. When it's full, you'll use it to fund a month of expenses right from the first of the month.

Let's address something psychological some people run into at this stage. For many, logging into their bank account can be a painful experience. They expect the balance to be low or for the money to be nearly gone by month's end. When you break the paycheck-to-paycheck cycle though, you will login and begin to see MONEY in your account at all times. You'll never login to see it at nearly zero or over-drafted, ever again. This requires a mindset shift. Those who've been "bank balance budgeters," who decide if they can make a purchase based on how much money is in their bank account, will need to build in protections against themselves in some cases so they don't sabotage and spend the money simply because it was there. Viewing these funds as your runway, peace protectors, and a buffer between you and life, is essential to staying ahead of your money.

Free Refills

Now, here's the part when the pool fills itself up every month.

Remember: You just "paid" yourself for the whole month. That means you don't need to touch any paychecks or income that come in during the month. If you just started May with a Month of Money, your May paychecks will just hang out in your bank account until you use them to fund all of June's spending. Just like that, you're a month ahead, every month.

A Little Extra Cushion

You might have gotten a little worried when we said you needed to have $1,000 in your Starter Rainy Day Fund. You feared that wouldn't be enough.

As we explained, we suggest $1,000 for your Starter Rainy Day Fund because it will be a good cushion between you and life, but it's not so thick a cushion that it'll take forever to build up. Also, you'll feel how thin it is when you stop and think about it, and that'll motivate you to get out of debt so you can build it up higher.

For those of you who think the $1,000 Starter Rainy Day Fund is a little *too* thin for your liking, the other benefit of getting ahead of your money like this is that it grows the amount of cash on hand you have at any moment, allowing you to take on slightly larger emergencies.

If an emergency comes up that's over $1,000 dollars, you also have your Month of Money — the paycheck(s) — just chilling, waiting for the new month, to help cover the emergency.

Your Month of Money plus your Starter Rainy Day Fund provide a custom-tailored cushion for emergencies that relate to your unique stage in life. Let's look at two examples:

- A single person, straight out of college, renting an apartment, is probably going to have smaller emergencies, as well as a smaller Month of Money they'll have on hand waiting for the new month. Perhaps in addition to their $1,000 Starter Rainy Day Fund, they have $2,800 in their Month of Money. Combined, they've got $3,800 if need be.
- A family with eight kids who lives in a house likely has a larger monthly budget, and when something (perhaps more expensive) happens, that larger Month of Money, alongside their Starter Rainy Day Fund, will cover it. In addition to their $1,000 Starter Rainy Day Fund, they have $8,500 in their Month of Money. Combined, they've got $9,500 if need be.

Emergencies aren't one-size-fits-all. Our approach offers unique protections for the varied states of life you might be in. What's great is you get this flexibility while still having that money *do* something for you — simplify your budgeting and spending — versus just having it sit around as a larger Starter Rainy Day Fund.

What Happens When an Emergency Comes Up?

Let's say you have a Starter Rainy Day Fund of $1,000 and you're one month ahead. You currently have $5,000 in Month of Money, for a total of $6,000. Your furnace goes out in the middle of February — you must get it fixed and fast. The repairs cost $2,500. What do you do?

Standing between the broken furnace and your financial plans are your Month of Money — with a total unique to you — and your $1,000 Starter Rainy Day Fund. The Starter Rainy Day Fund is the most fundamental block of your financial plan (it's also earlier in the Money Milestones). It is your last line of defense and should be protected when possible.

Let your Month of Money take the hit first, and pay for the furnace from those funds. You'll be left with a partial Month of Money of $2,500 (out of a needed $5,000), an intact $1,000 Starter Rainy Day Fund, a warm home, and not a penny of new debt.

To determine your next financial steps, consult the Financial Phases and Money Milestones (as always!).

You'll see that you are no longer a month ahead, so get back to work funding that Month of Money piggy bank. If you were working on a later milestone, like paying off debt, shift your attention away from that to your new, more fundamental goal. Now, if you're bummed to take your eye off that goal, you could decide to get creative and tap into Shark Mode (more on that in the next chapter) to build up your Month of Money and get back to the next Money Milestone.

Working with a month's worth of money at a time simplifies budgeting and makes working toward your goals easier, and simple and easy always help make you more successful. Amanda and I really felt the difference and made progress after we transitioned to budgeting a Month of Money at a time, and we're sure you will too.

Success Story
Macy Becker

My mindset before WalletWin was "Just make it to the next paycheck." I was constantly living in waiting, and had racked up so much debt on credit cards as a college student. I wasn't ever taught how to handle money, save, spend, or give.

Then I found out about WalletWin, and I wanted to break the cycle of spending above my means and using credit cards to make up the difference. I have been using WalletWin for a little over two years now and I am happy to say that as of November 14, 2020, I have paid off almost $10,000 of personal debt and got rid of all of my credit card debt! Next up, I am working on my student loans, and will hopefully be on track to pay those off and save up to pay cash for a car.

The financial freedom I have found in these past two years has been incredible. I never knew I could live well without having this debt hanging over me. WalletWin has been such a gift in my early young adult years. As I prepare for marriage and a family someday, I can do so knowing I have the skills to have financial peace and freedom to give generously.

Part III

Gain Momentum with Your Money

FINANCIAL PHASE 2

CHAPTER 9

Debt Payoff

"Owe no one anything, except to love one another."
— Romans 13:8

1 Money Mindset   2 Live with a Budget   3 Insure Yourself   4 Starter Rainy Day Fund   5 Get a Month Ahead   6 **Pay Off Debt**

▦ Establish Your Financial Foundation   ◠ Gain Momentum With Your Money

🐦 *Amanda*

On April 22, 2011, the day after Jonathan and I got engaged, we sat in my car chatting wedding details as it poured rain outside. We'd just hung up the phone with my childhood parish, locking our wedding date onto the calendar for exactly six months later, October 22, 2011 — the first-ever feast day of (then Blessed) Pope St. John Paul the Great. I'm not quite sure how the conversation turned, but the next thing I knew, we were talking about debt.

We hadn't discussed money in our relationship up until this

point, let alone how much debt we each were bringing with us. That was a mistake, and we were about to feel the repercussions of that in a big way. Naively, we thought that merging our money would be as simple as closing down separate bank accounts and having joint checking. We should've been working to get on the same financial page even while dating, through simple conversations about money habits, debt owed, and emotions around money.

But we hadn't.

Jonathan mentioned he had some student loans but didn't say how much … but then when he dropped the bomb on me that he had nearly $3,500 on a credit card he couldn't pay off, I nearly had a stroke.

I was raised in a household that didn't keep company with debt. My parents never had car payments or credit cards they couldn't immediately pay off. We weren't wealthy, but we lived comfortably within our means. Unfortunately, since student loans had become so indoctrinated into the culture, I did take some (we'll talk about that later), but credit card debt just wasn't something I was comfortable with.

I also had a great deal of shame around credit cards due to getting scammed into joining a multi-level marketing (MLM) business and taking on credit card debt when I was nineteen years old. While in college, I'd gotten tricked by a woman in her thirties into joining an MLM "to help my friend reach a sales goal" by putting $3,000 worth of makeup on a zero percent credit card for six months. The woman promised me she'd help me sell all my inventory in those six months — she even said I'd double my money since I was purchasing inventory at half off.

Well, you know the story. She met her recruitment and sales quota to hit the next level in her MLM, and ghosted me. My mom, aunts, and some friends had pity and purchased products, but two months later, my card balance still had about $2,300 on it with only four months to go until interest hit. Thinking about interest literally made me feel ill, so I went out and got two part-time jobs in order to pay the bill before it was due. Whew! I'd bootstrapped my way out of having to pay 18 percent interest on the credit card balance.

Now, hearing Jonathan admitting to a high balance that had been actively accruing 18 percent interest for a while? It triggered something deep inside of me. At that moment, I wasn't thinking rationally. I had more than that amount tucked aside in personal savings, so without thinking I transferred money to Jonathan and he paid off the credit card. I then had him promise to stop putting money on it again.

I thought I'd made everything right as rain, but little did I know, paying off his credit card bill like that was only a band-aid solution instead of a true fix.

As our wedding approached, many people gave us the advice to take a ten-day honeymoon and to spare no expense. Ten days felt like an awfully long time, but hey, other people said to do it, so we booked one of the nicest all-inclusive resorts in Mexico. We knew the price and had just enough money to pay for it, but we also had a lot of other wedding expenses coming up.

Someone suggested we open a new travel credit card with a generous cashback bonus, put the honeymoon on that, and pay it off over the next few months. Reluctantly we went with the plan since we had the money. But life began to happen, and we got sucked into the vortex of wedding planning and last-minute expenses we had never thought about. To be honest, I'd forgotten about the honeymoon even being charged to a credit card.

That is, until I got an email while on our honeymoon, stating that the bill was due in only two days.

Cue Amanda's panic-induced anxiety attack: honeymoon edition. I checked our bank accounts and there wasn't enough money inside them to pay the bill off. I was freaking out. "I am not a person who pays credit card interest" is what I kept saying over and over, shaming and wounding my new husband — who'd gotten caught in that cycle before. I called my dad, who had taken all the cash and checks given to us at our wedding, and I asked him to deposit them into my bank account that day. Mercifully he was able to, and the next day I paid off the credit card bill and closed the account, vowing never to get that close to the ledge again.

We proceeded to have a giant money fight on the honeymoon

— a fight that would have been prevented had we discussed our emotions around money, what money means to us, debt, how much debt, and how money was viewed by our families growing up. I'm not proud of the holier-than-thou stance I took when I demanded Jonathan provide financial details immediately upon returning home; but we did need to know what we were up against.

After finding all the logins and passwords and tracking down every last bit of information, we finally had the facts. Between credit cards and both our student loan balances, we were $25,000 in debt. The scarier number was that our combined take-home pay was only $2,900/mo., or $35,000/year. We were fundraising our income at the time, and it was obvious that we just weren't making enough money to make progress in any direction. Our debt was almost equal to a year of income … and if we didn't figure out how to manage our money, our lack of money would manage us.

Something had to change.

We started learning everything we could about personal finance. We decided that money wasn't going to be a source of division in our marriage; it was going to be a source of unity.

On January 1, 2012, married just over two months, we set out on our debt-free journey. We created a stretch goal of being able to get out in one year, and by golly, we were motivated to hit it. The first month we were able to knock out a couple of our smallest debts and it felt good! Just seeing our debt shift from a dozen or so creditors down to under ten was an incredible feeling. So we kept on hustling.

In late spring, we were comfortable budgeting our money and knowledgeable about how much we'd have per paycheck to toss at debt. But we were also getting antsy, because you can only cut so many expenses. We turned to the other side of the equation — boosting our income to accelerate progress. We began selling things we didn't use or need. When a gentleman came to buy Jonathan's bike, he eyed up the Super Nintendo and made an offer on it. I knew Jonathan was all in on becoming debt-free when he took the offer and parted ways with his beloved gaming system.

Eventually, we ran out of things to sell; so being in a college town as we were, Jonathan started looking in dumpsters to find the perfectly good items students were throwing away so he could resell them. He found a desk, a chair, a printer, lamps — you name it, he found it! And we sold it all on Craigslist for hundreds of extra dollars that month. By the end of May, we saw our debt drop below the $10,000 mark and we were jazzed.

During that time, we moved cross-country for work, so we sold off even more household goods, like furniture, and even sold my car since we'd be working at the same office in Denver and didn't need two vehicles. We lived simply over the summer and made fundraising appointments to work on getting a raise.

On August 15, 2012, the feast of the Assumption of Mary, we wrote our last check to Sallie Mae and closed the doors on debt. We celebrated by making homemade Debt-Free Doughnuts. We blew our original one-year stretch goal straight out of the water, and boy did it feel great!

It was tempting to view this as the finish line, but mentally we knew it was the starting line. There were far more financial decisions to make from that moment forward, but we'd experienced our first huge victory in watching our money work for us instead of someone else.

Why We Fought to Eliminate Debt

 Jonathan

As you just read, we worked *hard* to get out of debt. We sold things, said no to things, and got creative to pay off our debt in record time. We threw every available penny we had toward our goal of becoming debt-free.

But why? Why did we work so hard? Why was our "splurge" on my birthday Happy Hour 50-cent root beer floats at Sonic? Why didn't we listen to that voice telling us to live a little and take it easier?

We were 100 percent determined to eliminate all our debt as fast as possible because we clearly saw that debt was holding us back from living the life God intended for us. If we were stuck making debt payments for the rest of our lives, our income wouldn't be available to use for our family's priorities and goals. Being strapped down with debt would mean less flexibility and less availability to say "Yes" to whatever we might be called to do in life.

When we got married, we thought of all the fun and adventures we'd have together. The family we'd become and grow over time. As we thought about our future, debt payments were never a part of it. We had dreams, plans, hopes — and the only way they'd have a chance at becoming our reality was if we were debt-free.

Swiping Away Your Life

Debt of all kinds limits your freedom.

If you've ever been in debt, it's probably no mystery to you why the Bible says, "the borrower is the slave of the lender" (Prv 22:7). It stresses you out, steals your choices, and limits your freedom. Didn't Jesus come to set us free from slavery, and as such avoid falling into any form of slavery again? "Sure did," Paul writes in his letter to the Church in Galatia (see Gal 5:1).

Debt ties your money up in the past instead of letting it work for you in the present and for your future.

Read that again: Debt ties your money up in the past instead of letting it work for you in the present and for your future.

The past is past. It's over. It's gone. And so many people are still paying for it. But when you're busy paying for the past, you have less available to pay for your needs today, let alone preparing for and funding your future.

A 2020 study found that 42 percent of Americans carry credit card debt, and those who do owe, on average, $5,400. And it's not just due to overspending: Half of credit card debt is used for necessities like rent, utilities, and groceries.[1]

Carrying debt has dramatic effects on your life not only right now, but through the rest of your life. Over half (58 percent) of Americans say that debt has a moderate or substantial impact on their ability to achieve long-term financial security. Nearly a third have delayed saving for retirement, and 18 percent have delayed home buying.[2] We'll cover the importance of those steps in your financial journey — and how to handle them the right way — later in the book.

Debt traps you in the past and prevents your income from working for your present *or* future. It gives creditors permission to grab onto your income with their grubby meathooks and take it for their own.

And it's not just your money they take. It's your very life. Nearly 20 million Americans have delayed getting married because of their debt, and 94 million have delayed or are delaying having children because of their finances. When surveyed, 61 percent of Millennials have put off home buying because of their student loans and over a third have delayed starting a family![3] We've also had many friends who couldn't enter the seminary or religious life until they paid off their debts. These are *huge* life moments! It's the very stuff that makes up our lives, and people feel like they have to put it off because of debt!

Companies are getting rich off our debt. Credit is very lucrative — why do you think every store has its own credit card? Why does Amazon show you how much cheaper your order would be if you opened an Amazon credit card with them and got a signup bonus? It's not because they like giving away money! It's because they know you will (a) spend more and (b) inevitably come to a month when you don't pay it all off and owe interest (58 percent of credit cards used in the first quarter of 2020 did[4]).

What type of business would you say the Ford Motor Company is in? Selling cars and trucks? Partly. They also extend credit to dealerships to buy inventory and to customers when they take that inventory home. That's right, it's totally possible for a dealer *and* a customer to be in debt to Ford for the same car!

The plain fact of the matter is the average indebted American household carries over $26,000 of non-mortgage debt,[5] and it's ruining their lives.

Not All Debt Is Created Equal

When we work with our students, members, and coaching clients, and their debt, we put it all into one of two buckets: non-mortgage debt, and mortgage debt. But why is that?

Don't get us wrong: Eliminating debt of any kind is the end

goal. All debt keeps your income tied up and limits your choices. If you're paying down debt of any kind, you don't have that money available for anything else. However, a mortgage is a little different. Here's why:

- First off, it's going to be pretty dang hard for most folks to buy a house with cash. It's definitely possible, and it makes move-in day much simpler, but it's out of reach for most people (at least for your first home).
- A home also increases in value over time. Unless you buy during a housing bubble and sell during a recession, or only live in it for a short time, you'll almost certainly sell your home for more than you paid for it.
- And while interest rates aren't everything — more on that later in this chapter — mortgages usually have *very* low interest rates. So, with all that combined, getting into a home, even with a mortgage, is a wise financial move when taken at the right time. (We've got a whole chapter on that later.)

So, for the remainder of this chapter (and anywhere else in this book) when we talk about debt, we're talking about non-mortgage debt.

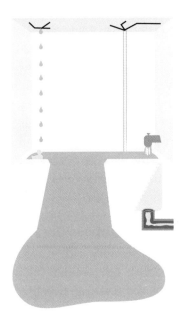

Knock, Knock! Anybody in There?

Join me for a second (metaphorically) in the bathroom.

Sorry it's such a mess in here! There's toothpaste on the counter, empty TP tubes on the floor, and the tub is overflowing onto the floor. I need your help. I need to drain the tub. I tried doing it myself, but couldn't get it. Now everything's getting wet and wrecked because of this tub issue. See, I pulled the plug to drain it, but it's draining pretty slowly. I don't think it helped much at all, actually. In fact I think the water's gotten *higher*!

What can I do? I need to get this tub drained because it's overflowing and ruining everything else!

The drain's clogged up with gunk? Yeah, that would make it drain pretty slowly.

And the roof is leaking into the tub, slowly adding more and more water? Yup.

What's that? The faucet's on! And it's filling the tub with water! I guess that needs turning off, doesn't it?

Let's pull back the curtain (eek!) on this metaphor and see what's happening.

Your tub is filling up with debt, and the effect of all those monthly payments is spilling out across your whole budget, ruining your chances at progress.

If you're not budgeting and getting intentional to clear the gunk from your spending, in order to accelerate debt payoff, then you can't drain your debt very quickly at all.

And when it comes to the water in your debt tub, your debt load grows in two ways:

1. The slow drip of interest accruing over time
2. The open faucet of new debt

You'll patch up the cracks in your ceiling one by one as you pay off your debts. There's not too much to worry about there. The more important thing to worry about — and the step you can take today — is turning off the faucet of new debt.

Think about it: If you saw a scene in your bathroom like mine, and your tub was overflowing (or about to), the first thing you'd do is run over to the faucet and turn off the water. It's the most obvious source of new overflow, and turning it off is the fastest, easiest action you can take to start fixing the problem.

If you have debt, you need to stop adding to your debt load.

If you want to get rid of your debt, the first, most immediate, easiest, and impactful step you can take is to turn off the faucet of new debt and vow: No new debt.

Say it with me: No. New. Debt.

NO NEW DEBT.

NO NEW DEBT!

NO! NEW! DEBT!

I got carried away a little bit there. But I'm totally serious about this point. You need to stop adding to your debt if you want any chance at getting out of the mess. In order to do that, you're going to have to get serious about planning — with a budget — how you'll use your money. You may need to get creative and find new ways to increase your income. But getting out of debt is totally possible, and you can do it.

When you're ready, **take the No New Debt Pledge at WalletWin. com/pledge**, print it, sign it, and hang it up somewhere you'll see it every day, like your bathroom mirror or your fridge. That piece of paper will serve as a reminder that you're taking a stand and changing your behavior so you can change your life.

Now that we've turned off the faucet of new debt, and cleaned the gunk from the drain with budgeting, let's drain it.

Do You Want to ~~Build a Snowman~~ Pay Your Debt Off?

Debt stinks, and it's best to pay it off as fast as possible and move on with your life. But how should you go about doing that?

A quick Google search can easily confuse you with a flurry of different debt payoff strategies, often with snow-related names. No matter the method, the fundamentals are the same. To make progress draining the tub, you need to make payments that are greater than the interest dripping into it. But which loans should you pay first? How many should you pay at a time? Does technique matter? Is there a strategy to it that will help you?

Let's discuss some of the most popular strategies you'll find out there, including the one that works with the way your brain is wired and is proven to be the best option.

The Flurry Method

One method of debt repayment is to take your debt repayment money each month and spread it across all your debts, making small progress on everything.

No bones about it: This method is terrible. The problem is that it spreads out your impact across all your debts, so in the end, you don't really feel like you've made any progress. All your hard work finding ways to cut back and increasing your income seems to be for naught. Eventually, you will abandon this method and go back to your old ways.

In order to make real progress paying off debt, you need to focus your energy (and funds) mostly on one debt at a time.

There are two main strategies that deal with paying off debt one loan at a time. Let's take a look.

The Debt Avalanche Method

This alpine-themed strategy has you order your loans by **interest rate**, and pay them off one by one, in order from highest interest rate to lowest. The idea is that by working to patch the largest cracks in the ceiling first, you'll have less water leaking into the tub, and in the end, have to drain less water overall.

This method seems like it would make sense, doesn't it? If your loans accrue interest every month, you should work to get rid of the ones that accrue the most interest first. If you do that, you pay off your debt faster and pay less overall.

That's the way it works — if you're a robot.

For the Avalanche Method to "work" best, you need to be a 100 percent rational being that is driven by numbers, data, cold, hard facts, and mathematics. Yes, if you pay off debt in interest rate order, you will save some money on interest and get out of debt sooner. But that's assuming that you have the same level of motivation and dedication to working your plan as on other methods, *and* that you end up paying the same amount each month as you would on other methods.

As behavioral scientists and economists find in study after study, we humans act like anything but rational beings. We don't always make the most straightforward decision. We often make choices — that extra doughnut, watching one more episode on Netflix, most hats — that turn out to be mistakes. These choices were *not* in our best interest. Why? Because we are moved by much more than cold, hard facts and figures. We are human, and are driven by a complex web of knowledge, emotions, and neurochemicals.

Thankfully, one debt payoff strategy takes advantage of it all.

The Debt Snowball A.K.A. Stack and Attack Method

The Avalanche had you list your debts by interest rate, with the largest on the top of the list. This method has you order your debts by **account balance**, from smallest to largest. You then pay off your debt in that order, paying off the smaller debts, working your way up to the larger ones.

This method is commonly referred to as the Snowball Method, or as Dave Ramsey has made famous, the Debt Snowball. It gets this name because as you pick off smaller debts, you add their minimum payment to what you now can pay toward your bigger debt. The amount you pay to your bigger debt gets larger over time, like a snowball rolling down a mountain. Instead of calling it the Debt Snowball, we call it the Stack and Attack Method. Here's why.

The snowball rolling down a mountain image works, and it *does* do a good job illustrating how you pick up momentum as you go along, wiping out all debt that stands in your way. However, it's a passive image. You set the ball rolling, and as it goes down the mountain it picks up weight and speed on its own. We want to emphasize your active participation in wiping out debt. We want to encourage you to get in the trenches, get dirty, and get free. We want you to understand you are at battle with your debt, and you will be victorious. We want you to *attack* your debt with tenacity and determination.

How Stack and Attack Works

Step 1 — Figure Out How Much You Owe

Before you can list your debts in order, you need to know what your debts are. Figure out who you owe and how much you owe them. You might need to sift through some paperwork, call the numbers on the backs of all your cards, and look up balances online, but this step is essential. You need to know what the mess looks like before you can clean it up.

I know this part might be scary. It might surprise you to see just how much you owe, all added up like that. But that's one of the tricks the debt industry, particularly credit cards, play on you. The further removed you are from real money (i.e., cash) — the more it's just numbers on a screen, or better yet for them, just a swipe with disregard for the amount — the more likely you are to spend. And you're likely to spend more.

You may also find it helpful to take note not only of who you owe, and how much you owe them, but also *why* you owe them. You owe Ford $32,454.98 for that truck you bought. You owe Target $2,582.11 for mindless shopping trips and retail therapy. You owe $942.07 to the repair shop because you were in a hurry, didn't look as you were pulling out, and hit a pole. You owe Navient $98,492.74 because you chose the private school halfway across the country versus the state school an hour away, since you didn't really know the difference in cost (or have the tools in hand to evaluate that financial decision) when you signed up. Knowing the reasons for your debt can help you connect your spending to real-life decisions and motivate you to work hard to pay it off.

When you see your numbers and reasons, you might experience any number of emotions. You might be surprised at the amount, never realizing your true financial situation. You might feel stupid or dumb for getting yourself into such a mess. You may feel overwhelmed, anxious, or despairing at the very thought of trying to pay it all back.

We've seen a lot of financial messes. And we've seen a lot of people clean them up. You are *not* too far gone. You are *not* too far in debt. You are not a failure, a lost cause, a screw-up, or too late to get started. Those responsible for teaching you about finances may have shortchanged you, you may have lost your way a little bit in the past, your credit score (more on that later) may be screwed up right now, and you might be getting started on this later than you or the numbers would have liked; but you're doing something about it now.

You are taking the responsibility to learn about money and try something different. You are finding the right way, *and* taking it. Your right actions will be reflected in your accounts soon. And you are just getting started. Yes, it would have been better to start five years ago. But it also would have been worse to get started five years from now. You are getting to work at the soonest possible moment: now. And all this is something to feel good about. We've done it. We've helped others do it. And we're looking forward to seeing you do it, too.

Step 2 — Stack 'Em Up

Now that you know who you owe and how much you owe, stack up your debts in order of account balance. Pay no attention to interest rate (we'll tell you why in a minute). Just put the smallest loan at the top of the list, and the largest on the bottom, like a big ol' pyramid of debt nastiness.

Step 3 — ATTACK!

Now it's time to go for the jugular. Here's how you're going to wipe these suckers out and have a bathroom that'll make the cover of *Real Simple.*

1. **Determine how much you have available to pay toward debt this month.** When you make your budget, Debt Payoff or Stack and Attack or Kissing Debt Goodbye needs to be one of your budget categories. Work your budget to make this category as fat and juicy as possible. The more you have in this category, the faster you'll knock out debt.

2. **Pro tip: Attack your debts as early in the month as possible.** If you wait until the end of the month, you'll be tempted (and perhaps give in) to whittling down that Debt Payoff category in favor of padding others as the month goes on. You'll not only be stunting your

self-discipline, but also robbing from your debt payoff, keeping you in debt longer. Use that money to deliver a right hook straight to Chase Bank's kisser at the beginning of the month, and you'll make sure you find ways to make the budget work as the month goes on.

3. **Pay minimum payments on everything.** This keeps you out of collections and keeps everybody off your back. Figure out your minimum payment for all your loans except your smallest one. Pay those amounts and move on. You've got fighting to do.

4. **Close your fists, clench your jaw, gird your loins, and deliver a solid uppercut to your debt.** The money you have left over after paying your minimum payments is your attack money. Take that attack money and throw it all at your smallest debt. If you have the option, apply the extra to your principal instead of your interest.

5. **Repeat this process, every month, until you're debt-free.** Be consistent, and you will see progress. Keep it up and pay it down!

6. **Celebrate your success with some Debt-Free Doughnuts!** The day we were debt-free, we were so jazzed we made doughnuts. That's right, we made doughnuts! And they were delicious! Now, every year on August 15, we have doughnuts. Some years, we make them. Others, we go to a doughnut shop. But they always taste better on that day than any other day all year. It's important to celebrate completing this Money Milestone — so if doughnuts aren't your thing (if that's possible) find something else you can do to celebrate all your hard work.

Why the Stack and Attack Method Works

Stack and Attack isn't the best debt payoff strategy just because we say it is. It's the best debt payoff strategy because it keeps you motivated to pay off debt, which gets you out of debt and does it faster.

It's the exact same method we used to eliminate all our debt. It's the method we watch our students, members, and coaching clients use to pay off their debt.

Stack and Attack isn't just "proven" by our experience. It's backed up by real-deal social scientists, time and time again. This method is proven to get people out of debt faster than any other.

In 2012, Northwestern University's Kellogg School of Management found that "people with large credit-card balances are more likely to pay down their entire debt if they focus first on paying off the cards with the smallest balances — even if that approach doesn't make the best economic sense."[6] And they admit that while the Stack and Attack Method is "suboptimal," the prevailing psychological advantages that the Stack and Attack Method provides through quick wins keep you working at getting out of debt, and ultimately reaching your goal. This happens because people are more motivated by knocking a debt account off their list than by making progress against the overall debt amount. Crossing a name off the list of "people I owe money to" is a more powerful motivator than saving a few bucks on interest.

A 2011 study from the University of Michigan found that participants displayed a natural "debt account aversion," choosing to pay off smaller loans instead of those with higher interest.[7] It admits that while the debt account aversion and methods like Stack and Attack may produce "nonoptimal behavior," that natural aversion to debt accounts keeps people working their plan to pay off debt. Stack and Attack may also provide other, non-financial benefits, like simplicity from managing fewer accounts, and may keep people motivated to use their money to pay off debt instead of extra spending.

And a 2016 study from the Harvard Business Review found that people who worked to pay their debt one loan at a time were more successful than those spreading payments across multiple accounts.[8] Paying debts one at time helped people work harder to pay more off, feel more motivated, and ultimately succeed in paying off their debt.

But *why*?! Why is it that seemingly going *against* the math would result in more successful debt payoff? Why does this method work better for us irrational humans?

This is Your Brain. This is Your Brain Using Stack and Attack.

Here's why it works so well:

Paying off a debt lights up your brain like it's the Fourth of July with positive, habit-building neurochemicals like dopamine. Paying off a debt — crossing off a name from your "people I owe money to" list — feels good. *Really good*. So good, you want to do it again.

After paying off a debt, you want to do whatever you can to pay off another and feel that way again. That makes it easier to make wise financial decisions — saying no to the guac at Chipotle, packing your lunch instead of going out, using free Spotify instead of premium — and frees up more money to throw at debt, which accelerates your progress toward paying off a debt, which makes you feel good, which makes you want to do it again, which makes you find more money for attacking debt, which makes you make faster progress, which … well, you get the idea.

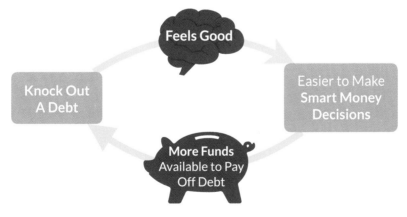

As you pay off debt, the amount of debt payoff money you're using on minimum payments decreases (fewer loans to make payments on), which grows your Attack Money over time, making your punch bigger and stronger as you go up against bigger debts, making it possible to continue seeing progress, even as the loans you're facing are larger.

And that's assuming your initial Debt Payoff amount in your budget stays the same. In our experience, and seeing that of our students, members, and coaching clients, thanks to the process diagrammed and described above, motivation only increases as time goes on. You become more motivated to get creative and find new ways to throw more at debt each and every month.

Other methods like the Avalanche Method don't produce these quick wins as reliably, and these quick wins can mean the difference between actually getting out of debt and staying stuck in endless payments the rest of your life.

#SharkMode

We want you to *attack* your debt with tenacity. You may have heard that when getting out of debt, you need to be intense like a gazelle. This image has its roots in the Bible. In the Book of Proverbs, it says:

> Give your eyes no sleep
>   and your eyelids no slumber;
> save yourself like a gazelle from the hunter,
>   like a bird from the hand of the fowler. (Proverbs
>   6:4–5)

It's a great image. And I'm not going to argue with the Bible. But let's dive in a little more. Save yourself "like a gazelle from the hunter" — who hunts gazelles (besides Teddy Roosevelt[9])? Cheetahs! You know, the fastest land animal in the whole world?

Gazelles flee from the hunter because they are literally running *for their lives.* They can escape the cheetah the vast majority of the time for two reasons:

1. They cut and corner and outmaneuver the cheetah.
2. A cheetah can only run so fast for so long. They tire out, and their prey escapes.

You're going to have to get creative to outmaneuver your debt. And you need to keep it up. You are going to outlast your debt. You are going to win. Remember: You are going to attack your debt with tenacity.

Like Amanda's legendary high school chemistry teacher/soccer coach Mr. Harris would say, "Get after that ball like sharks on a baby seal!"

We don't want you to be a gazelle, running away from a cheetah trying to eat you. You were prey in the past; now *you* are the one attacking the debt. You are the hunter, and you've got your debt in your sights.

Think of yourself as a shark eating a seal. You burst up through the surface of the water and even catch a little air as you chomp your prey in your jaws.

What does #SharkMode even mean? It's an intense picture, but it's more than just something to get you pumped up. Shark Mode is you taking every opportunity to put more toward paying off your debt. It's pedal to the metal. When I dug stuff out of the dumpster and sold it on Craigslist? Shark Mode. When I made the on-the-spot decision to sell my Super Nintendo and say goodbye to Mario Kart so I could pay off debt faster? Shark Mode. When you take on a side hustle and start bringing home extra income and throwing it at debt? Shark Mode.

Even if it's a few dollars here, a few dollars there, the money adds up. A shark's sense of smell is hundreds of times stronger than ours — some can smell blood that's up to a quarter mile away. When you're in shark mode, you can sniff out ways to increase your Attack Money like nobody's business. You save a few bucks, and throw it at debt. One bite at a time, and the debt is gone.

Shark Mode is especially appropriate when working hard to get out of debt, but you can tap into Shark Mode whenever you're chasing after a financial goal and want to get there as fast as possible. That said, you were not created to live in Shark Mode your whole life. Your resolve and commitment to healthy financial living will start to run down if you're in Shark Mode too long. Simply put: Use Shark Mode whenever you want to hit turbo on meeting your financial goals, but just don't try to go Shark Mode forever.

Making the Odds Be Ever in Your Favor

 Amanda

Oftentimes people get excited about becoming debt-free. They go all in. They strip everything from their budget to the point of deprivation and pay off loads of debt fast. But then life happens, and because old joys, comforts, and coping mechanisms have been removed from the budget, they snap and go on a spending binge, landing them back where they started or even deeper in debt. But wait, didn't Jonathan and I go #SharkMode and strip our budget down and pay off debt fast? Yes, but we didn't live in a deprived state, and that makes all the difference.

One way our method differs from popular financial advice is that we want you to love your life no matter what Money Milestone you're working on. Too often you'll hear the advice to cut, cut, and cut more out of your budget — all in the name of being able to get out of debt faster and get onto the life you'll love — later. But what if it didn't have to be that way? What if you could become debt-free without deprivation? To pay off all your debt and build your emergency savings while living a full, fun, and rich life?

Now, I didn't say you had to spend a lot of money or sacrifice your debt-free goals to make this possible. But it does take some creative thinking and willingness to do things differently — which

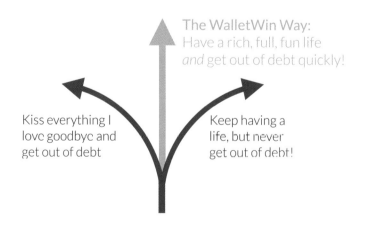

The WalletWin Way:
Have a rich, full, fun life *and* get out of debt quickly!

Kiss everything I love goodbye and get out of debt

Keep having a life, but never get out of debt!

happen to be our specialty. When life brings us to those fork-in-the-road moments with seemingly two possible paths forward, it's a good moment to stop and ask ourselves questions. Let's use getting out of debt as an example.

While standing at the fork in the road, the assumption is that you've got two routes you can take. Either you can pursue freedom from debt by eliminating *everything* from your budget that you don't absolutely need so you can pay off debt (rice and beans, anyone?), while hating your life in the meantime. Or, you can keep living it up and sacrifice nothing, while hating the debt you can't seem to get rid of.

When faced with two bad options, we like to look for the third way. We ask ourselves, "How can we make our dreams possible?" even though the paths forward seem diametrically opposed to one another. When it came to pursuing debt-freedom, we decided we wanted both. We wanted to aggressively knock out debt at a record pace. We also wanted to live life to the full. We were unwilling to spend our first year of marriage as exhausted, isolated penny-pinchers. But we didn't know anyone talking about living a rich, fun, and full life even in the midst of paying off debt … so naturally, we carved our own path forward.

While I could tell you hundreds of stories of how we did just that, one perfectly encapsulates our strategy.

In the winter of 2011/2012, *The Hunger Games* was all the rage. Jonathan read the books first and told me I had to read them too. Little did he know that meant I would spend an entire weekend locked in our bedroom reading! After reading the trilogy, we were excited to see the first movie coming out in March 2012. But wait, we were gunning to get out of debt ASAP, and seeing a movie in theaters would cost a cool $20 — if we did it up right with popcorn and candy, now we're talking $40! That was just too high a price to pay while blazing our way through debt, so we asked ourselves, "How can we see the movie without it costing us anything?"

We did some research and learned that the local movie theater had a rewards program. For every dollar you spent, you earned rewards that you could then use on anything — movie tickets, popcorn, candy, you name it! Now, in order to earn enough points to cover our tickets, we needed to find a dozen friends to go to the movies with us.

In a college town, it wasn't that hard to round up a dozen pals for a movie night. We kindly offered to buy everyone's tickets in advance before they sold out (see what we did there?) and were promptly paid back. On opening night of *The Hunger Games*, we walked in and used our points to pay for our personal tickets, and then as a thank you to our friends, we used more points to buy a couple of popcorns, some candy, and a few sodas to pass around (with individual straws, don't worry). It was an awesome night out. Not only did we have fun, but we also didn't have to sacrifice one bit of our debt pay-off goal to make it happen.

The third way was born. No longer was it a matter of this or that. The question we asked ourselves in every situation was "How?". And when you commit to asking *that* question, your brain opens up, expands, and can think of creative solutions forward. What started as a fun practice to help us live a full life while paying down debt, has now become a habit that's allowed us to accomplish a whole lot in a relatively short time.

But Don't I Need a Credit Card for ... ?

➤ *Jonathan*

"All this talk about no new debt is great, Jonathan and Amanda, but what about life in the real world? How am I supposed to get a hotel room, rent a car, maintain a credit score, or get a mortgage without credit cards?"

Yes, we've heard that before. I even said it myself at the beginning of our journey. This idea that you *need* a credit card to have any sort of a normal life is exactly what credit card companies want you to think.

While it can certainly provide more options and make things easier, you do not *need* a credit card in order to rent a car or book a hotel room. Do these companies prefer if you do? Sure — running up a charge on a credit card is an easy way for them to have a guaranteed form of payment if their property is unexpectedly damaged.

When it's a credit card, it doesn't matter if you don't have the money; they get paid by the credit card company, and now it's the credit card company's problem (yours, really) making sure you pay them back.

As much as hotel and rental car companies prefer having a credit card on file with them, what they prefer more is making money, so most have policies in place for serving customers who don't have a credit card.

Most hotels will allow you to book with a debit card and have a debit card on file for incidentals. The only catch is that they usually put a hold on your card, essentially calling dibs on a certain amount of money in your account in case they need to charge you for something later. If you don't go all Mötley Crüe and trash your room, the hold will expire and along with it, their dibs on your money. Most rental car companies do the same thing. These holds can be a few hundred dollars, and while the hotel or rental car company has dibs on your money, it can't be used for anything else. If your budget is tight, this *can* cause some problems. If you're looking to use your debit card like this, always call ahead and ask about the policies for that particular hotel or rental car location.

As far as getting a mortgage is concerned, yes, a "standard" credit history and high credit score will make the process easier and get you a low rate, but it's not impossible without it. If you don't have a credit score, you'd need to find a lender who will do a little more underwriting work, a.k.a. checking you out. A history of paying bills like rent and utilities, as well as steady employment and income are signs a lender can use to determine how risky (or not) giving you a mortgage is. We'll share more specifically about how your credit score can impact your mortgage qualification in a few chapters.

At the end of the day, no, you don't need a credit card. But you also don't need to feel like you're wearing a Scarlet Letter if you happen to have one — *if* you only charge expenses you've already budgeted for *and* you pay it off in full every month. If you aren't doing those two things, you're better off without 'em.

Credit cards are polarizing in the world of personal finance. Most experts land on the extremes — credit card rewards are either the be all end all, or credit cards are from the Devil. We don't fall into either of these camps, but we do have hesitations. There are responsible *and* foolish ways to use credit cards. There are pros (cashback or travel insurance) and cons (high interest or fees). Awareness and smart financial habits are key to using credit cards responsibly.

Speaking of awareness: Did you know that consumers spend more when they pull out the plastic?[10] How much more? According to one study, people spent up to 100 percent *more* when swiping their credit card opposed to paying in cash. Yowsers! While not every charge will be twice as expensive, most will be higher than had you used a debit card or cash. Every degree farther from spending cold, hard cash poses this risk, credit cards being the riskiest. And don't forget that over half of credit cards that carry a balance at the end of the month trigger interest payments. With the average credit card interest rate being 16.15 percent,[11] you can see how even the most lucrative "rewards" can end up being a net zero or a negative when you add up the overspending and charges. Factoring in the time you spent trying to keep everything organized … now the rewards aren't looking so lucrative. A well-paying side hustle easily could have been more profitable.

Credit cards aren't a sure path to financial peace … in fact, statistically, they're a stumbling block. For this reason, we don't teach them as a strategy … we teach the Financial Phases and Money Milestones because those will get you to your end goal *every time*.

Now that we've detailed how to blaze your way out of debt, are you picturing what life can look like on the other side? It's a pretty fun exercise to practice! Take a few minutes to consider how you'll spend, save, or give your money once it isn't being whisked out the door to Sallie Mae or Chase every month.

Once you're debt free, so much changes, but you're still vulnerable. While you've cut ties with debt, you're still at risk from the larger (and thankfully rarer) emergencies life can throw your way. Turn your eyes swiftly to beefing up and completing your Rainy Day Fund in the next Money Milestone — which is exactly where we're heading.

Success Story
Paolo and Liz Machado

Growing up, I was extremely fortunate that my parents took care of all things finance for my siblings and me — undergraduate education, living expenses, everything. Unfortunately, this set me up for some major failure when I moved to the San Francisco Bay Area — one of the most expensive areas in the US — with student loans and a desire for the newest iPhone. Before too long, I had gotten into credit card debt. When I met my now-husband Paolo, I was finally starting to learn about managing my finances and getting out of debt.

Due to a few crazy circumstances, including a long-distance engagement, we got married pretty quickly and put our wedding on a credit card. So by the time our first daughter was born, we were in about $85,000 of cumulative debt.

I started following Amanda and Jonathan and WalletWin in earnest while on maternity leave. Paolo and I both watched the videos and started budgeting — our biggest "Win" from those days was when we didn't need to put our groceries on a credit card. We were on a single income and did some crazy things to get out of debt, including living in a single room with two kids while the other room in our tiny San Francisco apartment was given to our au pair (God bless her!) for nearly two years.

By the time our son was born (our third child), four years into our marriage, we were debt-free and had made some big financial decisions with the help of Amanda and Jonathan's constant cheerfulness and outreach. Amanda, I remember, was so generous in her time and advice when we were about to pull the trigger on buying a home that would have saddled us with a 30-year mortgage and unsustainable monthly payment. Needless to say, we dodged a bullet! Now, five years into our marriage, we are slowly saving a decent down payment and budgeting, some months more successfully than others. We cannot thank Amanda and Jonathan enough for being the attainable example we really needed, and continue to look to them for encouragement and guidance.

CHAPTER 10

Full Rainy Day Fund

"Go to the ant, O sluggard;
consider her ways, and be wise.
Without having any chief,
officer or ruler,
she prepares her food in summer,
and gathers her sustenance in harvest."
— Proverbs 6:6–8

① Money Mindset ② Live with a Budget ③ Insure Yourself ④ Starter Rainy Day Fund ⑤ Get a Month Ahead ⑥ Pay Off Debt ⑦ **Full Rainy Day Fund**

▰▰▰▰ Establish Your
▰▰▰▰ Financial Foundation

Gain Momentum
With Your Money

🏴 *Amanda*

When we lived in Denver, I used to drive up a literal mountain every Friday afternoon to join Jonathan for daily Mass and lunch at the FOCUS (Fellowship of Catholic University Students) office. On September 15, 2015 — yes, I remember the date! — I quickly loaded our then 10-month-old daughter into the van because we were running late. As I picked up speed to merge onto the busy C-470 Highway, there was a strange sensation in the pedal: It felt like I'd temporarily lost power to accelerate. Weird. But I was late, so I kept driving.

Five minutes later, the sensation was happening again and again. All my dials and knobs looked fine, but I knew something wasn't right. I began to pull toward the right-hand lanes so I wouldn't end up stalling in the middle of the highway. As I began to merge right, the engine completely died. Mercifully there was an exit, so I coasted up and eventually pulled onto the shoulder, safely away from traffic.

I called Jonathan. No answer. I called again. No answer. Now I was getting angry since we have a rule in our family that if a spouse calls the other twice in a row, it means there's an emergency. But I am married to someone who has ADHD and frequently loses or misplaces his phone, so that "rule" was sometimes a bit of wishful thinking. I called the office receptionist, since Jonathan was likely already in the chapel waiting for us to join him for Mass. She tracked him down and got him on the phone. I told him that Josie and I were stranded on the side of the road and needed a ride home, and the car needed to be towed to a local shop.

Five minutes later he joined us on the side of the road and helped me entertain our busy toddler while making the necessary arrangements to get the van fixed. I called my dad, who has been a mechanic for over forty years and knows his stuff. He's our exclusive auto mechanic and won't let just anyone work on our vehicles. Within two minutes of asking me questions about what happened, he knew it was the transmission. He took it upon himself to call around to several shops in Denver to vet them with his sleuthing mechanic questions.

Most shops didn't meet his standards, but one had high competence and fair pricing, so Dad called us back with the details. We arranged a tow truck to come pick up the van, and boy, were we glad we'd had car insurance that included roadside assistance. I knew we'd use the locksmith at least three times per year between both our locking-the-keys-in-the-car track records, but I'd never really anticipated using insurance for a tow.

We moved our daughter's car seat to Jonathan's Jeep and followed the tow truck to the mechanic's shop to get everything settled. That evening they called us with the damage — well, after they'd called my dad first to go over it all with him, per his insistence! The van needed a total transmission replacement to the tune of $3,500.

Hearing that number flooded me with emotion but not for the reason you might assume. You see, a bill like that a few years prior would have financially destroyed us. We absolutely would have had to use a credit card to cover it, but we wouldn't have been able to pay it off without accruing lots of interest in the process. However, at this point in our marriage, we'd been completely debt-free for just over three years. We'd established a Full Rainy Day Fund of four month's expenses two years prior and thankfully hadn't touched it (though there was a close call when I got a case of granite-counter-top fever). The emotions flooding me that evening were ones of relief, gratitude, and peace.

The years spent saying "no" to getting guac at Chipotle and sipping PSL's at Starbucks, while saying "yes" to attacking debt and establishing savings, were paying off in a very tangible way. Instead of this unforeseen emergency wiping us out, it became a minor inconvenience that had no real bearing on our daily lives. We paid the bill without hesitation or worry. We fixed the van without a second thought and moved on with ease.

Welcome to the Hardest, Most Boring Milestone

We've talked about how important and vital saving a Full Rainy Day Fund is, but let's talk about a little known dark secret about this money milestone: It's often the hardest one to hit. Why? Well, if you think about the earlier money milestones, they're broken down into bite-sized victories. Examining your Money Mindset is something you can unpack in a few days or weeks. Same goes for creating your very first budget. Saving a Starter Rainy Day Fund can often be completed in under a few months. While eliminating all consumer debt can be a long journey, when you break it up by paying your debts off from smallest to largest, you're getting the rush of slaying debts and watching the balances fall every month. Even if that process takes years, your adrenaline is pushing you onwards for the next victory.

After all those milestones, you finally arrive at the time to start saving your Full Rainy Day Fund and it can feel like a letdown. There's no rush of adrenaline. You're just setting money aside and watching the balance grow month after month. Nothing seems to be "happening." As you're blazing through the earlier milestones, you're itching to get more lifestyle back in your life, if you reduced it while paying off debt. But completing these savings usually takes several months or maybe even a year. It's common to battle the desire to let the belt *way* out since you're debt free — but it's not quite time to do that just yet. Truth is, until this milestone is completed, you're not doing as well as you think you are.

The reason being, you're still financially exposed until you get these savings established. Job losses, furnaces going out, bones breaking, transmissions dying, pandemics … the infrequent yet massive emergencies you've escaped up to this point will be coming. If you don't complete this money milestone *before* dramatically upping your lifestyle, you're one major emergency from being back in debt. And unfortunately, we've seen it happen all too often.

Now, I'm not saying you shouldn't celebrate becoming debt-free. You should! Heck, we cash flowed a one-week trip to Rome a few months after breaking free of debt, while we were growing our Full Rainy Day Fund. But after that, we buckled down and began to home in on those savings. Looking back, we could've done a better job making smaller lifestyle upgrades we could feel in our everyday life. I remember months after becoming debt-free, with about two months of expenses saved, Jonathan said he felt poorer than when we were blazing out of debt. Rationally, this didn't make sense, but his brain was struggling with continuing to sacrifice lifestyle without the dopamine hits of paying down debt.

Make a few strategic upgrades in your lifestyle where it matters the most, but keep things simple and streamlined until you've got these funds established. Maybe you *love* seltzer water but have limited yourself to one can a day while blazing out of debt. Let loose a bit and drink a couple cans a day now. Find a simple yet very tangible lifestyle upgrade that actually matters to you. Or if you've avoided buying new clothes, set aside a budget to add some new pieces to your wardrobe. But don't spend hundreds per month on seltzer water, or go on shopping sprees with all your disposable income. Making lifestyle upgrades is a balancing act while you're working on this money milestone.

What *Is* a Full Rainy Day Fund?

To fully protect yourself from the bigger emergencies life is waiting to throw your way, you'll need four to six months of expenses set aside in your Full Rainy Day Fund account. As we discussed earlier, this is a liquid (meaning instantly accessible) bank account that is housed separately from your everyday checking account. If an emergency hits, you need to be able to use the funds without penalty. I know it can be tempting to pop that cash over into investments with the hope of earning interest, but say it with me: **Full Rainy Day Funds are more like insurance than investments.**

Insurance versus Investments

Insurance is something you pay for that protects you from being financially ruined should worst case scenarios rear their ugly heads. Investments are something you place money in to hopefully earn you more money with time, but there's inherent risk to all investments as they aren't a sure thing. Your Full Rainy Day Fund needs to be a sure thing. Just like we said about insurance in chapter 5, you have a Full Rainy Day Fund and hope you never use it, but boy are you glad to have it when something does happen.

Expenses Not Income

Notice that your Full Rainy Day Fund consists of four to six months of expenses, not four to six months of income. Reason being, if you suffer an emergency like job loss, the assumption is that you'll be cutting back on some of your everyday lifestyle expenses like going to the movies, saving for vacation, or driving through Starbucks a few times a month. When emergencies hit, you'll be operating in bare-bones budget mode — only what you need, until you reach a place of stability after the storm passes.

You can calculate this amount by going through your budget and making note of all the expenses you would still incur even in emergency mode. Tally those up and you have your number. Multiply that by four or six and you'll have your unique range of where your Full Rainy Day Fund should land. It's up to you whether you lean toward four months or six months, but our rule of thumb is this: How stable is your income? If you're an entrepreneur, freelancer, or gig economy worker, you'll likely be better off (and more at peace) with six months saved. If you're in a very stable job with a predictable income and it would be relatively easy to find another job in case you lost your current one, then you'll be just fine with four months.

Sometimes in the personal finance world you'll hear about experts recommending either no emergency savings, or a year or more of expenses in savings.

In the first situation, no savings is taught as a strategy to always be investing your money to create more cash flow. Popular author Robert Kiyosaki talks about being "cash poor," because he's always putting his money into other investments to earn more cash flow. But that's risky. If you hit an emergency and need to access funds, you have to sell something off or go through hoops to access your funds — which takes time and energy. What if you're sick and can't take the necessary steps? Life could get even messier, quickly.

On the flip side you have Suze Orman, who recommends a year of expenses in savings. Not only do we think this is a massive barrier for many people to reach, but it's excessive. You don't want more money sitting in savings than just enough to protect your family in emergency seasons. If you can be earning money on your money via investments or using it to reach other goals, that's more ideal!

Popular personal finance voice Dave Ramsey similarly says you can get by with three months saved ... but most major adjustments take *at least* ninety days for the dust to settle and I don't want this fund running shy on anyone. Which is why we prefer a balanced and just right Goldilocks-esque Full Rainy Day Fund of four to six months expenses saved.

Same or Separate Bank Account?

Almost all experts agree on one thing, though: Your emergency savings should live in a bank account that's separate from your everyday checking account you spend from. It's harder to accidentally spend the funds if they aren't attached to your debit card. Ideally you want to find a separate savings account that provides a tiny bit of interest, has no fees associated with it, and allows instant access to your money. That rules out options like a bank CD, where you're penalized for taking money out early, or accounts that would take several days to transfer the money.

When Emergencies Happen

It would be nice if we never needed our Full Rainy Day Funds, wouldn't it? A 2015 Pew survey found that 60 percent of households had a "financial shock" in the past twelve months, and half of those (or 30 percent of all households) struggled to make ends meet after their most expensive shock.[1] So, according to the research, stuff's gonna hit the fan, and probably sooner than you'd like.

When you use any portion of your emergency fund, your best next financial step is to pause progress on other goals and replenish those funds used. This ensures that you'll have the funds available should another emergency come up again down the line. When we paid for our transmission using our Full Rainy Day Fund, it took about ninety days to replenish the amount we'd taken before moving back to life as normal. But it's not always that easy. Sometimes it's a much harder journey if you used a significant portion or even all of the funds available.

That's where we found ourselves in October 2018. It was the hardest financial chapter we've ever faced. It tested all the skills we'd learned up to that point and proved what we already knew to be true: that we are money ninjas who always find a way forward no matter how challenging our circumstances may be.

A year prior, in October 2017, Jonathan lost his day job — for which, only one year earlier, we'd left an organization we loved and moved cross country. Ultimately, the Board of Directors ended the project he started, thus ending his employment. He came home in a state of shock, but I remember we looked at one another and said it was probably the best thing that had ever happened to us. Since getting out of debt in 2012, we'd been financially coaching folks at our kitchen table, on podcasts, and at live events for years. It brought us to life, and we absolutely loved every second spent doing it. As our family grew, time was tighter and we knew that if we wanted to keep coaching others, we'd need to take it online.

That fateful Friday evening in October, we knew this was the moment we'd been waiting for to start WalletWin. Up to that point we'd taken some online courses, organized our thoughts in outlines, and even taken a handful of students through a beta version of our program. We had no real launch date on the calendar because we were comfortable. I was a stay-at-home mom with two girls two and under, while Jonathan was bringing home a steady paycheck. But this moment popped the comfort bubble, and it was now or never. We knew we had a few more weeks of severance pay, and then four months of expenses saved and available should we need them.

Six weeks later we'd welcomed our first official WalletWin class and were off to the races. That brought in enough for our family of four to live on for a couple of months. But then we needed to welcome another class. And another. Eventually, we were so overwhelmed with all the tasks required to start and grow a new business that we couldn't keep welcoming new people in all the time, while keeping up with the students we already had, in addition to raising our babies at home. So we began to dip into that Full Rainy Day Fund to make up the gap every month.

Watching our fund slowly drain

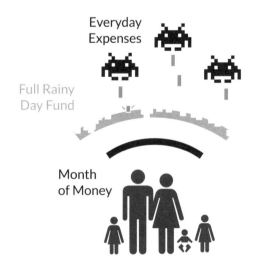

made me nervous, but I also knew we needed time and freedom to learn more about running a business. We needed occasional childcare, office space, cleaning help, technology, virtual assistance. Most of WalletWin's earnings needed to go back into running the business, not to be paid out directly to our family. We knew eventually the business would be able to pay us a higher income, but we had to really trust each other and work diligently to grow it to a point where it could perform at that level.

In June 2018 we received a surprise message asking us if we'd be able to adopt a biological sibling of one of our daughters, who had also come to our family through adoption. The baby was due in September, only three months away. Our business was only seven months old. Remember, we were making money, but still drawing from our Full Rainy Day Fund every month to make ends meet. We were afraid, because adoption is expensive and in a quick look at our bank account, we didn't have enough money available to say yes. But we also knew that we would be provided for because God's always taken care of us when we've said "yes" to His will in the past. We leapt in faith.

We had less than three months to figure out how we would welcome another child into our family, all while those emergency savings were dipping lower and lower. Many people in our life discouraged us from moving forward. They didn't see how this could work. They were stuck doing hard math instead of asking the essential question of, "How can we make this happen?" We felt at peace and knew that we could find a way. We planned around the clock for weeks on how we would welcome our largest class of WalletWinners yet, and bring in the funding needed for adoption fees.

That August, fueled by caffeine, God's grace, and the fumes of our dying Full Rainy Day Fund, we opened enrollment into WalletWin and held our breath. Four days later, as we closed up shop, we'd welcomed in just barely enough students to fund all the adoption expenses. The money never even hit our bank account, as we had to wire it immediately to the adoption lawyer. It was exhilarating, and we were so proud of what we'd accomplished. Over the following three weeks we flurriously nested and prepared our home and hearts to welcome home baby #3.

We were so exhausted, though, that we hadn't given a thought to life after bringing the baby home. That September, with three girls — ages 3, 1, and newborn — we sat down to pay final adoption expenses and make our October budget. Shockingly, we realized that not only was our Full Rainy Day Fund empty, but our month of money in our checking account and our Starter Rainy Day Fund were also G.O.N.E. It felt like the ultimate whiplash since we'd just had the highest-earning month yet in our business.

We paid ourselves from WalletWin for the month but knew it wasn't enough for everything our family needed. Only now, we didn't have those emergency savings we'd been comfortably siphoning off for a year. We didn't even have a Starter Rainy Day Fund anymore! It felt like we were walking on a tightrope with a giant abyss underneath us, but instead of having balancing sticks in our hands, we had three squirming babies and a mortgage.

Objectively, when we started our financial freedom journey back in 2011 with $25,000 in debt, no savings, and a negative net worth, we were in a worse position. But emotionally speaking, this chapter was far more painful. While we were debt-free and had a six-figure net worth between investments and real estate, we had unpredictable income, were back to living paycheck-to- paycheck, and had no emergency savings, all while having three very young children and many financial obligations! Replenishing our Starter Rainy Day Fund was our top priority, but only after we knew we had enough for our family to eat and keep a roof over our heads.

We sold things around the house: our wooden sleigh bed, my trusty crockpot, clothes, jewelry, paintings, and toys. We sold our second vehicle, Jonathan's beloved Jeep. We cut back on Chipotle. (I know that doesn't sound like a big deal, but if you knew how much we love Chipotle, it was!) We paused investments. We leveraged extra side hustles and freelance jobs. We steadily grew WalletWin's monthly revenue. In many ways, those lean days we knew while busting out of debt were back, because we knew they would keep us afloat as we built those Full Rainy Day savings back up. It was back to #SharkMode only this time it looked more like *Sharknado*.

It wasn't easy to replenish our savings, as we continuously balanced how much of our business income needed to be reinvested into the company versus what we could pay ourselves each month. We broke it down step-by-step and moved through the Money Milestones in order. After quickly setting aside our $1,000 Starter Rainy Day Fund, we built back our runway by getting a month ahead of our money, before turning our eyes toward the Full Rainy Day Fund of four to six months' expenses.

What had originally taken us a brief six months to save up back in 2013 before we owned a home or had children, took us the following eighteen months to build up for our needs as a family of five. We scraped, clawed, sprouted plenty of gray hair, and fought to get those savings back. Once we finally complet-

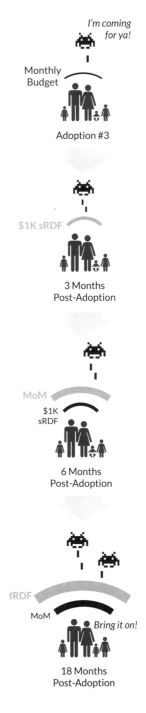

ed the Full Rainy Day Fund once again, we breathed a deep sigh of relief. We turned investments back on. We got back to Chipotle. We took a family vacation. We paid cash for a Class-A RV to make memories in. This was an extremely different rebuild from that first time we dipped into those Full Rainy Day Funds for the van's transmission. However, in both instances, our Full Rainy Day Fund had our backs when we needed it to. Without it, we would've been forced into debt, never have been able to start a business in the first place, or had to pass up saying yes to growing our family. It's unimaginable to consider those options looking back. This is why we're so thankful for our Full Rainy Day Fund and encourage you to get these emergency savings established as soon as possible. The consequences of not having them are limiting and painful but the options and possibilities they open up are tremendous.

So what do you do when you need to use your Full Rainy Day Fund? We just walked through it in story form but here's a recap of the practical steps to take:

1. Be discerning about when and if you need to use your Full Rainy Day Fund. If you can weather the storm with your monthly cashflow without touching your emergency savings, do it. But if you can't? Use the funds! That's what they're there for. There is absolutely no shame in using your Full Rainy Day Fund, if it's the right time to do so.

2. Use only as much as you need. Just because an emergency popped up doesn't mean you bottom out your entire Full Rainy Day Fund. Never take more than you need to get through the crises, as you don't know how long you'll need the fund to last you.

3. When the emergency is over and you are past crisis mode, take a moment to thank yourself. That's right! I know, it might sound cheesy but past you saved today you's tush. You said no in the past to prioritizing saving for this exact moment in the future, although you couldn't see it at the time. It took sacrifice and you did just that.

4. Assess what you took from your Full Rainy Day Fund and craft a plan to replenish the money as quickly as possible. Remember, you're never doing as well as you think you are until these funds are complete. It's a vulnerable spot to live in. Don't let the grass grow under you on getting these funds saved up. Get creative with selling items, taking side hustles, negotiating a raise, and so on, so you can get this done in haste. Your future self is literally counting on the Full Rainy Day Fund being there, and today you can make sure it's ready to go.

Now that we've completed our Rainy Day Fund chat, it's time to move onto a super fun, albeit complicated, next step: home buying. Buckle up, it's time to (responsibly) house hunt!

Success Story
Philip and Katie Zubrod

When we came across WalletWin, we were about to have our second child. We felt through prayer that the Lord was leading us to become debt-free. We started with about $36,000 in debt ranging from credit card balances, student loans, and auto loans. For the first year and a half we were flailing along on our own and managed to pay off $12,000 of our debt, mostly because of large tax returns and an insurance settlement. Jonathan and Amanda and WalletWin came along at the right time for us and became such a blessing.

One of the biggest benefits of WalletWin for us was that it gave us a language and an opportunity to get on the same page about our money. Honestly, we did not know how we each thought about money, except that we needed it, we did not have much, and we owed people a *lot* of it. Through WalletWin, we learned how much our past experiences growing up shaped how we approached money in the present. Talking about all of this lit a fire under us and gave us great hope and encouragement to persevere in this journey.

The encouragement was tangible and personal coming from Jonathan and Amanda. They made money matters fun for us in our marriage, and cheered us up and on especially through their videos. These gave us a mental boost to persevere through the hardest part: making a *real* budget and giving money a purpose. Seeing our plans and goals on paper filled us with a realistic excitement that it was *possible* to get out of debt and not live like hobos. Moving with this excitement, we forged ahead. We were blessed with an opportunity to increase our income and develop a side hustle. Through concentrated effort and grace, we were finding at least an additional $1,000 per month to throw at the debt. Then the mini celebrations started. First the credit card balances — gone! Student loans up next — done. Finally, the cars — done and DONE!

With the help of WalletWin, we were able to pay off $24,000 of debt in eighteen months. We did not stop at that goal. We switched our efforts to building up our savings to reach our goal of a fully funded emergency fund of $16,000, which we proudly attained in August 2020! Although we still struggle with that pesky budget, we are extremely grateful for our WalletWin!

CHAPTER 11

Save a Down Payment

"When Christ took flesh through the Blessed Virgin Mary, he made his home with us. Let us now pray that he will enter this home and bless it with his presence. May he always be here with you, share in your joys, comfort you in your sorrows. Inspired by his teachings and example, seek to make your new home before all else a dwelling place of love, diffusing far and wide the goodness of Christ."
— *Catholic Household Blessings and Prayers*[1]

① Money Mindset ② Live with a Budget ③ Insure Yourself ④ Starter Rainy Day Fund ⑤ Get a Month Ahead ⑥ Pay Off Debt ⑦ Full Rainy Day Fund ⑧ **Save Down Payment**

Establish Your Financial Foundation · Gain Momentum With Your Money

🏳 *Amanda*

In fall 2013, we'd just wrapped up saving our Full Rainy Day Fund but we weren't sure what our best next financial step was. We were two years into infertility treatments and had no clue if we would ever welcome children into our family. Home buying seemed like the best next step, but I'd always imagined buying a home *after* becoming parents. Emotionally, this was a very taxing season of life as we cycled through hope and despair continuously. We couldn't see the forest through the trees any longer. Ultimately, we knew we had nothing but good options ahead of us. We'd paid the price and won. The future, at least financially speaking, was bright even though we were arguably in the darkest emotional chapter of our lives thus far.

How we handled the next steps was up to us. We could ramp up retirement investing and take a couple of years to save up a down payment. Or we could prioritize saving a down payment at warp speed and *after* buying a home, ramp up investing. Since we lived in the notoriously white-hot market of Denver, Colorado with homes, in some cases, going up tens of thousands of dollars in mere months, we chose to prioritize home buying.

After saving our Full Rainy Day Fund (the first time) with our belts let out just beyond when we were paying off debt, we buckled down again and tightened things up. It was aggressive, but we wanted to have our down payment saved in six months flat. Having an extremely concrete and tangible goal once again reignited our excitement and passion for personal finance.

Join me as I share the story of how home-buying played out in our journey. We learned a whole lot — and we'll break down the practical stuff at the end of this chapter so you have a step-by-step guide for smart home buying.

Tip of the Iceberg

If you've turned on HGTV for more than a second, you know the drill — young twenty-something couple, he walks dogs on the weekends, she works part-time at a daycare, all-in budget of $1.2 million. While we all know that's unrealistic, what's not obvious onscreen is that the home buying process seen on these shows is merely the tip of the iceberg. And it's what's underneath the water that could sink you.

There is far more to buying a house than house-hunting. If you want home ownership to be the American Dream instead of the all-too-common nightmare, you must carefully prepare and plan.

There are many steps to master if you want to buy a home with peace of mind, and these steps take time.

Diving In

As we dove under the surface and into all the ins and outs of preparing for home buying, I found the process a welcome distraction from all the disappointment we were experiencing with growing our family. While adoption and my fertility seemed completely out of our control, this was something I could take steps toward and see direct outcomes.

One of the first steps we took that fall was choosing a Realtor. Months before we were ready to pull the trigger, we began interviewing Realtors. If you're like most people you have a friend, neighbor, or relative who's a real estate agent. I'm not saying you should never hire them. But more often than not, you should skip the nepotism when it comes to choosing an agent. If your cousin or pal from church happens to have a ton of experience and is a professional full-time real estate agent and closes multiple deals per month, that may be the exception. Most people with a license in real estate are hobbyists who do it part-time and only close a handful of deals in any given year. That's not who you want steering the ship in dark and iceberg-filled waters.

We set up interviews with several recommended real estate agents, but something stood out with one in particular — she was experienced, enthusiastic, driven, and hardworking. She didn't ask us anything about the actual home buying straight away. She took us out for coffee and asked us about who we are, what we value, and our personal finance journey. She took an interest in our lives. At the end of that initial meeting, she asked very basic things about the home-buying process. We told her our timeline of starting to look in May, and she gave us the advice to hold firm to that and to not go out looking beforehand. I knew we would be in good hands with her.

The other Realtors? They were nice enough, but within minutes of being on the phone (with no attempt to meet us in person) they were trying to set us up so we would get emails about houses as they came on the market. One even tried to get us to go house shopping that very weekend. We didn't even know our price range yet! We had no clue what we wanted in a home. They didn't ask about our timeline. They didn't ask about who we are. They didn't care about our financial goals and where home buying fit into our plans. We thanked them for their time and let them know we were going in a different direction. An agent who viewed us as a quick path to a payday just wouldn't cut it.

We asked the agent we liked to connect us with a few of her past clients, and called them. We wanted to choose her but needed to do our due diligence to check references for the good, bad, and ugly. We called a few couples she'd recently worked with and they all provided well-rounded feedback and overall had glowing reviews. They were raving fans of her and her team's service. This gave us confidence in moving forward with her, and provided us peace knowing we'd fully vetted the professional we'd chosen.

We chose to work with her in January, but our buying timeline wouldn't begin until May. That winter and spring was dedicated to education! Our agent invited us to her office one evening for a several-hour, personalized class on the entire home buying process. I could hardly believe she provided this type of service, but we were so grateful as we were first-time homebuyers and knew literally nothing. We were able to ask questions and she and her team were patient and wouldn't move on until we completely understood their answers. It was obvious by her actions, patience, and desire to help us understand home buying that she had our best interest in mind.

Choppy Waters

After interviewing, vetting, and choosing our real estate agent, the next step was the mortgage pre-qualification, where we ran into a hiccup. I checked our credit score and what to my wandering eyes did appear but a years-old speeding ticket and many loud jeers.

 Jonathan

I used to have a bad habit of speeding. Take it from me (and my wallet): Don't speed cross-country on holiday weekends. Or ever, really. It's dangerous and just not worth it. Now, I had paid this ticket, but somehow Indiana never got my money, and three years later, the money order receipt was long gone. Anyway, the ticket went to collections without me knowing. That is, until Amanda discovered it … which isn't exactly how I wanted it to go down! I paid the ticket (again) and the collections agency swore they wouldn't report it to the credit bureau.

🏴 *Amanda*

But of course they did. This meant that the mortgage interest rate we would qualify for would be higher. There was no way we were going to pay upwards of $75/month for potentially over a decade in interest because of some fluke speeding ticket that ended up in collections.

Just a note here that a FICO credit score has nothing to do with creating financial freedom or building wealth. There are many factors that influence it: payment history, credit mix, length of credit history, new credit, and balances owed. Each of these carry a different weight but ultimately represent your estimated ability to pay your bills and debts back. Companies use this number to assess their risk level in lending you money. Regarding home buying, you either want to have no credit score or an excellent credit score. In between is where you get into trouble. After recently becoming debt-free and having paid all our bills in a timely manner for years, our credit score was excellent. This collections account was throwing us into the middle, so we had to proactively fix it or be willing to accept a higher interest rate for the life of our mortgage.

While credit scores aren't representative of how well you're managing money, they are something you need to consider. If for some reason you don't have a credit score, while you'll still have mortgage lending options, they will be more limited. This isn't a bad thing, but you will need to find a bank willing to do a thorough manual underwriting to qualify you for a loan. If you've got less-than-stellar credit, there are many ways to improve your score, so don't despair. While I can't get into all the available strategies here in this book, the WalletWin Method is a great place to start as you'll be paying down debt, decreasing your credit utilization as a whole, paying your bills every month, and eliminating the need to charge unexpected expenses — all of which greatly impact your number for the better. For a deeper dive into the importance of your FICO score and strategies to improve it, **download our free resource available at WalletWin .com/fico.**

By now you should know what we did when our credit score was subpar! I dove in and made phone calls, faxed letters, begged, emailed, and so on. It took two and a half months to clear that ticket from our credit report, but we managed to get it done just in time for our May buying timeline. Whew! Now we could finally go through the mortgage pre-qualification process.

To make sure we got the best rate possible, we wanted a few different mortgage quotes. Shopping around ensures you're getting the most competitive rates, and we strongly recommend you never skip this step whether you're qualifying for a mortgage, applying for auto insurance, or hiring a drywall contractor.

Our first quote was with a local independent mortgage broker recommended by our Realtor. It's common that Realtors will have relationships with brokers in your area, but always inquire about any referral fees that might be involved in their recommendation. We were blown away by the recommended broker's customer service, dedication, swiftness, and that heart of a teacher quality that is so rare. She wanted to help us meet our goals by getting a 15-year fixed rate mortgage with between 10–20 percent down. Her rates were also very competitive, since independent brokers bring many lenders to the table to offer their very best rates to try and gain your business. This is a huge advantage — if you show up at your local bank or credit union, they're only going to show you their rate. It's in your best interest to make sure many banks are putting their best foot forward to win your business. While we found our broker through our Realtor, there are a growing number of websites that perform similar functions, making it easier to get access to highly competitive mortgage rates.

The second quote was from our credit union. The first red flag was when they told us we could "afford" a house $200K over what we were considering. Then he said, "Since you have no other debt, more of your income is available for a mortgage payment." To which I replied, "Yeah, if we want to be house poor, and never adopt, send our kids to college, give generously, or retire!" We would *much* rather live in a modest home below our means than live in one that sucked our income dry every single month and cramped our ability to pursue dreams and hit other goals. We still love our credit union for the banking services they offer, but banks often don't have the best rates because they're not shopping around. They're simply offering you their rates.

Let the House Hunt Begin!

After choosing a Realtor to work with and getting prequalified for a mortgage, it was finally time to begin our house hunt! This is when the fun began. The first time we hopped into our agent's car, she had water and treats waiting for us — so sweet and thoughtful! That afternoon we looked at seven houses, and in each one our agent was continuing to provide an education. She wasn't going to hold her opinion back. She wanted us in the right house and that's all there was to it. Anything that needed to be said, she said. Early on she described herself as a "real-estate mom" and she lived up to the title.

That day we learned a few things:

1. Photos always look better online. Spaces can appear brighter and more spacious in a well-edited picture.
2. You can't smell the house in photos! Smoke, cats, and mildew scents are hard to get rid of.
3. Location, location, location. We saw a "deal" online only to find the house faced a ginormous domed road salt storage facility.
4. Assess what you can change versus what you can't change. Carpet and paint? No big deal. A little bit of creativity with some fresh materials can radically transform a space. Living on an extremely busy road, being thirty feet from a drainage ditch, or a house layout you can't stand? Those are things you can't do anything about.

We didn't find anything we loved that day and quickly found our-selves going from excited and pumped up to discouraged and ex-hausted. In my state of desolation and frustration, I started to fudge a bit on our boundaries. I began looking at houses outside of our price range. A few days later we got picked up to go looking again. The first property was a town house that was beautifully remodeled inside, and the second was a mostly updated brick ranch with an immaculate yard and cozy sunroom.

Now we were just confused. You couldn't have found more op-posite properties for us to fall in love with. The town house would be a short-term strategy since it was 2 bedrooms, 2 baths, 1,300 square feet, and no garage. The ranch could be where we'd raise a family, with 5 bedrooms, 2 baths, a 2-car garage and nearly 2,700 square feet.

The town house was a no brainer. We could easily afford it and keep saving for things like adoption, retirement, and future home purchases. We could do a 15-year-fixed-rate mortgage with more than 10 percent down, and the payments would not be greater than 25 percent take home pay. Easy-peasy-lemon-squeezy.

The ranch (with its gorgeous plantation shutters) was out of our price range on a 15-year fixed rate mortgage. Even upon pulling up, our Realtor looked at us and said, "Are you sure you want to go in there?" She knew it was a temptation in the making even by see-ing the exterior alone. Even though our brains were sounding the alarms and saying "NO!" we decided to go in anyway. Of course, we loved it. Comparing a townhome with half the square footage (and half the price) wasn't really fair. But the beautiful ranch would require us to do a 30-year mortgage, and even at that the payments would be 35 percent of our take home pay.

Jonathan and I went home and talked strategy. Were we going to follow the boundaries we'd already agreed on, to incrementally work toward the eventual dream home? Or would we jump into the dream home, and sacrifice other lifestyle and savings goals for the immediate gratification?

The decision about our strategy wasn't actually that hard. In twenty minutes I realized that when we were talking about the town house, we were excited and happy. On the same page. A team. It felt easy. In talking about the ranch, we argued. Got defensive. Lost our peace. Worried about having the funds to invest, give, or grow our family. I turned to Jonathan and said, "If this is what life looks like in the dream home, I don't want it!" I refuse to have money fights. We don't have money fights and I don't want to start. Also, our dreams of adopting, traveling, and giving are too important to us to be compromised. The entire point of the journey we'd been on for the previous three years was *financial peace*. We wouldn't trade it for anything.

So, we chose the town home! The next step was to put forward an offer. Our agent advised us to go back to the neighborhood we wanted to buy in and spend time walking the sidewalks and talking with people before formally submitting an offer. Buying a home only to find out we loathe the neighborhood would be rather frustrating! Jonathan and I hopped in the car, went back to the town house development, and walked around for over three hours. We met lovely people and asked them *lots* of questions. We wanted to research the good, bad, and ugly before we committed to live there.

After walking around and confirming that we loved not only the townhome but also the larger community, we were ready to move forward with the offer. We were nervous though, as we watched dozens of others tour the same town house while we walked around the complex. When we called our agent that evening, she already knew there were three offers on the table (all higher than the asking price) with anticipation of four more by the end of day … and they were going to take offers for two more days. She gave us suggestions and strategies we could use to make our offer as strong as possible without simply offering more money. I hadn't realized that sellers don't always take the highest offer — and there are nuanced ways to write a home offer that can offer the seller peace of mind, safety, time, and confidence in a way more money can't provide. It was yet again another reason we were so glad we'd spent time vetting our agent up front.

Long story short, the homeowners chose us and we beat out not one, but two cash offers for more money! Once your offer is accepted, the next phase of home buying can be a blur. It's full of moving parts, quick decisions, and signing many documents. Putting an earnest deposit down, scheduling home inspections, negotiating results and repairs from what came up during the home inspection, locking in your interest rate, signing mortgage paperwork, getting title insurance, and scheduling a closing date are just a few of the to-do's before you can walk through the front door and call it home.

Looking back, I'm proud of our first-time home buying experience. It's easy to get house fever, to get swept up in emotion and wind up in situations that compromise your long-term goals. Heck, we almost did, and we were being super intentional! It's hard to set boundaries and then follow through on keeping our commitments to ourselves. But we're so thankful we did just that.

We didn't know it at the time, but mere weeks after closing on that first home purchase, we were privately matched with a birth family to adopt our first child. If we had been financially pinched by our home, there's no way we would've been able to cash flow over $25,000 in adoption-related expenses over the following three months. Because we said "no" to extending ourselves beyond our home buying financial guidelines, we were able to say "yes" to our deepest desire — growing our family.

Two years later we sold that first home for a whole lot more than we paid for it. Not only did it keep our initial down-payment savings nice and warm, it proved a wise investment and gave us a sizable down payment for our next home. We've never regretted sticking with those initial boundaries we set and ultimately the peace it's given our family in addition to the dreams it's made possible.

While we shared about those boundaries in the story above, let's dive into each specific guideline in detail and chat about why it's important.

Mortgages: 15 Versus 30

 Jonathan

Thirty-year mortgages account for almost 90 percent of mortgage applications,[2] while 15-year mortgages account for only 5–8 percent. Why do we recommend such a seemingly unpopular type of mortgage?

The simple reason is that a 15-year mortgage drastically reduces the price of your home compared to a 30-year. As LeVar Burton says, "But you don't have to take my word for it." Let's take a peek at the numbers.

Let's imagine you're shopping for a home and have two different loans to consider:

Price: $250,000
Percent Down: 20%
Amount Down: $50,000

MORTGAGE A	MORTGAGE B
Principle: $200,000	Principle: $200,000
Term: 15 Years	Term: 30 Years
Interest Rate: 3%	Interest Rate: 3.5%
Monthly Payment: $1,380	Monthly Payment: $900

Note: Monthly payments and totals do not include taxes, insurance, or HOA dues, as many real-life mortgages would, along with less-rounded interest rates. Numbers have also been rounded. These modifications have been made for simplicity and to more easily illustrate the difference in the loans.

The first difference you notice is that the 30-year mortgage hits you with the one-two punch of both higher interest rates *and* a longer loan. You're paying more interest for longer — not a great combo.

Now, the 30-year has a lower monthly payment than the 15. But remember, you're paying it for *twice* as long! Let's see how those payments really add up over the decades.

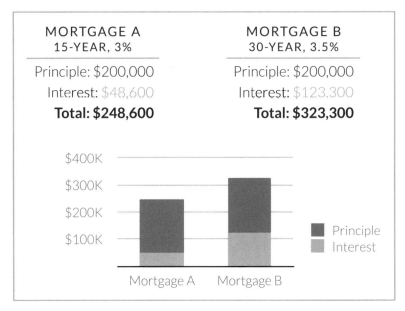

You pay *over two and half times as much interest* on the 30-year loan. Choosing a 15-year mortgage on this house instead of a 30-year is like using a 20 percent off coupon! For this house, that's $74,700! I'm happy to use *any* coupon and on something as big and expensive as a house — that 20 percent off is HUGE!

But you don't have to wait fifteen years to see the difference.

Dude, Where'd My Money Go?

Let's hop in the "What If?" Machine. The last eight years have been quite a ride: Your family's grown, your job has changed, or you've always wanted to live somewhere else. Whatever the reason, it's time to move! Only eight years in a home before moving may seem short, but you're right in line with the national average.[3]

Thankfully, your house value has gone up the typical 3.4 percent a year, and you sell it for market value, around $327,000.

What do your two mortgage choices look like now?

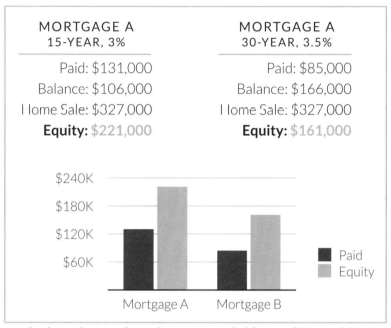

MORTGAGE A 15-YEAR, 3%	MORTGAGE A 30-YEAR, 3.5%
Paid: $131,000	Paid: $85,000
Balance: $106,000	Balance: $166,000
Home Sale: $327,000	Home Sale: $327,000
Equity: $221,000	**Equity:** $161,000

Like the earlier numbers, these are rounded for simplicity and do not include things like Realtor fees.

After selling the house and paying off the balance of your mortgage, you're left with equity, or money in your pocket, most likely to be used for your next home. If you chose the 15-year mortgage eight years ago, you'd have an additional $60,000 of equity versus the 30. You might think it's pretty straightforward that the higher payments of a 15-year mortgage will build more equity in eight years than the lower payments of a 30-year. But it's more interesting than that!

Extra $14,000 in Equity!

Compared to 30-year Mortgage B, you've paid an additional $46,000 in mortgage payments over the last eight years. It's natural to think you'd only have $46,000 more equity, too. Or maybe a little less, since a chunk of your payment goes toward interest. But check it out: You've paid $46,000 more in payments, but have $60,000 more in equity! That's an extra $14,000 versus Mortgage B.

How did that happen? Let's look at where your payments went:

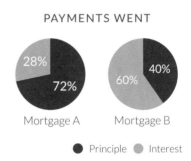

Your mortgage payments pay down both the principal (the amount you borrowed) and the interest on the loan (thank you very much for lending me some money, Mr. Bank, here's some for you to keep).

One way to look at it is, money paid toward the principal stays warm and cozy in the home's value and returns back to you when you sell the house. Interest payments disappear forever into the bank's pockets.

The 15-year mortgage above is the clear winner because out of the $131,000 paid over the last eight years, you only lost $37,000 in interest payments, and are essentially getting the rest back now in equity after the house sells.

While you paid less in total payments with the 30-year ($85,000 versus $131,000), you actually paid *more* interest. Nearly $51,000 has disappeared into the black hole of interest payments, never to be seen in your pockets again. So, while you've paid $85,000 toward your $200,000 loan, you'll only get back $34,000 of it in equity.

The lower interest of a 15-year mortgage means you build equity faster, and that not only saves you loads of money, but also gives you more options when it comes time to sell.

I'll Pay It Like a 15!

Let's address an elephant in the room. Some people get a 30-year mortgage initially since the payments are lower, thinking they'll pay it off in fifteen years. Good intentions aside, this rarely happens. Why? Because life happens instead. You might decide to keep that extra payment instead of send it off to the bank and instead take a vacation. Or maybe it's time to upgrade your kitchen. Or finish the basement. What about a new wardrobe? Maybe the cars are wearing out. Whatever it is, there's always a reason to spend that money somewhere else.

When you have a 15-year mortgage from the get-go, you won't be tempted to use that money for something else. You've got built-in accountability to get your house paid off in half the time!

Why 10–20 percent Down?

While at a dinner party years ago we overheard a guy bragging about how he recently bought a home with 3 percent down using an FHA loan and that some mortgages will even allow you to put zero percent down. While he was sharing all this information to prove how smart he was, he was revealing how little he actually knew.

Putting 10 percent down helps guard against changes in home values, so that it's very unlikely you'll end up in a situation where you'll owe more on the house than it's worth. In the unexpected event that you'd need to sell your home and move toward the beginning of your mortgage, starting off with 10 percent equity allows you to weather changes in home value and fees paid when selling. It also means you're starting off halfway to having 20 percent equity in your home. Why is this important?

If a homeowner has less than 20 percent equity in the house, something called Primary Mortgage Insurance or PMI is added to the loan until the loan-to-value ratio is below 80 percent. This insurance is not for the borrower, but for the lender in case the borrower doesn't pay their mortgage. In other words, a buyer with less than 20 percent down is a riskier investment for a lender, so they insure against the likelihood of not being paid. And they make you pay the insurance bill!

The easiest way to avoid PMI is to start with 20 percent down. If you started out with less than 20 percent down, make sure you call your lender as soon as you hit the 20 percent threshold. PMI will automatically drop off once you hit the 78 percent loan/22 percent equity threshold, but you can request it be taken off when you hit the 80/20 mark. Why pay any more PMI than needed? Make that call!

Conventional Mortgage

While there are many contributing factors to the financial crisis in 2008, the market's appetite for cheap loans fueled the fire. There was great demand for a number of new investment products made up of mortgages. Because of the great demand for mortgages, it became quite lucrative to create mortgages and sell them. This led to lenders getting "creative" with the mortgages they created and the clients they sold them to.

Non-conventional mortgages were a big reason why people were losing their homes in the crisis. Remember that a mortgage lender is always balancing risk. In order to balance out the risk of giving mortgages to people with less than desirable credit, they created an upside with the types of mortgages they were providing. When creating loans for people with bad credit, they'd often sign them up for an adjustable-rate mortgage or ARM. These mortgages would often have low "teaser rates" at the beginning of the mortgage, with the interest rate shooting up in one-to-three years.

A number of these mortgages were so-called interest-only mortgages, which had payments that only paid the interest (and not the principal) during an initial period of a few years. Not only did their payments increase after this introductory period to reflect both increased interest rates and payments on the principal, but the "missed" principal payments were due all at once in a "balloon payment." So, the person whose finances are so tight they can't get a regular mortgage, and can only handle a "teaser rate" that only includes interest payments is going to magically be able to cover not only the increased payments but make a lump-sum payment, too? What world were these mortgage officers living in?! One of greed and disregard for the well-being of their clients/victims, it seems.

All this is to say, get a conventional, fixed-rate mortgage. If a lender won't give you one, or you can't get one at a rate that works for you, there's probably a reason. It's likely a sign that your finances need to be in a healthier spot before proceeding to take out a mortgage and buy a home.

Do the work. Save a larger down payment, increase your income, get a longer history of paying your bills on time, and so on, so you can qualify for a conventional, fixed-rate mortgage. You'll be happy you did.

Why Less than 25 percent of Your Take Home Pay?

All right, so 10–20 percent down makes sense. Getting a 15-year mortgage makes sense. Getting a conventional, fixed-rate mortgage makes sense. But having the payment (including insurance and taxes) be 25 percent or less of your take home pay — where does that come in? And why 25 percent?

If you look around online you'll find a number of different recommendations for how much mortgage you can afford. Some are pre-tax, some are post-tax, others take into account your other debts. Forget all that: We recommend 25 percent of your take-home pay for a few reasons.

It's easy to figure out.

You don't have to dig up your paystub. You don't need to determine how health insurance premiums and other benefits may or may not be "counted" as take-home pay. Simply look at the number on your paychecks, or the amount of your deposits for a month, and divide by four.

It keeps your mortgage from eating the rest of your life.

If your mortgage payment is too high, you don't have any money left to do anything else. Remember when one lender wanted to give us a much larger mortgage than what we were looking for? The rationale was we had no other debts, so we could supposedly handle a higher debt-to-income ratio. This misses the fact that the whole point of getting out of debt is to be able to use your income for other goals! What's the point if we're just going to get it tied up again? We wanted to save for adoption and grow our family. You have goals, too. And you'll want as much of your income as possible available to help you reach them.

If you look around online, you'll find people saying that you can handle a 40 percent debt-to-income ratio, meaning you can "safely" spend 40 percent of your take-home pay on debt payments. And if you don't have any other debts, then you can load up on a huge mortgage. No way! That might work for the "average" consumer, but you're not average. You have plans for your money. You have a purpose here. You can't afford to weigh yourself down with such a large mortgage, no matter what.

You have other Money Milestones to work on. You have retirement to contribute to, maybe your children's education savings to fund. If you have a nice house, but you can't save up to replace an old, dying car, contribute to your retirement, go on decent outings or vacations with your family to create memories, or afford healthy food, you're what's called *house poor*. And sticking to a mortgage payment of 25 percent or less of your take-home pay is a great way to avoid that.

It keeps you nimble.

Let's imagine you have a $5,000 take-home pay. Twenty-five percent of that is $1,250. If you load up on a mortgage that's 40 percent of your take-home, you'd have a $2,000 payment. That's a difference of $750 each month! The most immediate thought is that you have $750 less to fund the other areas of your life, and that's certainly right. But think about the trickle-down effects. You have an additional $750 in monthly expenses versus if you went with our advice. Now let's think about your Full Rainy Day Fund of four-to-six months of expenses. In order to accommodate your larger mortgage payment, you'd need an additional $3,000–$4,500 in your Full Rainy Day Fund.

If you get sucked in by some nicer, larger, more expensive home than

ONE MONTH OF EXPENSES

LARGER MORTGAGE'S EFFECT ON RAINY DAY FUND

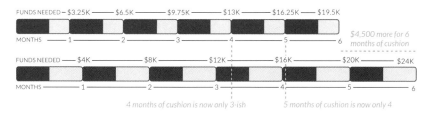

you were planning on — like we almost did — I can almost guarantee at least one of two things will happen:

1. You just chopped down the size of your Full Rainy Day Fund. It used to be 6 months of expenses, and you felt secure. Now it's four or less, and you're feeling anxious. Or maybe you were at four months already, and now your suit of armor against life's emergencies is feeling more like a thin jacket.

2. You need to stop any and all progress you were making — or were about to make — on further Money Milestones and build your Full Rainy Day fund up to a size you're comfortable with. But how long will it take to build back up, since so much of your money is going toward your new mega-mortgage? How much will retirement and education savings suffer because you aren't able to contribute to them and didn't have the money

in there to take advantage of interest?

Keeping your mortgage payment at 25 percent or less of your take-home pay keeps everything manageable, so you can both pay your mortgage and live your life. You're not trying to figure out the absolute maximum mortgage possible for you. You're trying to find a mortgage that will serve all of the goals you and your family have.

Buying a home is one of the largest financial decisions you'll ever make. Doing it right helps ensure any home can be a dream home instead of a nightmare. When you're ready to interview real estate agents, **grab our free list of interview questions at WalletWin.com/realestate.**

Part IV

Grow Your Wealth

FINANCIAL PHASE 3

CHAPTER 12

Contribute to Your Retirement

"And God is able to provide you with every blessing in abundance, so that you may always have enough of everything and may provide in abundance for every good work."
— 2 Corinthians 9:8

🚩 *Amanda*

We were 25 and 26 when we became intentional about our re-lationship with money. By all accounts, we were young. But when we learned about the power of compound interest and began investing only a couple of years later, I felt behind. There was a bit of righteous anger brewing in me. Anger that basic financial foundations weren't taught to me earlier in life. Anger that I'd gotten tangled in student loans and tied my disposable income up in payments before I'd gotten my first real job. Anger that I had no guidance to avoid debt and begin investing from my teen years onward.

Of course, it was a lie that I was "behind," and there was no reason to beat myself up. We can't change the past. What mattered was that we were finally ready to invest for our future and it was exciting. That is, until we began sifting through the alphabet soup of investing.

A Long-Term Play

👉 *Jonathan*

You may have heard a lot of different things about investing. People can invest in all sorts of things in all sorts of ways for all sorts of reasons. Some of them are smart and should be emulated; others are foolish or unwise and should be avoided.

But what is investing? To put it simply, you buy something (or part of something) in hopes that when it is, hopefully, worth more later, you can sell it (or your part of it) for more than you originally paid. When this all works according to plan, you make money. However, it doesn't always work according to plan, and it is certainly possible to lose money investing.

The guidelines we'll outline in this chapter are *not* guaranteed to be successful. In order to guarantee it, we would have to know the future. What we can do is give you sound advice that, given the history of investments, seems like it will work out well for you. All investment involves taking on risk. By personally investing, you take that risk upon yourself.

What's an Investment and What's Not

You may have heard phrases like "it's an investment in …" or "well, it's an investment" thrown around before. Some things really are investments. Others are not investments, even if some people would like to pretend they are — in reality, they're expenses cloaked as investments to make someone feel better about their spending.

Put simply, if things go according to plan, investments should go up in value over time. If it doesn't go up in value, it's not an investment (or at least, not a good one). If it's not reasonably expected to go up in value, it's not an investment.

A car, for example, is not an investment because it goes *down* in value over time.

What about that rookie card of that player everybody loves? While it might go up in value from the time you bought it in a pack of baseball cards their first year in the majors, it's not an investment. It's a lucky break. Baseball cards, in general, are not expected to go up in value. Some do, but overall they just become pieces of cardboard.

A piece of furniture is not an investment. As you might see by scanning Craigslist or Facebook Marketplace, old furniture is worth less than new furniture. Now, a nice piece of furniture, or a nice pair of shoes, might last longer than cheaper ones, and because you paid for quality up front, they might last longer than a few rounds of cheaper replacements. But even if you save money in the long run buying one expensive thing versus blowing through five cheap ones, don't call it an investment. It's just an expensive thing that lasted longer than a cheap one. Might be a smart buy, but it's not an investment.

What about a share in a company that's well managed and performs well? Now, that's what I'm talking about!

Stocks

The most common way to invest in a company is through buying stock. A publicly-traded company is one that issues stock that's available to buy. Each share of stock is a share in the company. If the company issues 1,000 shares, each share is worth one thousandth (or .1 percent) of the company. If you were to own 10 shares, you'd own one percent of the company. If you owned 500 shares, you'd own half of it. (FYI: These are smaller, easier-to-understand numbers: Companies usually issue millions of shares.)

If this company with 1,000 shares was worth $10,000, each share of the company would be worth $10. If the company was worth $20,000, each share would be worth $20.

You make money when you sell your shares of a company for more than you paid for them. If I had invested in Amazon even just five years ago, I would have paid about $535 per share. Amazon's stock is now worth over $3,000 per share.

On the other side, I could have purchased stock in Kodak five years ago for about $15 per share. If I sold them today, I'd lose money since they're only worth about $9 as I write this.

The price of a stock is determined like the price of anything else: supply and demand. There are X shares of a company available, so the amount each is worth is based on how much people are willing to pay. Now, what determines how much people are willing to pay? All sorts of things: financial aspects you might expect like the company's expenses, revenues, and profits, or things like sales growth; but other things too, like how much profit people think the company will make in the future. The price can also shift for a myriad of other reasons. For example, the company announced a new product and investors think people will buy a lot of them, making the company a lot of money, so they buy more shares of the company, sending the stock price up. Or the founder said something controversial online and investors think the called-for boycott is going to hurt business, so they sell shares and make the stock price go down. Or some investors are interested in the new board members of a struggling video game retailer, and talk up their investments on Reddit, and a ton of traderbros pile on.

Bonds

Another very common type of investment you may have heard about before is bonds. Bonds are essentially loans between the investor and the company (or government). Essentially, you agree to give a company, municipality, or government some money today under the agreement that they will pay you back with an agreed-upon amount of interest on a certain date in the future.

Bond rates are usually determined by how trustworthy the borrower is. Think of it this way: Your friend Dan is very trustworthy. If he asks for $20 and promises to pay you back $21 dollars next week, you know he's good for it and you'll get your money. Your return is low because it's a pretty sure thing.

If your less-reliable friend Adam asks you to spot him $20, you might not want to, because you know you may never see that money again. To encourage you to lend him the money, he agrees to pay you back $25 next week. You agree to the more risky investment because the potential reward is higher.

And when your neighbor Larry, who has "borrowed" a bunch of your tools that you'll probably never see again, asks to borrow $20, you really don't want to. Buying a "bond" from Larry is *very* risky, and because of that, he offers you $50 next week. You may as well kiss your money goodbye. But if you take this high risk, you just might get rewarded for it.

Bonds are rated in order to help people understand how trustworthy a particular bond is. The ratings range from AAA to C or D (depending on who's rating it) with ratings like Baa2 or A- mixed in. Bonds like Larry's are considered "junk bonds" because the risk is so high and are rated BB+/Ba1 and lower.

Due to the nature of bonds (you give me X"\ amount of money today, I'll give you X + interest later) they are very predictable, and depending on which bonds are invested in, relatively safe. The right bonds will usually provide a positive return on investment; however, that return won't be very high.

Mix It Up

So, investing in companies, whether through stocks and/or bonds, can be a good thing and earn you money. But what if all your money was in one company? A downward shift in share price based on one bad financial report could wipe out a big chunk of your retirement nest egg. If your investments consisted entirely of stock in Jonathan's Popcorn Company, your investment account balance is directly tied to how well my popcorn company is doing. If there's a popcorn shortage and I can't get ingredients to make popcorn to sell, or a competitor comes along and takes away a ton of my business, they take away a lot of your investment, too. This can happen even if you're invested in multiple companies in the same industry:

If you're too heavily invested in coffee growers, your money could disappear when everybody decides to drink tea instead.

To protect your investments from getting completely wrecked by events outside of your control, it's a good idea to spread your investments around. Investing in not only different companies, but different types of companies, is called diversification. It simply means you're spreading out your money across different types of investments.

The idea is that when one company or industry is struggling, another will probably be doing well, and that will balance out your investments so you have more steady, even, and consistent growth. It's generally recommended to diversify not just across companies, but types of companies too. By diversifying, a bump in the road for American-based food producers is balanced out by your strongly performing European medical manufacturers. Or when your stock in American hotel chains and movie theaters got hit because of COVID-19, growth in your stock in Zoom and disinfectant manufacturers makes up for it.

That type of diversification spreads your investments out across different types of companies. It's also helpful to consider spreading your investments out across different types of investments. There are many more types of investment choices than just stocks and bonds, but let's stick to those for now.

Typically, younger investors with more time before retirement have a greater tolerance for risk (and more time for fluctuations in the market to smooth out), so they invest more heavily in stocks, which in the past have generally had a larger return on investment over the long haul than bonds. However, older investors with less time before retirement typically don't want to risk their nest egg on stocks that might go down in value, so in general, they lean more heavily on the relative predictability of bonds. Younger investors are usually more interested in the potential for growth, and older ones are usually more interested in predictability, so the way their investments are diversified reflects that.

"Diversification sounds like a great idea, Jonathan, but going around and investing in a bunch of different companies and stocks and bonds and all that sounds like a lot of work." You're right! And many other people agree with you! That's why the financial system has come up with ways to do most of the work for you.

Mutual Funds and ETFs

Not only would buying a bunch of different stocks take up a lot of your time, you'd also have to diversify your investments one investment at a time, and with prices of some investments, that could take a while, leaving you exposed in the meantime. This is where financial products like mutual funds and ETFs come in.

Mutual Funds

Mutual funds work like this: A bunch of investors get together and throw their money into one large pool of money, which is *mutually funded* by all the investors. The fund manager then takes that giant pool of money and makes different investments. The investors don't need to think about what to invest in, the fund manager does that for them. Mutual funds may be invested in hundreds of different investments, giving their investors built-in diversification.

There are two main types of mutual funds: actively managed and passively managed. An actively managed fund is run by a fund manager who is actively making decisions about the particular investments the giant pool of money is invested in — the manager is making decisions on what to invest in and when to invest in hopes of getting a better return than the rest of the market. Investment decisions for a passively managed fund are usually made according to what you could call a set of rules (instead of the gut instincts of a fund manager). For instance, an index fund is a passively managed fund that is designed to mimic the performance of a particular stock index[1] — it's passive because the decision on what to include in an index fund isn't up to a fund manager. Instead, the very nature of the index fund makes those choices — for example, an index fund that follows the S&P 500 must include Apple, because it's part of the S&P 500 index. Because there isn't much for a fund manager to do in order for these funds to exist, these are considered to be managed passively.

In an actively managed fund, because there's a real, live person whom you need to pay to make decisions about investments, the fees are usually higher. The hope is that the fund manager is really good at their job and more than makes up for the higher fees; however, that usually isn't the case.[2] So why do actively managed funds exist, and why do people pay higher fees for poorer performance? Sometimes, an actively managed fund does outperform the market (better hope it outperformed enough to pay the higher fees!). Other times, people want to feel clever and smart by finding people they think are clever and smart who will "beat the market." Also, active management allows the fund to charge more fees and make more money.

A mutual fund will usually have a particular focus: American companies of a certain size, companies in a particular industry, tracking a particular stock index, and so on. So, by diversifying in a number of different mutual funds, you've just diversified your diversification. Awesome!

Exchange-Traded Funds or ETFs are very similar to mutual funds. There are some technical differences in how they work, but in the day-to-day or decade-to-decade life of the average investor (i.e., you), you can think of them the same way. ETFs usually are more like passively managed funds, and also usually have *very* low fees. Typically, you'll see ETFs used by roboinvestors. Robowhat? Don't worry, we'll come back to these. ETFs have gained popularity because their super low fees help increase returns for the typical buy-and-hold investor.

Target Date Funds

Some mutual funds help you diversify your investments across multiple companies, industries, countries, and so on. And that's really helpful. But what about when it comes to diversifying in *types* of investments — simply put, stocks and bonds — like the younger and older investors we mentioned earlier? Most every younger investor will become an older investor, and as time goes on your investment strategies and preferences may change. What are you to do?

You could manually realign your investments based on your

preferences, and many do. There is also a category of mutual funds and ETFs called *Target Date Funds*. These funds change their investments over time, based on a targeted date of retirement. So, let's say you plan to retire in the year 2055. You might invest in a 2055 Target Date Fund. Generally, a fund like this would, over time as retirement nears, shift from being stock-heavy to being bond-heavy.

Other investment choices like roboadvisors may have similar functions or features that rebalance or shift your investments like this over time, even without using a target date mutual fund.

Target date funds can help simplify the investing process, but sometimes that simplification can come with increased fees. Be sure to check the fees before signing up for one of these — or really any investments. While these fees will be only a few percentage points (or tenths of percentages) of the value of your investment, those small fees add up over the decades and a (seemingly) small difference in fees can have a large impact on your returns over time. If you have questions, find a financial advisor in your area you can trust.

Speaking of retirement — for most of us, most of our investment activity will be focused on retirement, so let's turn to investing for your "golden years."

Building Your Nest Egg

The term "nest egg" has been around for centuries. It comes from the practice of a farmer leaving an egg, real or artificial, in the nest, which (supposedly — I'm no chicken expert) encourages the hen to lay more eggs.

The theory here is that money left in your investment accounts turns into more money (via growth and interest) that can be withdrawn and used, just like how the nest egg encourages the hen to lay more eggs, which could be taken out of the nest by the farmer and sold at market or scrambled for breakfast. But the idea is that you leave the nest egg alone since it's driving the growth.

So how *do* you grow your nest egg?

You will see the best results saving and investing for retirement if you do it over the long haul. Time is your friend, here. You'll have a much easier time (and a much better retirement) if you start investing for retirement when you're 35 versus when you're 55, and better still if you're 25!

That said, you need to follow the Financial Phases and Money Milestones and begin investing for retirement at the right point in your financial journey.

Let's take another look:

As you can see, it's not time to start investing for retirement until you understand you and money, are budgeting, are debt-free, have a Full Rainy Day Fund, and have saved a down payment (if house-buying is for you). Investing for retirement before then will only serve as a distraction that slows your progress through the other phases (and slow progress and delayed wins may derail your entire journey!).

Once you're ready to contribute to retirement, we recommend you contribute 15 percent of your pay toward retirement. We recommend 15 percent because it's a high enough amount to put away to build up a decent chunk of change for your future, without making your current reality miserable. There's also a pretty good consensus on this amount in the personal finance world, and a study from the Center for Retirement Research at Boston College[3] found that 15 percent was a pretty good target for most people.

But where should you put that 15 percent, and how should you divvy it up? We'll cover a few practicals and then go through a simple step-by-step plan.

Free Money

Most employers will match, up to a certain percentage of your pay, what you put into the company-sponsored retirement plan — 401(k), 403(b), and so on. So, if your employer has a 3 percent match, they will double every dollar you put into your retirement account, up to that 3 percent of your salary mark. This is free money, and free money is one of our favorite kinds of money. It should be one of yours, too.

Any employer match should be considered the cherry on top, the gravy, the icing on the cake, whatever food topping analogy floats your boat. Consider it your responsibility to take care of that 15 percent. Any match you get will just make your retirement fund that much more funded.

When Would You Like to Pay Taxes?

You have two different types of retirement account options: Traditional and Roth. Both are tax-advantaged versus a regular investment account. The difference between these two options comes down to when you pay taxes.

In a regular investment account, you put in the money after you've paid taxes on it, and the deposits are not tax-deductible. You also pay taxes on the growth (your re-

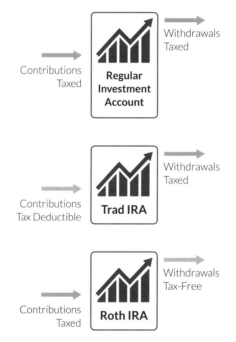

turn on investment/the money your money has made) when you take a withdrawal.

Thankfully, there are some special provisions in the US tax code designed to encourage people to invest for their retirement.

Funds deposited in a traditional retirement account go in before they are taxed (or are tax deductible if funded with after-tax money). This is nice, because you'll have more money to invest since you didn't pay taxes on it first. You'll pay the taxes later when you withdraw the money in retirement.

A Roth account is funded with after-tax money.[4] It grows tax-free and you pay zero taxes on it when you withdraw the money during retirement. This is nice because you know all the money in your retirement account is yours, and it'll generally be better to pay taxes now on your money when you put it in, versus paying taxes on it later once it grows bigger. In the majority of situations, a Roth account is the way to go.

Where does the money go?

As great as free money is, your employer-sponsored plan is probably not the best place to put all your retirement savings. This is because your choices will be limited to a small number of options for your investments, like a handful of different mutual funds. Quite often, the funds in employer-sponsored plans have higher fees than elsewhere. For that reason, you'll want to grab up that free money by investing up to the match amount, and then heading elsewhere to finish hitting your 15 percent.

Our Plan

While your individual situation may have unique needs or options available, here's our recommended plan for most people:

1. Invest in your employer-sponsored plan up to the match amount.
2. Invest in a Roth IRA[5] using investments with low fees (like ETFs) until you hit the IRA limit.
3. If you still haven't hit 15 percent yet, go back to your employer's fund until you reach the limit there.
4. If you still haven't hit 15 percent, start using regular investment accounts.[6]

Let's take a look at a real-world example with some numbers.

Julie makes $85,000/year at her job and her employer offers a 3.5

JULIE
Annual Salary: $85,000
Employer 401(k) Match: 3.5%

15% of Income to Invest: $12,750
3.5% Employer Match: $2,975

percent match. Fifteen percent of her income is $12,750.

First, Julie will tell her job to put 3.5 percent of her income into the Roth option for her 401(k), which her employer will match. Gotta love that free money!

Now, Julie has $9,775 (or 11.5 percent of her income) left to invest, and she'll turn to a Roth IRA.

Julie contributes the maximum amount (as of 2020), which is $6,000. She now has $3,775 left to invest.

She'll turn back to the employer-sponsored 401(k) and increase the amount she's putting in there to complete her 15 percent.

Now, she's not making two different contributions to the 401(k), but has simply split the contribution into matched and not-matched chunks to figure out her amounts.

Here's Julie with all her investments:

JULIE
Annual Salary: $85,000
Employer 401(k) Match: 3.5%

15% of Income to Invest: $12,750
3.5% Employer Match: $2,975

Investments
401(k) at work: $2,975 + $3,775 = $6,750
Roth IRA: $6,000

401(k) Match: $2,975

Total Investments: $15,725 (15% of income + 3.5% Match)

Again, the order of divvying up your 15 percent we suggest is:

1. Matched account with your employer up to the matched amount
2. IRA (probably a Roth) up to the limit
3. Non-matched account with your employer

Here are some visuals with the same info:

Welcome Our Robot Investing Overlords?

Now that you have a plan for your investments — namely, how much of your money you'll invest and in what types of investments — you need to determine where and how you'll invest. None of us can just call up Amazon or hop on their website and buy some stock. We need to work with a financial advisor or other intermediary to get the job done. You have a few options, and we'll cover them quickly.

- You could try DIY-ing it. You could open up an account with a firm like Vanguard and be in charge of where all your money goes — which funds and how much you put in each. You might avoid some fees, but you'll be doing all the work of searching through thousands of investment options and balancing your portfolio over time.
- You could load your life savings into a trading app and manage your retirement one swipe at a time. On top of the hassles of evaluating all your choices and keeping it balanced over time, those apps usually don't handle retirement accounts, so you'll be missing out on tax savings.

- You could also do what's called a self-directed IRA. That *really* opens up the types of things you can invest in (land, gold, water rights, etc.). However, all that freedom comes with more risk, and way more time and energy needed to make it work out well for you in the end. Frankly, it takes too much work and carries too much risk for most folks.

All these options *may* have an upside but are weighed down with just too many downsides. So, it seems, that working with an advisor is much better.

When it comes to advisors, you have some options. Let's start by categorizing advisors into two big categories: humans and robots. (The future really is here, huh?)

Let's start with the humans.

There are all kinds and types of investment advisors out there, with all sorts of different names and titles. No matter who you're looking at working with, we recommend you work with someone with the following traits:

- **Fiduciary:** This means they are required to work in your best interests. Shouldn't *all* financial advisors work in the best interests of their clients? Yes, they should, but not all do. When things like commissions, quotas, or other incentives are thrown in the mix, a temptation for the advisor to do well by themselves first can creep in. If they don't say they are a fiduciary, or it's not listed on their website, ask them. If they are not, don't work with them.
- **Fee-only:** You will pay a professional fee for their services. This could be a flat rate, or a percentage (maybe 1 percent) of your portfolio. You want a fee-only advisor because they are paid only by you, instead of through commissions. *Fee-based* might sound like the same thing, but that means you pay them *and* they can earn commissions. Typically, fee-only advisors also act as fi-

duciaries, but you'll want to make sure.

- **A helpful guide and teacher:** This one's less straight-forward, but you'll want someone who will help you make decisions about your investments, not keep you in the dark and insist you simply trust them to "do their job." It's your money after all! Certainly lean on their experience and advice, but lean on it to help you make your own decisions. Working with a good advisor will leave you knowing more about your investments, how they work, and why they're a good choice for you.
- **Experienced and good at their job:** You'll want to make sure you are working with someone who has a fair amount of experience. Having years of experience can help them gauge current conditions and experience with lots of clients, especially those similar to you, can give them insight on how to help you best.

Now, the Robots!

As investing — along with everything else, it seems — moves online, a new type of advisor has been created: the roboadvisor. Roboadvisors use algorithms and data analysis to make investing decisions for you. You tell the roboadvisor platform how you'd like to invest — your tolerance for risk, your target retirement date, and so on — and it goes to work without any pesky human emotion getting in the mix.

The good thing about roboadvisors is that they are really easy to set up — you can do it in a few minutes, typically — and they are super cheap. As of writing this, the most popular roboadvisors charge around a quarter of a percent of your assets to manage them, and most don't require much of a minimum of funds to get started.

The downside to roboadvisors is that they are robots, and sometimes you'd like more personal attention and advice. In keeping things simple, you don't have as many choices for your investments as you may like. Some platforms allow you to schedule meetings with real live human advisors for an additional fee.

We like roboadvisors, and use them ourselves. We're always

evaluating them to find the best one, so if you're interested, **check out our latest recommendations at WalletWin.com/advisors**.

No matter if you work with a human or a robot, it's important to work with an advisor that you trust will do a good job and put your interests first. A good advisor can be a trusted partner and an important part of your financial plan.

Terms and Definitions

Investing is full of lingo, and we've just thrown a lot of it at you. If you're not familiar with the vocabulary, you might feel confused pretty quickly. So here's a quick review of some of the more common terms you may run into, defined in plain English, to equip you for your investing adventures:

- **Exchange:** A market where different things like stocks, commodities, and so on are bought and sold. Some have real physical locations, while others are entirely virtual.
- **Share(s):** A share is a tiny slice of a company. If a company issues 1,000,000 shares of stock, each share is worth one millionth of the company. Own 500,000 of those shares, and you own half the company.
- **Stock:** Used to describe owning shares in a company. If I have ten shares of Company A and fifteen shares of Company B, you could say I own stock in two companies. You could also say I have two stocks.
- **IRA:** Individualized Retirement Account — an account that has certain tax benefits (as outlined in US tax code) and is used for retirement savings.
- **Bond:** A loan made between an investor (the lender) and a company, municipality, or government (the lendee), payable at an agreed-upon date at an agreed-upon interest rate.
- **Traditional IRA**: An IRA that is funded with pre-tax money (or contributions are tax-deductible) — up to certain income limits. The money grows tax-deferred

and is taxed upon withdrawal as income.

- **Roth IRA**:An IRA that is funded with money you've already paid taxes on, and your contributions are not tax-deductible. But because you've already paid the taxes on that money, it grows tax-free and you pay no taxes when you take it out.
- **Index**: An index measures a particular part of the financial market. For example, Standard and Poor's S&P 500 index measures the stock prices of 500 large companies in the US stock market; the Dow Jones Industrial Average follows only 30 large companies; and the FTSE 100 (or Footsie) follows 100 companies listed on the London Stock Exchange. You cannot invest in an index, but it is possible to invest in mutual funds or ETFs that are constructed to reflect an index.
- **Mutual Fund**: A Mutual Fund allows investors to pool their money together to make investments, giving them the ability to easily diversify their investments, as the fund will invest in many different stocks, bonds, and the like.
- **Exchange Traded Funds or ETFs**: Exchange Traded Funds or ETFs are similar to mutual funds in that they are invested in multiple companies, but these trade on exchanges like any other company. In the real life of the typical investor, they serve a nearly identical function to mutual funds.
- **Target Date Funds:** A mutual fund or ETF that changes its composition on a timeline to lower risk levels as your target retirement date approaches. As a simple example, many change the stock/bond ratio from being stock-heavy early on to being bond-heavy in later years.
- **Roboadvisor:** Investing platforms that use algorithms to make investment decisions versus a human's intellect and/or gut feel. Due to the fact that you don't have to pay robots to work, fees are often very low.
- **401(k):** The provision of the US Tax Code that outlines

the tax benefits of particular types of investment accounts offered by employers. These accounts are often
referred to as 401(k)s.

- **403(b):** Pretty much exactly like a 401(k) but for
  non-profit organizations.
- **Thrift Savings Plan (TSP):** The retirement plan offered
  by the US government to members of the military, government, or civil service.

While it may not be exciting right now, investing for your retirement
is one of the best ways to prepare for long-term financial success.
Work hard to get to this Money Milestone as quickly as you can. Unfortunately, a lot of us have been delayed from reaching this Milestone as we paid off student loans. While we can't change the past,
we *can* help our children make better financial decisions when it
comes time for their education, and that's where we're heading next.

Success Story
Sebastian and Leslie Fisher

My mindset about money before I started WalletWin was one of unease. I am always afraid that financial ruin is just one bad decision away. I used to leave all the financial decisions to my husband and think of it as "his department." WalletWin's method of budgeting and working toward concrete goals has been enormously helpful. I no longer have the feeling in the back of my mind that something bad financially could happen to me. We plan out our spending and stick to our budget. The idea is simple, but it can be hard making the right financial decisions day after day. Seeing progress is what kept motivating me. We paid off about $10,000 in debt after going "shark mode" and I feel so relieved! We are working toward other financial goals now and I feel like I am in control of this area of my life.

CHAPTER 13

Save for Your Kids' College

"Education is the food of youth, the delight of old age, the ornament of prosperity, the refuge and comfort of adversity, and the provocation to grace in the soul."
— Saint Augustine[1]

🏳 *Amanda*

Every year we graduate the next most indebted class in history. Student loans have become a defining factor in young Americans' lives — and not for the better. By the time Jonathan and I started college back in 2003 and 2004, student loans were a way of life, completely normalized and commonplace. The assumption was that everyone had student loans unless they were uber smart and scored a full-ride scholarship, or had wealthy parents, and/or a trust fund. While these aren't true, neither of us considered a different route through college.

As we look back, both of us realize that we indeed could have completely avoided student loans had we been more intentional and educated about our options.

Personally, I took less than $15,000 total in all five years I was in college (yes … nursing school at the time required an extra year). Had I done summer school while living at home or worked a part-time job every year I was in college, I could have avoided loans altogether. But I wasn't familiar with the research[2] that shows college students working part-time jobs excel in their studies, and ultimately I valued my social life more than my financial health. It wasn't a conscious choice, but nobody had ever taught me to really think about money beyond the here and now.

Jonathan

The amount my parents had saved for my education would have totally covered one of Pennsylvania's many smaller state schools. But I just didn't like the few we visited, and the dumb rebellious teenager part of me bristled at the idea of going to the same school as my parents. I ended up going to an out-of-state school, with an out-of-state price tag (and student loans), to get a degree I've never really used.

Amanda

When it dawned on us that our student loans were ultimately a result of our own poor decision-making, it was incredibly humbling. We'd strapped balls and chains on our legs unnecessarily — and so many others have fallen into this same trap. On another level it was angering. At age 17 or 18, students are signing on the dotted line for tens of thousands, sometimes hundreds of thousands of dollars in debt, with no real understanding of or connection to their requirement to pay these back. The adults in their lives oftentimes aren't educating them on the realities they'll feel when that first student loan payment comes due. Colleges, universities, banks, public and private lenders alike certainly aren't going to spell out the details. It's in their *interest* (ba-dum ching) to keep the process simple and streamlined, so the students barely notice what they've signed up for.

Student loans have defined an entire generation and it's time that same generation declares, "NO MORE!" It's time to interrupt the crippling student loan generational cycle.

I know what some of you might be thinking, though:

- "I had to pay for college myself! It built character!"
- "We don't make enough money to help."
- "I have more children than the average bear."
- "Will college even be relevant anymore when my kids grow up?"
- "We're too late … my kid is heading to college next year!"

While we've heard comments like this, they're often rooted in fear.

I have no doubt that paying for college builds character … but taking copious amounts of student loans in the process doesn't. Teaching your child money management skills and how to find creative solutions around debt will build character, not to mention a variety of other extremely beneficial life skills they'll need to succeed. It's also worth noting that back in the day, it was feasible for students to work part-time during the school year and full-time on breaks to cash flow their education without debt. For better or worse (probably worse), those days are long gone in higher education.

As for not making enough money, it's a valid concern. But more often than not, it comes from parents still in debt from their own student loans, and stressed out about money. They're underestimating the power of a solid financial game plan and how it could turn around their entire family financial situation. Or if parents have many children to save for, it can feel like they're trying to put a fire out with a squirt gun, as the money they can set aside to save gets so spread out it effectively does nothing. These parents are underestimating the power of strategic college conversations with their children and creating individualized plans for each one. They also might not realize what options exist for financial aid or in winning scholarships.

If you've got a child heading to college in the next year or so, don't panic. While you might not have compound interest on your side, there are many valid options for you to navigate paying for college. Sure, it won't be as simple as if you'd started eighteen years ago, but hey, better now than never.

Lastly, while college trends will certainly shift and change over the decades to come, there will always be professions that rightfully require a collegiate education. Even if higher education isn't the right fit for one child, it will be the right fit for another. This is also where guided discussions with your children come into play, so you can make sure to align your education savings with what will likely be the best path for each unique kiddo.

While this chapter is written to parents, it's equally beneficial for students. We'll tackle what parents need to know and how to equip both yourselves and your students for this transition. Then we'll move into three different strategies to use to secure a debt-free degree: savings, work, and scholarships.

As we've already mentioned, our twelve Money Milestones are to be done in order. If you're reading this and you aren't yet budgeting, have debt, or have no emergency savings established, this is NOT your best next financial step. You need to put your own oxygen mask on first before you take care of others. Even if you've moved further up the milestones and you're debt-free and own a home, if you aren't investing for retirement, you're not ready for this milestone. There's no use helping your child secure a debt-free degree if it jeopardizes your future and possibly lands you back in debt because you didn't save enough for retirement.

The College Discussion

Before we dive into the strategies, you first need to discuss a college plan with your spouse and child(ren) as they enter high school. You need to begin with the end in mind so you can work backwards from the end goal and craft your plan for helping them graduate without student loans. For example, if you attended a private school and want the same for your children, you're obviously going to need to come up with far more money than you would for a state school, a local community college, or some combination of both. Or if you've got kids with wildly different personalities and desires (one Ivy League bound for a master's in engineering and another a skilled videographer with entrepreneurial aspirations), you may choose uneven saving amounts for each.

Knowing where you envision your kiddos ending up (and when they're old enough, where they envision themselves) will help tremendously as you work the plans backwards and set goals for how much you need to save, how many hours per week they need to work, and what kind of gap they need to make up with scholarships.

Here are a few questions to guide your discussion(s):

- How many children do you plan to save for?
- Do you plan to pay for none, some, or all of their education expenses?
- Do you plan to pay for none, some, or all of their room and board expenses?
- Which types of schools are you considering? Public, private, in-state, out-of-state?
- How many years are you planning to fund? Two, four, grad school?
- Will you be eligible for any financial aid?
- Are your children willing and eager to pursue scholarship funding?
- How many years away are you from paying for college?
- Will there be outside funding sources available? Grandparents, other relatives?
- How much can you afford to save toward this goal every month without harming other saving priorities?

I can't stress how important this discussion is for parents to have with each other and their children. Getting clear about answers to these questions provides the foundation on which the entire paying-for-college plan will stand. Once you've had the discussion(s) and gathered relevant numbers and information, it's time to craft a plan for your kid's debt-free degree.

Savings

The average cost of college has jumped an incredible 3,009 percent over the last fifty years.[3] Yeah, you read that right! While inflation typically rises about 4 percent each year, college tuition usually jumps about 8 percent.[4]

Not only has tuition increased in that time frame, but so have room and board, books, and fees. Anyone seen the new high-rise luxury apartment buildings/dorms present on many campuses nowadays? I count myself lucky to have spent a year in a cinderblock dorm from the seventies that cost a fraction of the price! Thinking about saving enough to help one, let alone several children get through college without debt can feel like a daunting task.

Parents today have many options when it comes to saving and investing for their children's future education. While we could detail out every possible strategy, we're going to keep things simple and stick with the tax-favored strategies we personally use for our girls as we plan and prepare for their schooling: ESAs and 529s.

Education Savings Account (ESA) or Education IRA

A Coverdell ESA (named after the late Senator Paul Coverdell) allows you to save and grow your money for educational purposes. While similar to 529s, as they're both investment vehicles, ESAs have some restrictions and a couple of major differences worth mentioning.

An ESA has a contribution limit of $2,000 (after tax) per year, per child. It also has income restrictions — you can't contribute to an ESA if you make more than $110,000 (single) or $220,000 (married filing jointly). The amount also must be used by or for the beneficiary by age 30 or else transferred to a sibling.[5]

The funds can be used on both elementary school or high school education, in addition to college expenses. The money grows tax-free (you know we like that phrase) and allows you to choose from a wide variety of investment options. While you won't receive any tax benefits upon contributing to these funds, there won't be taxes to pay when you take them out later on, meaning the money grew without requiring you to pay taxes on it, which is pretty cool.

529 Savings Plans

A 529 savings plan (named after its section of the US tax code) is an investment account offering tax advantages that allow you to set aside money for qualified educational expenses. While similar to the ESA, 529 savings plans have their own set of restrictions and differences you should be aware of.

If you want to save more than $2,000 per year for your children's college education, or if you exceed the income limits for an ESA, a 529 savings plan is the way to go. Important note: There is a prepaid tuition 529 option, but we don't recommend that route. Most 529 savings plans are run by states — and no, you don't have to open one in the state you reside or where you plan to attend college. This means you can take advantage of the state plan with the best investment options and the lowest fees!

Anyone can contribute to a 529 (need a birthday gift idea, Grandma?) and there are no income or age limits on contributions. Due to recent changes, in some states you can even use the funds in some 529 plans for K–12 education expenses, including homeschooling. Compared to an ESA, most 529 savings plans have limited funds available and auto-adjust based on the age of your child, giving you less direct control over your investments.

You might be wondering if there's a point where it no longer makes sense to use an ESA or a 529 to pay for education expenses. The answer? It depends. The truth is that there are many factors to consider. Even if you have a high-schooler who is college-bound in a matter of months, your state may offer tax advantages that outweigh the fees associated with opening an ESA or a 529. There may be advantages even if the money is simply channeled through these accounts, as opposed to being deposited for long-term growth. There is no universal line in the sand as to when it's "too late" to get started. Each family has to look at all sides of the equation from their unique circumstances to decide what's most advantageous.

Work

Studies show that students who worked a part-time or full-time job while in college had average earnings up to $20,000 higher than those who didn't work throughout school.[6] They also reveal that students who work less than twenty hours per week have higher GPAs than both students who worked more hours or who didn't work at all.[7] The mentality has predominantly been that students ought not work so they can "focus on their studies" since being a student is their job. This attitude is missing a big opportunity for students' preparation for the real world, though.

When you think about it, it makes sense that students working less than twenty hours per week would be excelling. An attribute of successful people is the ability to manage their time well amongst competing priorities. Shark Tank's Kevin O'Leary, a.k.a. Mr. Wonderful, loves to share this adage, "If you want something done, give it to a busy mom."[8] From the outside that makes no sense — why give a busy person *more* to do? The secret is that a busy mother has learned task management, project oversight, prioritization, strategic decision-making, and she has developed strong critical thinking skills. Because of this skillset, a busy mother's capacity tends to be higher than the average bear. So it goes with a student who's using a small portion of their week to work. This requires them to figure out when they're going to study, socialize, and work, developing strong skills early in life that will accelerate their growth and leadership abilities compared to their peers.

Another quality of successful people is stretching oneself by taking on responsibility but not overwhelming oneself by tackling more than can be managed. This speaks to why more than twenty hours of work per week can lead to lowering GPAs. Anything more no longer leads to peak performance, but sends the student constantly running around in a state of stress. We're helping our students learn boundaries and what their personal capacity is by inviting them to stretch themselves while still protecting their time, mental health, and ability to rest. Learning these boundaries earlier in life, as opposed to later, is beneficial not only in college but post-graduation. How many adults have you met who continuously bite off more than they can chew, while simultaneously underperforming in many areas of life? Getting addicted to busyness and becoming overwhelmed is a very real risk. It makes people feel productive even though they're anything but. They're simply running around achieving tasks with no real merit or meaning, faster and faster. Again, if we can help our children learn the difference between being busy and prioritizing action, we do them a great service.

Earning a bachelor's in nursing was challenging — it definitely wasn't one of the "easy majors" on campus. Balancing the hours of studying (I'm looking at you, Anatomy!) with various leadership roles on campus was truly my first taste of balancing competing priorities, and it's served me well over the years. Economically speaking, a paying job would've helped me begin learning about money, instead of just sticking my head in the sand about all things finance. While I was busy and learned many time management skills, I do wish I'd known about the power of working less than twenty hours per week.

Scholarships

Last and certainly not least: scholarships. When I was in high school, I subscribed to the thinking that you had to either be Einstein or Michael Jordan to score a scholarship. While I'm "life smart" as Jonathan and I like to call it, I'm not very book smart. I figured the path to a scholarship via academics was a dead end for me. That left athletics, which was something I excelled at. I played several sports — softball, volleyball, swimming, and soccer. As high school went on, I began focusing on volleyball in particular. I played during both the regular season and on a club team. Being only 5'4", I knew I was never going big places at the net, so I began focusing on playing defense well.

During the summer of my junior year, I began to receive letters from small rural colleges about possibly playing volleyball on scholarship at their schools. They requested to come see me play that fall of my senior year. I'd never given serious thought to playing volleyball in college but this perked my interest. When I returned to the varsity volleyball team that fall, though, there was an emphasis on the team rebuilding and growing young varsity talent who could hopefully win a championship a couple of years down the line. This meant that my nearly permanent spot was as a benchwarmer. I tried talking with my coach about the real possibility of playing in college and that recruiters needed to be able to see me play but it fell on deaf ears. It wasn't part of the coach's plan for the team, and that's all there was to it. Hurt and confused, I erased all thoughts of an athletic scholarship from my mind. Looking back, I wish I'd have fought a bit harder and communicated more clearly with my coach, knowing how big an opportunity that was. Truthfully, I was afraid of being different and going to a small college anyway. Attending the University of Nebraska-Lincoln and joining a sorority felt more important to me at the time. If only I could go back and talk some sense into that young girl about why allowing "coolness" to affect major life decisions was a bad idea.

With both academic and athletic scholarships scratched out in my book, I figured there were no other options left on the table. Boy was I wrong.

Years later, I had the pleasure of meeting Jocelyn Pearson from *The Scholarship System*. In high school her parents sat her down and told her "You're either gonna have to figure out paying for college, or you're gonna have to take out student loans." She knew she never wanted to look at a giant ball and chain of debt, so she started finding and securing scholarships to pay for college. From her experience she wrote a book about how she secured six figures in scholarships throughout her entire college career, and ultimately launched The Scholarship System.

My jaw dropped upon hearing her story. It was so frustrating that I hadn't even considered the tactics she'd used! As a guest on The WalletWin Podcast, she singlehandedly busted many of the myths that surround scholarships and make them feel inaccessible. If you have a student in high school or in college already, do yourself a favor and craft your plan to a debt-free degree watching her free training over at **WalletWin.com/scholarships**.

I'm guessing you've also accepted a few of these myths as fact too … so let's play a round of MythBusters: Scholarships Edition!

Myth #1 — You must score all your scholarships before heading to college.

Did you know that a student doesn't have to win all his scholarships *before* college? He can apply for them at any point in the game — in high school, as a college sophomore, or even in his final semester! If you've got a child in college and you or she has taken loans so far for her education, you can put an end to that right now and help her begin securing scholarships instead. Neither one of you needs another student loan, and it's never too late to get started. In fact, Jocelyn told us that of the six figures in scholarships she won to pay for college, the final check she secured was cashed on her way home from graduation.

Myth #2 — Scholarships are for the mega-smart or mega-athletic.

Are there really scholarships available if you aren't Isaac Newton or Tom Brady? When most people think of scholarships, merit-based ones often come to mind. It's easy to assume that you either need a high GPA/ACT/SAT score or to be a child sports prodigy to earn a full ride for a college education. While there are many merit-based, school-specific scholarships available, there are far more scholarships available from private organizations that use wider criteria to choose winners. There are more scholarships out there that are won by students with average GPAs and not a single athletic bone in their body, proving that a kid doesn't need the perfect GPA or a great throwing arm to get a debt-free education.

Myth #3 — I make too much for my child to qualify for scholarships.

You fill out the Free Application for Federal Student Aid (FAFSA), or government financial aid, and it comes back saying you make too much and your child doesn't get any funding. So naturally when your child is applying for scholarships, if it says "financial aid required" she can't apply. Right? Not necessarily. If the scholarship specifies that the expected family contribution (EFC) must be zero, meaning you will not be paying anything for education expenses and qualify for maximum aid, then you cannot apply for those. However, most of the time, they will say you must have an "unmet financial need" in order to apply. In this situation, if you or your student would have to turn to student loans for any amount of her education expenses, this is an unmet need. Most families will fall into this middle category of technically being able to contribute something toward college but not everything, especially if they have multiple children.

Myth #4 — If you don't score the Big Kahuna, there's nothing left.

It's easy to think that the only scholarships available or worth applying for are ones that provide a full ride through college. Reason being, these are the ones with the most publicity and status, so they feel like the only ones out there. In reality, these don't make up most of the scholarships available. The majority of scholarships don't have a giant price tag attached to them, but they have the potential to really add up when combined.

Going back to Jocelyn's story — she secured six-figures in scholarships to cover her four-year degree, but the largest one she received was only $4,000! She only won $2,000 each year from her university, and the rest of her scholarships were won through outside organizations. After trial and error, she figured out a way to go after the smaller-dollar, low-hanging-fruit scholarships to pay her way through college. You don't need the Big Kahuna when you have a systematic way to win a few thousand here and a couple thousand there. Paying for college can be death by a thousand papercuts with winning these types of scholarships. Lest you be tempted to think $2,000 isn't worth going after, Jocelyn told us that the average student might only put ten hours into applying for that initial scholarship. When you calculate the return on investment (ROI), that's $200/hour! That's definitely worth your student's time.

While I've had moments of kicking myself, wishing I'd known the truth about scholarships long ago, I'm relieved to know about them now. In 2036 we'll have a college freshman, sophomore, and senior. At our current savings rate (which we began the month each of them was born) we probably won't have enough to fully cash flow their entire education (which will be about a billion dollars a semester by then). But I'm not sweating: As our girls approach college, I'm confident knowing we have a multi-pronged approach to pay for college without debt — if that indeed is the best next step for them to make. A combo of careful planning, our savings, their work, and scholarships, is our family's path forward — and it's relieving. I hope you also feel a weight being lifted off your back now that you know there's another way that doesn't involve debt, debt, and more debt.

Once you've got a plan to make sure you're not saddling your children with crippling student loans, it's time to tackle your final payment: the mortgage. At this stage, total financial freedom is no longer a distant dream — it's so close that it's palpable!

Success Story
Hannah Crites

I graduated college in 2017 with over $134,000 in student loan debt. I knew I took out a lot of money each year of school — I was present during the phone calls with the student loan company. But my mentors assured me that I would be able to pay it all off within a few years of graduating. What a lie.

I cried when I added it all up. I did not expect so many zeros. There was no way I was going to be able to pay off that amount with my measly $35,000 take-home pay. I wasn't sure how I would cover my minimum payments. I worked for a struggling Catholic apostolate and lived in a city with a high cost of living.

I discovered WalletWin a few days later after listening to Amanda on one of my favorite podcasts. She talked about hope and freedom. She talked about the plan that she and Jonathan taught inside the WalletWin course, that led to becoming debt-free and attaining financial peace. I signed up right away.

When my first payment for student loans was due in January of 2018, I had a plan. I had a written budget. I had a goal to be debt-free by 2023. I felt confident and ready to tackle it. I paid off $15,000 in the first seven months.

I picked up side hustles to boost my income. I started babysitting again, which I hadn't done since high school. I delivered groceries through Shipt. I started freelance writing. I worked at a weekend farmers market. I took my marketing and project management skills and started working as a virtual assistant.

It hasn't been easy. Nine months into my journey, I was let go from my job due to downsizing. Two years in, my twenty-year-old car went kaput on me and COVID-19 hit. But I absorbed the blows, paused Stack and Attack when I needed to, and then started up again once things were steady.

I have sacrificed and worked hard while still living a very full, joy-filled life. Money conversations that ended in tears are now making me feel in control and empowered. I am proclaiming from the rooftops, I AM BIGGER THAN MY DEBT!

I have since paid off $75,000. I still have about $82,000 to go (thank you high interest loans), but I'll likely pay it all off sooner than 2023.

CHAPTER 14

Pay Off the House

"By wisdom a house is built,
and by understanding it is established;
by knowledge the rooms are filled
with all precious and pleasant riches."
— Proverbs 24:3–4

1. Money Mindset 2. Live with a Budget 3. Insure Yourself 4. Starter Rainy Day Fund 5. Get a Month Ahead 6. Pay Off Debt 7. Full Rainy Day Fund 8. Save Down Payment 9. Contribute to Retirement 10. Save for College 11. **Pay Off House**

Establish Your Financial Foundation   Gain Momentum With Your Money   Grow Your Wealth

🚩 *Amanda*

Back in 2009, I trained to run my first half-marathon. Up to that point, I wasn't what you would've called a runner. In fact, I never voluntarily ran, and preferred team sports or basically any other form of exercising *except* running for my workouts. I knew it wasn't going to be a walk in the park, so I downloaded a detailed 16-week training protocol to help get into runner's shape. I spent that entire spring going on runs in the sleet, rain, snow, and eventual sunshine. Somehow,

239

as the weeks passed, running got easier. My body experienced that mysterious "runner's high" and I fell in love with running.

When it came time for race day, I was nervous. In my training I hadn't ever actually run a full 13.1 miles, so I wasn't sure how it would turn out. Thankfully I had friends also running, and they kept me distracted from the butterflies. During the race, I felt great. Everything was going off without a hitch, but around mile 9, I made a terrible mistake. Instead of getting a drink of water, I accidentally grabbed Gatorade at a drink station and downed it before I could realize what I'd done. One of the rules I had learned early in running was that if you didn't train with it, don't do it on race day — and I had only trained with water.

By the time mile 10 came around, I knew something wasn't right. My stomach began to cramp up and I could feel the cramps descending further down my digestive tract. It was around this time I had to peel off the path and hit my first of several port-a-potties. When mile 11 came, I was deteriorating rapidly. Psychologically, I was thrown and whatever zone I'd been in was gone. My hips were numb. My legs, dutifully plodding into the pavement, felt like they weren't even attached to my body. Everything hurt … but there was no way I wasn't going to finish the race, so I blasted a pump-up jam and kept moving forward.

Something strange happened on the final stretch. Just before entering the University of Illinois' Memorial Stadium where the race ended, my legs began going faster. I saw the finish line about a hundred yards out and instinctually tapped into some hidden adrenaline as I kicked things into overdrive. While I am sure it wasn't my fastest sprint, I was giving that race 110 percent of what I had, and finishing strong became all I could think about. Seeing the finish line gave me strength to give everything I had.

That's the visual I want you to have in your mind's eye as you arrive at this Money Milestone. When you arrive at this final milestone, it's important to look back and see the journey you've been on. What started as an exciting adventure to begin winning with money (even if you hadn't budgeted a day in your life!) led you to paying off debt, building emergency savings, protecting those you love, and cultivating a spirit of generosity. Like my Gatorade-induced digestion challenges, I'm sure you experienced bumps in the road that tested you. There were likely times you wanted to give up. But you didn't. And you're in the home stretch.

This final Money Milestone of the Grow Your Wealth Financial Phase is the equivalent of those last 100 yards on half-marathon day. It's time to trust yourself, tap into adrenaline, and sprint toward that finish line. It's time to get creative and kiss the mortgage goodbye, securing total freedom over your number one wealth-building tool — your income.

Imagine paying that last and final mortgage payment on your home. In one moment, everything shifts. Suddenly that stroll in the backyard with your first (or seventh if you're Lorelai Gilmore) cup of coffee in hand feels a little more peaceful. Sitting in front of the fireplace and reading a book, more soothing. Rocking your babies and grandbabies to sleep in the nursery, more secure. Nothing around you has payments attached to it. Take a deep breath, sit back, and soak it all in with gratitude.

Paying off your mortgage is one of the final milestones of creating financial freedom in your life. The power comes not only in the fact that your income has a lot more flexibility now that it's not obligated to a large monthly payment, but also in the emotions. Mortgages, while typically low in interest, still represent risk. Dave Ramsey likes to say that "100 percent of foreclosures are on homes with mortgages,"[1] and it's true. This milestone allows you to free up your monthly income while leaving a large portion of your net worth warm and cozy in your paid-off home. This new financial freedom and peace of mind opens doors to giving, investing, and spending that extra money on things that matter most to you and your family.

Discerning This Milestone

You'll notice this milestone is part of the third Financial Phase: Grow Your Wealth. Paying off your mortgage exists alongside other milestones like saving for education expenses as well as your retirement. What good does it do you to have a paid-off house, yet you had to turn around and take (or had your child take) student loan debt? Or if you couldn't retire because you'd been neglecting investments in the name of paying off the mortgage? Not a whole lot of good.

Your approach to this Financial Phase truly does depend on where you are in life when you arrive at it. If your kiddos are very young and college is more than a decade away, you might save 15 percent toward retirement, some toward education, and then aggressively hit the mortgage so it's gone in under five years. In that situation, you'd have your income to help cash flow education expenses in addition to what you've saved, as a mortgage wouldn't be clogging things up anymore.

However, if your children are only a few years from high school, your priorities might flip. You might save 15 percent for retirement, and aggressively save for education, putting only a little extra at the mortgage, if any at all.

The important thing to remember is that you're most likely doing each of these alongside one another as they are long-term goals. This is unlike the other milestones we've discussed that are shorter-term in nature and completed consecutively, one after the other. Knowing your own situation is important for discerning how you'll personally tackle the Grow Your Wealth Financial Phase and address each individual milestone.

Think of the execution of the Money Milestones in the Grow Your Wealth Financial Phase this way: Start them one at a time and when you're satisfied with how that one's going (and will continue to go), start the next. First, start contributing to retirement and get your contributions up to 15 percent of your income, before moving on to education savings. Once you're contributing 15 percent for retirement *and* you're satisfied with how much you're putting away for education, *then* start discerning how to tackle paying off your mortgage early.

Start one, get it to a good place, and keep it running while you start the next.

Now that you're contributing 15 percent of your income to retirement, and are on track for education savings, it's time to focus on tackling the mortgage.

But What about My Tax Deduction?

 Jonathan

Before we dive into exactly how to do just that, let's address a hotly debated topic: the tax deduction. There are personal finance "experts" out there who discourage paying your mortgage off, because you'll lose the tax deduction on the interest you're paying. But let's run some easy math on how this shakes out in practice.

If you have a $200,000 mortgage at 3 percent interest, you'll pay between $300 and $5,000 in interest each year, depending on how long you've had the mortgage (the principal/interest ratio of your payment shifts over time). On average, you'll pay about $3,000. That gives you a $3,000 tax deduction, meaning your taxable income on your taxes will be $3,000 less.

Using 2020 numbers, if you're married, filing jointly, and have a household income of $85,000, you'll be paying $10,280 in federal taxes before any deductions or credits. Paying $3,000 in mortgage interest payments lowers your taxable income by $3,000 to $82,000. Your federal tax bill is now $9,620.

MORTGAGE INTEREST TAX DEDUCTION

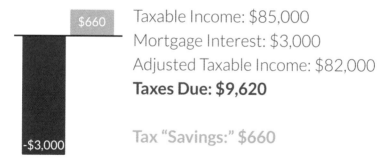

Taxable Income: $85,000
Mortgage Interest: $3,000
Adjusted Taxable Income: $82,000
Taxes Due: $9,620

Tax "Savings:" $660

While I enjoy a tax break as much as anybody else, if you think keeping your mortgage around so you can get a tax deduction is a good deal, you just paid $3,000 in interest to save $660 in taxes. And if you really want a tax deduction, you (and the world) would be better off if you were free and clear of your mortgage and you made a charitable donation of $3,000 — which would get you both a deduction *and* do some good with the money.

You also might run into people who discourage paying off your mortgage because they say you can make money by borrowing money at a low interest rate on your house and investing it in the stock market. But by the time you adjust for risk (Remember that line about foreclosures? Or that time the market halved in a week?) and taxes, you don't come out ahead. Don't borrow on your home for the sake of investing.

The "Secret" to Paying off Your Mortgage Early

Now, let's chat about how to accelerate your mortgage payoff.

When you reach this Money Milestone, the top-secret, super sophisticated strategy that you'll use to make it happen is: paying more money toward your mortgage.

It's not fancy. It's not even a "secret." It's just simple common-sense math. If you pay more money toward a debt, you'll pay it off sooner — and when interest is involved, you'll pay less.

You'll run into some services or programs that sell themselves on helping you pay your mortgage off faster, but you don't need them. There's no super special secret you're missing out on. Every mortgage payoff strategy is just a slightly different flavor of "pay more toward your mortgage."

But that's not to say it's boring. Or that it's not something to lean into. Think about it: This is your very last debt. You pay this off and you owe nothing to nobody. *All* your income is yours to determine what to do with.

You've run the race and done it well to get to this point. You are Amanda running her half marathon. You've been running for a while, your legs might be getting pretty tired, you might want to quit.

But you're not going to.

You're coming around the bend, and the finish line is in sight. Think about when you were paying off debt earlier in your financial journey. You did everything you could to get rid of that debt. You got creative; some might even say you were a little crazy. You were in full-on Shark Mode.

It's time to get back in touch with your inner Jaws. Time to sharpen those teeth and start taking big fat bites out of that mortgage.

This one last debt is between you and full financial freedom. No more payments. No more owing anything. Let's go after it.

For a little motivation, let's look at the numbers. Let's assume you bought your home ten years ago. We'll run the numbers on a 15-year mortgage (since that's what we recommend) *and* a 30-year, since that's what the vast majority of mortgages are (perhaps yours). The only differences in these mortgages are the length of the mortgage and the interest rates. Both were for $200,000 ten years ago.

MORTGAGE A	MORTGAGE B
Term: 15 Years	Term: 30 Years
Interest Rate: 3.0%	Interest Rate: 3.5%
Payment: $1,381.16	Payment: $898.09
Time Left: 5 Years	Time Left: 20 Years
Balance: $62,399.67	Balance: $149,409.68

Let's see what happens when you pay an extra $500 a month toward the principal:

MORTGAGE A	MORTGAGE B
Term: 15 Years	Term: 30 Years
Interest Rate: 3.0%	Interest Rate: 3.5%
Payment: $1,381.16	Payment: $898.09
Extra Payment: $500/mo	Extra Payment: $500/mo
Time Left:	Time Left:
~~5 Years~~ 3 Years, 8 Months	~~20 Years~~ 11 Years, 2 Months
Total Interest:	Total Interest:
~~$48,609.55~~ $46,921.91	~~$123,312.00~~ $95,065.55

MORTGAGE A	MORTGAGE B
Term: 15 Years	Term: 30 Years
Interest Rate: 3.0%	Interest Rate: 3.5%
Payment: $1,381.16	Payment: $898.09
Extra Payment: $1,500/mo	Extra Payment: $1,500/mo
Time Left:	Time Left:
~~5 Years~~ 2 Years, 4 Months	~~20 Years~~ 6 Years
Total Interest:	Total Interest:
~~$48,609.55~~ $45,388.20	~~$123,312.00~~ $79,593.82
Money Saved: $3,221.35	Money Saved: $43,718.18
Debt-Free Earlier by:	Debt-Free Earlier by:
2 Years, 8 Month	14 Years

You'll see two big changes: the length of time left on the mortgages, and the amount of money owed. We're paying more toward the principal of the loan, so there's less interest, and with less interest (and principal) to pay off, we get out faster. Well over a year faster on the 15-year — that's being debt-free 25 percent faster! And you save almost nine years and twenty-eight grand on the 30-year!

And that's only paying an extra $500 a month. Weren't we going to go Shark Mode on this thing? What if we pay an extra $1,500 a month?

We cut the time left on the 15-year down to *less than half* — just over two years to go — and save over $3,000 in interest. And when it comes to the 30-year? You save over $43,000 *and* you're totally debt free *almost a decade and a half sooner.*

Fourteen years. You'd be totally out of debt fourteen years sooner. You'll find yourself over $43,000 richer. Think of the time spent with your family in those thirteen years. That's most of watching a child or grandchild grow up. Think of how having your full income available to you for *an extra fourteen years* will allow you to be generous with your loved ones and make a difference in the world.

That's the power of managing your money well and applying the WalletWin Method to your personal finances. It won't happen overnight. This isn't a sprint. It'll be step by step, Money Milestone by Money Milestone. A burst of speed at the end, and financial freedom is yours to use to really lean into answering the call God has put on your heart to make this world a better place.

Part V

Live Financial Freedom

FINANCIAL PHASE 4

CHAPTER 15

Live Generously

"Each one must do as he has made up his mind, not reluctantly or under compulsion, for God loves a cheerful giver."
— 2 Corinthians 9:7

 *Amanda*

When we worked for FOCUS, we fundraised our entire income. One of the primary ways we did this was giving talks after Mass at the home parishes we grew up in. After Mass, Father would invite us to share about our mission work. If folks in the congregation wanted to support us, they could fill out a contact card and drop it in a basket so we could follow up with them. After going through our new contacts (which often included joke cards filled out by children … you wouldn't believe how many Seymour Butts wanted to chat with us!), we would call to set up an in-person visit to invite them to support us on an ongoing monthly or annual basis. Now, it didn't always work out this way. Some people didn't want to meet and just wanted to hand us cash after Mass.

In December 2011, six weeks after getting married, I had Jonathan join me in speaking at my home parish in Omaha, Nebraska. We'd never done this together before, but I was excited to introduce all my support partners to him. I was also excited for him to speak alongside me since I'm a nervous public speaker and he's a rather charismatic one.

It was either Advent season generosity or Jonathan's engaging personality, but we had more cash given to us after Mass than I'd ever experienced before. This was a great thing, as we had just decided the week prior that our New Year's goal for 2012 was to establish our initial emergency savings and get out of debt. We were finally on the same financial page and committed to making smart decisions with our finances. These cash donations surely were given to us by God so we could get started strong.

At the seventh and final Mass of the weekend, I saw the collection basket coming our direction. I saw Jonathan reach into his pocket where the giant wad of cash people had given us was located. I figured he'd pull out a few twenties and drop them in. We hadn't been married long enough to really discuss our giving habits. I was rather calculated and donated a tenth of my income to my local parish and charities I loved, but no more. Jonathan was freer with his giving and was very generous, but sometimes to the harm of his other obligations. Little did I know, our giving personalities were about to collide.

As I saw him pull the cash out of his pocket, I quickly realized it was the entire wad in his hand. I passed him the basket and he proceeded to drop ALL the cash in. It was probably close to a thousand dollars, and he gave it all away without a thought. I immediately shot him laser eyes of death to communicate my feelings, but what was he supposed to do, take the money back out? Removing money or making change from the collection basket isn't necessarily encouraged.

The drive home wasn't pretty. I accused Jonathan of being *laissez-faire* with money, and giving no consideration to our recent conversations about being on the same financial page. He accused me of being a Scrooge and so calculated with the purse strings that maybe I was missing the point of giving entirely. We were both right about the other. Jonathan admitted that we should've chosen together how much to donate back to my parish in an act of thanksgiving. He also needed to make sure our giving was prudent. I should strive to be as generous as possible (without harming legitimate obligations) and view my calculated ten percent as a starting line, not the end — and to see giving as a joyful occasion and not a box I check off.

While Jonathan was naively yet heroically dropping the Benjamins into the basket that day, I had forgotten a fundamental truth — *we can never outdo God in generosity*. He always gives us far more in return than we can give to him. No, I am not saying that if you send $100 in to that mega-church on TV, God will send you back $1,000. But God did choose to honor Jonathan's trust that day and provided us with many fruitful meetings with our new contacts over the following week. We were able to increase our monthly support by several hundred dollars per month, which helped us meet those big goals we had of establishing emergency savings and becoming debt free in 2012. The Lord provided for us more generously than what we offered him (begrudgingly in my case) that December day, and I'll never forget the lesson.

The Need Is Great and the Response Is Lacking

➤ Jonathan

There is great need in the world for those with means (even if they are meager) to give to those with less. Even without seeing the commercials on TV or hearing a missionary come speak at church, we know there is great suffering in the world. And so many of us are able to do something to help, even if that help might feel small to us. Unfortunately, only a little over half of US households give to charity. And of those who do give, the median amount given in a year is only $1,000.[1]

Why don't more of us give, and give more? While there are dozens of possible reasons, from personal experience and in working with thousands of individuals and families, I've noticed two common causes: greed and fear.

Greed chokes out generosity because you want more money and possessions. Greed doesn't like limits or boundaries on these and it encourages the endless pursuit of more for the sake of more. This greed may not be a conscious choice, and I would think it most often is not. But a greedy undercurrent to your thinking can slip in unnoticed and take up residence in your heart, especially in financial matters.

However, I believe greed is only a small reason people aren't giving. Fear plays a larger role in tempering our generosity. It's hard to be generous and provide for the needs of others when you're unsure of meeting your own needs. Now, these fears need not be entirely rational. You might have a well-paying job and have no real risk of going without a meal, but without a handle on your spending, you seem to only squeak by every month, and every paycheck is badly needed when it arrives in your account. In short, poor money management can easily make *any* income not enough. And the fear generated by that situation can make any income feel like there's not enough to spare for giving.

The solution? Following the WalletWin Method we've mapped out in this book. Our big goal for getting you financially healthy is for you to be as generous as possible.

Giving is your opportunity to make a difference in the lives of people in your own town to those on the other side of the world, and can be very personal. Like the rest of the topics in this book, we look at them with a Catholic worldview, and believe it offers wisdom and guidance for everyone, not only Catholics. We'll do the same with giving, especially in this section. In desiring to live a financial life fully integrated with our deepest-held beliefs, we must ask the question, what do God and the Church teach about giving?

Quite a lot, and as Mr. Food says, "Ooh, it's so good!" We'll only scratch the surface here.

Don't Be a Goat

Jesus tells us explicitly that we must give to others. In the twenty-fifth chapter of Matthew's Gospel, Jesus tells us that when he comes at the end of time as judge, he will separate everyone out "as a shepherd separates the sheep and the goats."

The "sheep" get to come into heaven, because when they saw Jesus hungry, they fed him. When they saw him thirsty, they gave him drink. Whenever he was in need, they came to his aid.

The "goats" go to hell because when they saw Jesus suffering — hungry, thirsty, a stranger, naked, sick, imprisoned — they did nothing to help him.

Both ask the Lord when these things happened. When did we see you hungry and feed you? When did we see you sick or in prison and not minister to you?

And Jesus replies to them: "Truly, I say to you, as you did it not to one of the least of these, you did it not to me" (Mt 25:45).

The Lord makes it perfectly clear that taking care of others is an essential part of living a Christian life.

A Work of Restoration

Giving is our chance to participate in the work of restoring things to how they ought to be. When we see images of children starving or hear of girls in developing countries missing out on an education because they have to walk all day to get water, or see the poor sleeping on a cold sidewalk under a thin blanket, we think to ourselves, *That's just not right! It shouldn't be like that.* When we give to programs to feed the hungry, build wells, or shelter and educate the homeless, we're upholding and protecting the dignity of those helped, playing a role in the important work of setting things right.

Pope St. Paul VI wrote, "The hungry nations of the world cry out to the peoples blessed with abundance. And the Church, cut to the quick by this cry, asks each and every man to hear his brother's plea and answer it lovingly."[2] Those of us who have much — and chances are if you're reading this book, you have quite a bit, compared to the rest of the world — have a responsibility to help those who do not. Scripture and two millennia of Church teaching agree on this truth.

In fact, it's incumbent upon us to use what we have for the good of others. God gave the earth to all mankind, and anything and everything we can do to help others is not only a contribution to restoring the way things should be, but also a recognition, acknowledgment, and honoring of the humanity in those whom we help. St. Thomas Aquinas, a Catholic priest and philosopher in the thirteenth century, says it this way: "Man should not consider his material possessions as his own, but as common to all, so as to share them without hesitation when others are in need."[3]

So ... how much?

The desire to give is innate. Perhaps the last section was simply a good pep talk for something you already knew or believed. The real question usually isn't "Should I give?" but "How much should I give?"

This is an important question, especially if you believe there is a moral imperative to give. You want to make sure you give enough. There wouldn't be a question if there wasn't a tension there. Let's explore it quickly.

What holds you back from giving absolutely everything you have to others? Many legitimate reasons — you and your family need to eat, you need shelter, you need clothes, you need to plan and prepare for your children's education, and so on. You have real needs that you must use your money to provide for. No one, not us, and especially not God, is asking you to skip feeding your own children so you can feed someone else.

In his encyclical *Rerum Novarum*, Pope Leo XIII wrote, "no one is commanded to distribute to others that which is required for his own needs and those of his household; nor even to give away what is reasonably required to keep up becomingly his condition in life. … But, when what necessity demands has been supplied, and one's standing fairly taken thought for, it becomes a duty to give to the indigent out of what remains over."[4]

Then, the question is what does it mean to "keep up becomingly [my] condition in life" or exactly what *does* necessity demand and when have I supplied it?

That, my friend, is for you to determine. I can't give you an amount. I can't give you a percentage. And neither will God.

But what about tithing?

Ah yes. The practice of giving the first 10 percent to God. It's a great idea. It's a good thing to do.

But God doesn't want you to tithe. When has God ever wanted only 10 percent?

Nobody shares the story about how they were going through a hard time, had a spiritual experience and encounter with God, and then decided to give him 10 percent of their life. I was giving 10 percent of my life to God back when I didn't know anything and hardly believed in the guy!

God doesn't want 10 percent of your money (or your life).

He wants it all.

Just like how giving him our whole lives doesn't mean we're in church praying twenty-four hours a day, I'm not saying you need to put your entire paycheck in the collection basket at church.

When we, as Catholics, give our whole lives to God, that means we live our lives in a way that gives God glory at all times, no matter what we're doing. German priest, theologian, and Servant of God Romano Guardini said that even the way we climb a tree should show our love for Christ.

Similarly, the way we use every cent entrusted to us should be influenced by our faith and give glory to God. That's why 10 percent just isn't a good enough bar for our giving.

For some, 10 percent really is too much, and they wouldn't be able to give at that level without dipping into "that which is required for his own needs and those of his household." For others, giving 10 percent is barely noticeable.

A good, though fuzzy, rule of thumb is that you should give at a level that's noticeable, even a little uncomfortable. You should feel the difference that giving makes in your budget.

Turns out that for most people, in line with historical wisdom, a good starting line is 10 percent. Some in a tough financial spot simply won't be able to give that amount of money and still put food on the table. If that's you, give financially as much as you are able and find additional ways to live generously via your time and talents. But for most households, 10 percent is a good starting line for your giving discernment. If you aren't giving at least 10 percent, try it out (or begin working up to it!). You may be surprised at how much you can give and how much joy it truly does bring. If you're giving 10 percent and it literally has no impact on your life … try increasing that amount. You may even consider a staircase approach to giving if you have a high income (more on that coming up!).

Whatever the amount is for you, I encourage you to give and give generously of your time, talents, and treasure, but certainly your treasure.

What Generosity Is — and Isn't

☞ *Amanda*

Now that we've shared about the need and call to live generously, I want to turn our gaze toward how it looks when practically lived out. Let's play the Is/Isn't game again.

Living generously is your life's mission.

We were created to live generously. To both receive the gift of others and fully give of ourselves in return. Like one big lifelong inhalation and exhalation. It's woven into our very essence as humans, made in the image and likeness of God. Since the dawn of time, it's what makes us fully alive and brings us the most joy. Just think of those paradoxical seasons of life where you have immense responsibility to others. Dawn to dusk, you're serving others with everything you've got, yet somehow, in your exhaustion, feeling more alive than ever. We all know times like that and the deep fulfillment we feel in those chapters of life is the result of living generously.

Living generously is all-encompassing.

Living generously is far more encompassing than calculating a tenth of your income and donating it to church or organizations you care about. We could explore all the ways in which we could live generously (e.g., bringing others a meal, checking in on our elderly neighbor), but since this is a book about personal finance, we're zeroing in on money. Now, since money touches everything in our lives, we'll explore a wide range of how financial generosity could manifest itself.

Living generously is a reflection of your unique person.

Some of our most fun acts of generosity haven't even been traditional giving examples you might think about. Of course, those typical opportunities are wonderful, but oftentimes it's the smaller and more individualized acts of generosity we love most.

One Christmas, we decided to send a special gift to a friend of ours who'd recently joined a religious community. If you aren't familiar with religious communities, most take a vow of poverty to imitate the life of Christ. Choosing to live this way means they don't receive the extras in life unless they're given as gifts from others. When we got the Costco catalog and saw a gourmet 7-tier chocolate tower, we knew we wanted to send it to our pal and his community. Weeks later we got a call thanking us for the tower and how it was such a hit — as soon as it arrived, it drew everyone's attention and they proceeded to swarm it and share all the delicious goodies inside. Knowing our money gave their community that moment of respite, sweetness, and memories meant a lot to us. It was far better than if we had bought the tower for ourselves.

Another time, back in the Spring of 2014, I found myself in an infertility community. I nervously applied to join a small virtual support group and worried about if I would gel with any other women on the call. I was delightfully surprised that our group instantly connected. It was as if we were long-lost BFFs who'd just never met in real life. In a welcome and wild turn of events, only months after we began chatting, three of us wound up adopting our first babies only weeks apart from one another. The fourth ended up conceiving in that time frame and welcomed her first baby a few months later. While it wasn't huge, I wanted to send a gift to each of these women as they transitioned into motherhood. I spent a couple hundred dollars on swaddle shirts they could use to bond with their babies, as well as to have their hands free during the day. Again, it wasn't some huge price tag, but it was something Jonathan and I chose to financially prioritize even though we ourselves had just adopted and wiped out most of our savings. We absolutely could've found ways to use that money to ease life for our own family, but we committed to living generously and trusting that we'll never be able to outdo God in that.

Living generously is about giving *and* receiving.

There are two sides of the generosity equation, and if you experience one without the other, you're missing a vital component. On the one hand, there's *being* generous with others: giving of yourself to another whether it be time, money, emotions, shelter, talents, and so on. This is what people most often think of when they think of generosity — giving to others. But on the other hand, there's *receiving* generosity from others. This is an equally important aspect of living generously, and it's oftentimes this side that makes people uncomfortable.

There's a temptation to believe that *being generous* toward others is better than *receiving generosity* from others, and it's just not true. Both are equally important, and you'll always be missing something if you have one but not the other.

For better or worse, there's a certain stigma that to be self-sufficient means you're wiser, smarter, and/or better than others. But the truth is that we will all have times in our lives when we're called to give, and times we're called to receive. None of us are self-sufficient. We need one another. No man is an island, and anything or anyone that tries to tell you otherwise is hogwash.

Now that we've covered what Living Generously Is, let's finish by diving into Living Generously Isn't:

Living generously isn't altruism.

Like Saint Paul says, "If I give away all I have, and if I deliver my body to be burned, but have not love, I gain nothing" (1 Cor 13:3). Giving is *not* about the giver being good. It's about the goodness and dignity of the recipient, made in the image and likeness of God. The goal of living generously isn't to make yourself feel good or appear altruistic to others. That's selfish use and exploitation of the poor. Don't pat yourself on the back after being generous with others — feel honored to have had the opportunity to serve them and offer your time, talents, and/or treasure back to God who gave them in the first place.

Living generously isn't a chance to get rid of your junk.

All too often I see people ready to give themselves a gold star for giving the poor their old clothes, beat-up 2005 iPhone, and DVDs after they'd received blu-rays. I'm just gonna say it — stop Marie Kondo-ing your house and giving the poor your junk. Now, before you mishear me, it's not a bad thing to donate items you are no longer using to those who need them. But if *all* you give to others is your leftovers, there's some room to do more. You need to do both. If you habitually upgrade your lifestyle and pass along your downgrades to others, you're missing a chance to live generously. In addition to giving items you no longer use or that need a second chance, challenge yourself regularly to go shopping to buy nice items for the purpose of giving them to others.

Living generously isn't a power play.

As you build significant wealth, there becomes a temptation to want influence over organizations and causes you are giving to. This isn't all bad, but it's something you must keep in check. Wanting to lend your expertise so your donations can be used prudently and efficiently is a good thing. However, if your giving starts to come with expectations, guarantees, or favors, it has now slipped into self-service, which is the opposite of generosity. Again, so much of this boils down to your motives and requires deep self-knowledge and reflection. Are you giving so you can secure that board seat or get access to a respected leader? Are you donating with a "scratch their back so they scratch mine down the road" mentality? These are dangerous territories and it's important we actively work to give from a clean heart with pure and unattached motives.

Jesus said it best in Matthew 6:5–6: "And when you pray, you must not be like the hypocrites; for they love to stand and pray in the synagogues and at the street corners, that they may be seen by men. Truly, I say to you, they have their reward. But when you pray, go into your room and shut the door and pray to your Father who is in secret; and your Father who sees in secret will reward you." The same goes with giving.

Intense and heavy stuff, right? We believe that giving is the most fun you'll ever have with money. While it can be uncomfortable to dive into our motives underneath the surface, it's worth getting them right. Now that we've discussed what giving is and isn't, next I want to dive into how others' generosity has shaped us as persons.

Why Receiving Others' Generosity Is Vital

Our own personal financial journey and desire to be generous with others has been deeply shaped and impacted by how others have been generous toward us — and had we not received their gifts, we'd be lacking.

One of our earliest encounters of receiving the generosity of others was fundraising our income while working for FOCUS. It appalled some friends and family members that we were "professional beggars" inviting others to join us in mission with a donation to support our work. We knew that our support partners weren't giving simply to us. They were giving to God to support our missionary work on college campuses. We had no reason to feel shame for inviting others to support our mission work.

Another early exposure to generosity that changed us to the core was when we were married about six months and needed to move cross-country to find a new place to live. Joe and Evette (a couple in Colorado) invited us through a friend of a friend to come and live with them. They didn't know us from Adam, but they and their sons opened their home to us. We lived with their family for just over two months, but it didn't take long to realize they were who we wanted to be when we grew up.

The first night we arrived (after having driven cross-country from Illinois, which is at sea level), we showed up to this beautiful home on a literal mountain top in Colorado. Evette had made dinner and we were invited to join them on the back porch, overlooking the Front Range of the Rocky Mountains. Joe prayed for us and thanked God for our safe travels and, over the next couple of hours, we each shared the Cliff Notes versions of our life stories. They welcomed us and made us feel like family.

Over the next couple of months, we shared meals, Joe taught me how to give Jonathan a haircut (huge #WalletWin right there!), we watched football (and rooted for their team, the Steelers), they introduced us to Costco, we went on walks to watch those gorgeous Colorado sunsets over the mountains, we played games, and we had many meaningful discussions and good laughs. We even became debt-free while living with them and we made our now infamous Debt-Free Doughnuts with one of their sons, whom we roped into celebrating with us.

Their generosity influenced us greatly during that first year of marriage. They didn't have to host us. They were a busy family with many responsibilities, yet they chose to prioritize making their home a blessing to others in need of housing. More than that, they certainly didn't have to invite us to dinner, game nights, sports games, Mass, or walks with their family. But they did — they opened not only their home, but their hearts. They were far more than simply financially generous. They were living embodiments of generosity with their entire lives.

A Dinner to Remember

It was a Sunday afternoon in the spring of 2013 when we got a call from a friend. She explained that her roommate's parents had reservations to take ten FOCUS staff members to a restaurant called Texas de Brazil. Two of the original staff invited had to cancel at the last minute and she wanted to know if we wanted to come in their place. We had no clue what Texas de Brazil was, but said "sure!" When we arrived, we were escorted to our table and as soon as our server began explaining the green and red cards, I realized it was one of those fancy Brazilian steakhouses where they shave the meat right onto your plates.

Over the next several hours we ate more meat than I ever thought imaginable, enjoyed many bottles of wine, and shared a lot of laughs. So much joy and laughing! It was one of those meals where you forget time even exists and you're completely in the moment, enjoying this respite from the grind of daily life.

While Jonathan and I lived comfortably, we never chose to go out to eat at fancy restaurants. That spring, we were knee-deep in infertility treatments and saving every spare penny to cash-flow those. And the stress we were under? We were nearly at a breaking point as every month yet again resulted in disappointment. This dinner was arguably the nicest meal we'd had since getting married almost two years prior. It was also the most carefree and joyful we'd been in months. We felt so honored to be invited to join in — all because this older couple wanted to bless others with an enjoyable evening out. They could have used that money a thousand other ways, but chose to use it to make memories with their daughter and her friends. This is living generously.

Safe Harbor in the Storm

Another chapter where receiving the generosity of others changed us to the core was when our second daughter was born. Her birth mother made an adoption plan with us in September, and she was due in Little Rock, Arkansas in early December. We knew literally zero people in the entire state of Arkansas, let alone in Little Rock. I went into a Facebook group for adopting families to find a local housing connection in the area. I won't go into all the reasons here, but staying in a real home with people who know the area as opposed to a hotel or empty Airbnb is a far better arrangement for adoptive families. I posted in the group when we would be in Little Rock, and lo and behold, someone had a cousin who lived there. She connected us and it was instantly the perfect connection — not only had they been foster parents before, so they knew the world of adoption, but she was a certified financial planner and a Dave Ramsey fan! We couldn't have gotten a better match!

Once we arrived, we realized how they lived generosity through and through. All our family hoped for was a simple bedroom to sleep in together while in Arkansas. But when we showed up, they gave us a stall in their garage and led us to a private guest suite for our family to stay in. They had custom built their home a few years prior, and because generosity is so central to who they are, they designed it in a way that would welcome guests regularly and give them a comfortable and beautiful place to stay. It was nothing overly fancy, but it was so hospitable. Where many would've chosen to create an office space or an exercise room, they made a space to welcome others and nurture relationships in their home.

But that space wasn't what encapsulated their generous hearts. It's what happened in the following weeks that showed us how truly blessed we were to have found this family. When our second daughter was born on December 14, 2016, on a rainy Arkansas afternoon, she couldn't breathe on her own. Within a half hour of birth, she was sedated and intubated so they could get her body the oxygen it so desperately needed. That evening we got the diagnoses: persistent pulmonary hypertension of the newborn. I'll be honest — I Googled her condition once (and only once) because when I read that as recent as the year 2000 only 40 percent of children with this diagnosis made it, I was tempted to despair. She needed me to be hopeful and to fight for her.

The family we were staying with came to the hospital and picked up our newly two-year-old daughter who was exhausted from the long day. They fed her, bathed her, and put her to bed that night, freeing us up to focus on our newborn who was fighting for her life in the NICU. Over the following weeks (we were in Arkansas a month!) they helped us take care of our two-year-old, brought us food to make sure we were eating, and even welcomed us to join them in opening presents with their family on Christmas morning. (We'd left all our gifts at home in the chaos. I'd ordered things on Amazon … but with shipping delays, the only gift to make it in time for Christmas was a nose hair trimmer for Jonathan!) When they found out I was having trouble sleeping, they offered melatonin and valerian root with some essential oils. When they knew I was stiff from sleeping on the hospital couch, they gave me special Epsom salts and their master bath to soak in. If they were picking up dinner for their family, they asked for our order as well.

They had no reason to do any of this, but they chose to live generosity in every way, and it blessed our family immensely. It also inspired us with how we want to show up in the world. While we aren't ready to custom-build a home with a guest suite, you better believe it's part of our long-term plans. The generosity they extended will ripple out beyond them, through us, to others, in a cycle which I hope continues to repeat itself on and on and on again. If we'd closed ourselves off to this, we wouldn't have experienced all that beauty and the chance to be inspired ourselves. We were financially in a position where we could've afforded a hotel or an Airbnb, even for an entire month. But we would've missed out on the relationships forged through their generous offering and our reception of their generosity.

Steve and Janet weren't the only ones who bathed us in generosity though during that NICU stay. Local breastfeeding moms pumped and brought me frozen milk to make sure our little one had the best nutrition possible as she battled for her life. One of them even surprised me with my favorite Starbucks order along with the milk. We had friends send gift cards for lunch and dinner. We had people from all over the country sending us cards and Christmas decor for our daughter's room so it would feel like a cozy and healing place full of love. And believe it or not, Chipotle blew us away with an act of generosity on Christmas Eve.

Burrito Bowl-ed over by Generosity

Days before Christmas, the hospital's pediatrician told me she wanted her Christmas gift to be me holding my daughter for the first time. (Because of the fragility of her situation, we hadn't been able to even hold her yet.) I remember waking up excited on Christmas Eve, knowing that was the day they were going to extubate her and we could finally hold our girl. I had stayed the night back at the house to spend some time with our oldest in the morning. Jonathan called me around ten to let me know she'd just had her tubes removed and was breathing on her own — a miracle! I spent a few more minutes with our two-year-old and then headed back to the NICU to trade off with Jonathan.

While I was driving, though, he called again to tell me something wasn't right. Charlotte was having labored breathing. He also mentioned they just lost her umbilical IV and needed to find another access point, but were having trouble. I focused on getting to the hospital as quickly as possible. When I walked in and saw half her head shaved from attempted IV's (there's (usually) an accessible vein on each side of the head), I burst into tears because I'd missed my baby's first haircut. It didn't seem logical but I was wrecked. I also noticed she was having chest retractions and her breathing was very loud upon expiration. I knew it wasn't looking good.

Before I knew it, her oxygen saturation levels were dropping again just as they had in the first half hour after she was born. Fifteen doctors, nurses, respiratory therapists, and techs swarmed the room for yet another emergency intubation. Within a few minutes, they had successfully intubated her, but they'd lost that IV line, meaning she had no more sedation and was waking up and beginning to fight the breathing tube. It became a race against the clock to get that IV access.

Five pokes turned into ten, which turned into fifteen. Special tools, different nurses. You name it, they tried it. Around noon they told us she needed an emergency transfer to Arkansas Children's Hospital as they'd reached the end of their scope of care. The Angel Flight transport team was there within minutes and they began the very thorough process of setting up a transportable incubator/ventilator to load her into the ambulance.

It was close to three in the afternoon before I realized I hadn't eaten yet that day, and I was shaking because of the stress of going through everything on zero food. We were gearing up to get into the ambulance and there was no way I wasn't riding along with my daughter. Jonathan got in our van and decided to call Chipotle to see if they were open. It was Christmas Eve, so he wasn't sure. They answered but unfortunately had *just* closed their store. He explained what was going on in our family, that his wife has food allergies and that it's hard to find hospital food or other takeout that works, and boldly asked if they'd let him order something quickly. Not only did they let him order food, but when he got there, they slid it across the counter, told him they were praying for our daughter, wished him a Merry Christmas, and told him it was on the house. Jonathan got to the car and just started bawling and laughing. Even Chipotle was taking care of us on this NICU roller coaster. Weeks later, by God's grace, our daughter made a full recovery and we traveled home.

How Has Generosity Shaped You?

That was a lot of stories about our family receiving the generosity of others. Each was deeply impactful on shaping us as persons and grew our hearts exponentially. The way our family chooses to live generously now, and in the future, will always be influenced and linked to these early and formative receptions of others' generosity toward us.

As you can see, we are big fans of generosity. Being open to both ends of generosity has shaped so much of our lives, and we invite you to do the same. As we wind this chapter down, take a minute to reflect on the following questions:

- When have you encountered generosity?
- What deep and lasting impact did receiving that generosity leave on you?
- Has there been a time you failed to receive the generosity of another?
- What got in the way of your receptivity?
- What could you do to ensure you remain open to receiving generosity from others?
- When have you been able to give generously to another?
- How did you feel when you made that gift of yourself (financial and beyond)?
- What can you do to weave more generosity into your everyday life?
- What are ways in which you'd like to be generous with others but never thought you could?
- Name a few causes, charities, or changes you'd like to support generously. Why those?

Generosity is the reason we started WalletWin and the reason we want to help you get your finances on track. When you're financially stable, you can more fully live generously. And when you've grown wealth, you can really lean into it. Speaking of wealth … that brings us to our next (and final) chapter.

CHAPTER 16

Be Wealthy (Without Losing Your Soul)

"Every one to whom much is given, of him will much be required; and of him to whom men commit much they will demand the more."
— Luke 12:48

🏴 *Jonathan*

We've come to the end of this book. And now, it is incumbent upon us to give you this word of warning:

If you follow the plan we laid out in this book, build great wealth, and do it only for yourself — well, we think you'd honestly be better off had you never read it at all.

Let us explain.

We just spent an entire book breaking down our financial playbook. By reading our book and learning our method, you are Frodo finding the One Ring, Luke discovering his sensitivity to the Force, Lucy coming across Coriakin's spell book and that which could make her beautiful "beyond the lot of mortals," Peter Parker learning that "with great power comes great responsibility."

Amanda

Sounds like a big deal — because it is.

At the start of our journey, we promised to share what is needed in order to win with money without losing your soul. Chapter by chapter, we dissected strategies to help you gain control of your finances, eliminate debt, and begin intentionally building wealth. We believe that when you leave money stress behind, you can more fully become who you are meant to be and change the world by living generously. More money, more impact.

If we didn't also provide ample warning about the possible dangers ahead, we'd be failing you. Remember, money is neutral. It's neither inherently good nor bad. It's a resource given to us by God to manage. But just because something is morally neutral doesn't mean it can't be misused or bring us harm.

The truth is, if you don't build healthy boundaries as you build wealth, it can destroy you.

He's Not Wrong

Remember what Jesus says in Matthew 19:24? "It is easier for a camel to go through the eye of a needle than for a rich man to enter the kingdom of God." He's not wrong. Like we talked about in the first couple of chapters, money — just like virtually anything else in life — has the potential to be a blessing or a curse. Which one it will be for you is determined by your financial habits, how you relate to money, and where you draw your identity from.

Jonathan

The whole point of this book is to help you be successful with finances and grow wealth over the course of your life. The work we do at WalletWin is to help stop money from being a distraction in your life and free up your finances to work for you and your family's goals while allowing you to be as generous as possible in the world.

We'd be remiss if we didn't stress the importance of developing boundaries with money as it grows. Financial boundaries help protect you and ensure you're managing your money instead of your money managing you.

Pope St. John XXIII said, "all men without exception both individually and in society, have a life-long obligation to strive after heavenly values through the right use of the things of this earth. These temporal goods must be used in such a way as not to jeopardize eternal happiness."[1]

Money, especially as wealth grows, *can* pose a threat to eternal happiness. Let's dive into a few of those threats, and more importantly, discuss how we can guard against them.

Bigger. Better. More. Especially More.

 Amanda

If you've ever sat down with a Costco-sized bag of Nacho Cheese Doritos, you'll understand that *more* is never enough. These addictive chips are scientifically designed[2] to keep you coming back time and time again.

Ecclesiastes 5:10 says, "He who loves money will not be satisfied with money; nor he who loves wealth, with gain." If you love money, you will never have enough money. If you love wealth, you will never be wealthy enough. If your happiness and desires are on the other side of *more*, it is there they will be, forever just out of reach.

Jonathan

And we're not just talking money. If you love clothes, and your wealth allows you to be able to buy a lot of clothes, you may find you always need just one more outfit, or that latest pair of shoes. If you love tech and you have the wealth to buy a new gadget whenever it catches your eye, there will always be another gadget to buy, one more piece of gear to get before your setup is complete.

There will *always* be one more thing when *more* is in the driver's seat.

How Much Is Too Much?

Not gonna sugarcoat it: I like things. I think stuff is really neat. When I was younger, I live-streamed Apple product announcements (oh, when the iPhone was announced!) even though I didn't have the funds to buy any of that stuff. I really like presents. And free things.

I just plain like *stuff*.

The things of this world (and you don't have to be religious to see things this way) have a particular relationship with money. Things — power, sex, thrills, food, prestige, and more — can typically be found more easily, in more abundance, or of higher quality when you have more money.

And if you have a particular inclination to any of these or some other fleeting pleasure — and I imagine most of us do — it will be harder to avoid indulgence and find moderation when "more" or "better" is easy as pie.

Let's think of food (which I do quite a bit, as you can tell by all of the food analogies in this book). If you're a foodie or even an aspiring foodie, having wealth means you will be confronted with the question of just how much is *too much* for a bottle of wine, or a dinner out, or whether a $300 steak should ever enter your mouth. The $300 steak for someone who isn't a foodie is an easy no. The $300 steak for a foodie who is in poverty is an easy no. The wealthy foodie? A tougher decision.

Amanda

Can we define what "excessive" means for you? Not really. You'll have to discern for yourself with God's help, and context always matters.

In John 12, Mary (Lazarus and Martha's sister) takes a "pound of costly ointment" to anoint Jesus' feet. His disciple Judas (who was a thief and about to betray him) bemoans, "Why was this ointment not sold for three hundred denarii and given to the poor?" (Jn 12:3, 5). Was Mary being excessive? Gosh, she could've sold the oil and solved world hunger … seems like a bad use of some pricey oil, right? Wrong. Anointing Jesus in this special way, just before he was arrested, beaten, and killed was an intimate display of thanksgiving and love, an act of worship for a God who literally gave us everything, to the point of his very life. Jesus goes on to say, "The poor you always have with you, but you do not always have me" (Jn 12:8). Her use of these extravagant resources was appropriate given the situation.

It's tempting to want to make black and white blanket statements like, "I would never drive *that* kind of car," or "anyone who lives in a house that costs *that* much or vacations *there*" is being excessive. However, as few things are, it's just not that simple. Many factors are in play, from net worth, to income, to motivations, to context, as we just examined above. All of these, and more, must be factored in.

At the end of the day, we are responsible for ourselves, our own hearts, and our own choices and behaviors. It's easy to point fingers and judge what others are doing (or not doing) with their money without putting in the work to ask ourselves the hard questions.

Am I saying we can't hold others accountable or *charitably* ask hard questions regarding their money? No, we absolutely should. But at the end of the day, we can't control their actions or know their hearts. We can only control our own actions and know our own hearts. Just as Jesus commands in Matthew 7:5, before we can remove the splinter from our neighbor's eye, we must remove the board from our own. Before I show up on Jeff Bezos's front doorstep and kindly invite him to loosen his grip on the literal hundreds of billions of dollars he has and judge his spending decisions, I need to ensure I've asked myself the hard questions and hold myself to comparable standards.

Wealth Can Insulate You from (Some) Suffering

🏳 *Jonathan*

They say money can't buy you happiness. And it can't … but it *can* help, to a point. Multiple studies and surveys have found that money does indeed improve happiness. Mostly, money can improve happiness when it helps take care of everyday needs.

If $10,000 more a year means you don't have to clip coupons five hours a week in order to squeak out dinner each night, you'll be happier. If $15,000 more means you can quit that second job and spend more time with your family, you can bet it's going to make you happier. But the effect peters out at a certain point. Somewhere between $65,000 and $95,000 a year, according to current research, though I'm sure that would depend on the size of your household and your area's cost of living.

In these cases, money increases happiness because it is taking away suffering. Once "inexpensive sufferings" like good food on the table and being able to both work *and* enjoy time with your family, are taken care of, the emotional impact of more money is diluted.

The next tranche of sufferings, what could be considered "expensive sufferings," require a much higher income to alleviate. While most could be considered annoyances, they *are* sufferings, and wealth can make some of them go away.

Hate waiting in line at airport security or on layovers? Fly on a private jet. Hate going to the grocery store, picking up your dry cleaning, or a variety of other tasks? Hire a personal assistant. Can't stand scrubbing toilets and vacuuming? Employ a maid to keep your home spotless. Don't like cooking? Hire a private chef. Have a driver take you places so you don't have to stress behind the wheel in traffic. Tired of college admission standards? Hire Rick Singer to get your kid in (too soon?).

We can see that these expensive sufferings are on a different level than inexpensive ones. In a sense, addressing inexpensive sufferings allows you to *live a normal life* without excessive amounts of stress and worry, while addressing expensive sufferings allows you to *escape a normal life*.

And that is where the seed of trouble can be planted in your heart. There will always be suffering in our lives, and for most of us, our natural tendency is to try to avoid it. We must find the balance between alleviating suffering in our lives, while accepting it as an opportunity to grow while uniting it to the sufferings of Jesus on the cross as a redemptive act for the good of ourselves and others.

Typically, most inexpensive sufferings — needing adequate necessities to live your life — should be addressed. Like most issues of discernment, the ends of the spectrum are easy: yes to making sure your family has enough nutritious food to eat, no to a private jumbo jet. The middle is where it's up to you and your conscience to determine the answer. And it is the act of discerning which sufferings you willingly accept that will help you find peace. Striking a balance that allows maximum fruitfulness in your life is a worthwhile effort.

Avoiding suffering can be another appetite that is never satiated. There will always be some suffering, however small, to avoid, to stamp out, some annoyance you don't want to deal with, and will try to find a way not to. And this neverending quest for a perfect life here on earth will never end, except in misery and disappointment. You know that YouTube or Instagram influencer that has a *perfect* life? No, they don't. No matter how carefully we curate our feeds, suffering is always part of life this side of heaven.

Let's return to that idea of addressing inexpensive sufferings in order to live a normal life and addressing expensive ones to escape a normal life. That may be something worth considering in your discernment. "Does addressing this suffering allow me to freely focus on God and my vocation/enter more fully into life, or might I be running away from life by trying to escape?" For example: While knee-deep in diapers and work deadlines, hiring a bi-weekly cleaner could be the difference between "anxiety-crippled Mom" and "joyful/peaceful Mom." When Mom isn't run ragged by trying to do it all and prudently outsources some of her tasks, it frees her to be more present in other aspects of life. On the flip side, if Mom outsources her tasks so she can instead escape, numb out, or misuse her time (#beenthere), using it neither for the service of God nor those entrusted to her via her vocation, this becomes problematic.

Eliminating suffering and annoyances, or attempting to, in order to escape a "normal" life, can lead to another danger. By making moves to eliminate sufferings and live a "better" life, you may be tempted to think you are better, or that you deserve a life without much suffering. Beware of this lie and keep guard against it creeping into your heart.

Wealth Can Make Others View and Treat You Differently

When you've built wealth, folks tend to take your opinions more seriously. Your money (in their minds) may be a sign that you know what you're talking about. Interactions with others are more likely to go in your favor. If something goes awry at a restaurant, the server will be more likely to take care of things quickly because they don't want to lose your business, or perhaps they're looking for a large tip.

And this is where things can start to turn. Yes, you're being treated better than you might otherwise be — but not because you are a better human being. They are treating you well because you are a human being in control of a lot of money, and perhaps by treating you well, there might be perks for them.

Some will treat you poorly. Perhaps folks who knew you before your wealth are jealous, or think you don't give enough. Perhaps those who don't know you at all will operate out of a stereotype of rich people they've cooked up in their heads and assume a snootiness or greed that just isn't in you.

You may be approached for donations by every charity and organization that knows your name or can find your phone number. You may be treated like an ATM by your loved ones.

There will be a temptation for others to look beyond your humanity and see primarily your wallet. In the minds of many, *you* will be thought of less and less, and your wealth will be thought of more and more, sometimes consciously, sometimes subconsciously.

Wealth Can Infect Your Identity and Self-Image

It is not only others who may view and treat you differently. You, too, must be careful of how you think about yourself. You, who get the best seat at the restaurant. You, who hasn't had to go grocery shopping for yourself in years. You, who go to amazing places on vacations. You, who buy whatever you want whenever you want. You, who donated a whole new playground to the park and started a scholarship fund for at-risk youth.

You are a pretty great person, aren't you? You deserve the finer things in life. Your opinion matters more, doesn't it? Because it's a better opinion — because it's your opinion! What do you mean there are no more tickets available? Even VIP passes? First Class is full? But it's you who's asking!

Wealth can make a lot of things possible in your life. You can live where you want. Do what you want. Buy what you want. Make things happen. Minimize suffering. Even create massive change for good in the world and improve the lives of many.

But despite all this, and even if other people think that you must be more important than others, you must remember you are not. Even if you have an easier go of things, get your way more often, if others treat you better, you must remember that your wealth does not define you. Your money might be able to make some things happen, but the power is not yours. Even if you worked harder or smarter than others to earn your living — it doesn't mean you are more worthy or have more dignity than anyone else.

Remember, the money isn't even yours. It's God's money, and he's asking you to manage it for him. And you must manage it well. You are a humble manager, that's all, doing work in a vineyard that isn't yours, in a world that you will live in for only the blink of an eye.

Ensure Being Wealthy Stays Healthy

Amanda

We've just dropped some heavy stuff that might have you hesitating regarding winning with your personal finances. But when you build healthy boundaries into your relationship with wealth, you have *nothing* to fear. When these safeguards are in place, money is no threat to your salvation.

We're going to break down our four-pronged approach to keeping money in its proper place: a financial examination of conscience, generosity, reviewing our role, and building a life of virtue.

1. Your Financial Examination of Conscience

We frequently use a financial examination of conscience to make sure the motives behind our money are in the right place. This helps identify potentially problematic motives like jealousy, envy, sadness, stress, anger, pride, covetousness, and the like, to name a few likely offenders. Spending, saving, or giving money from these motives can tangle up your finances fast. A financial examination of conscience helps unmask any unhealthy vices lurking in the background, before you make a money decision. In that state of awareness, you can pause everything and do the inner work to root out the unhealthy motives, making sure healthy motives are paving the way.

If you'd like a copy of our financial examination of conscience, head on over to WalletWin.com/examination.

2. Generosity: The Antidote

As you read in the title of this book, what we do at WalletWin is help
people attack debt, build savings, and change the world through
generosity. We don't just add that last part on because it sounds like
a nice sentiment. Not only do we believe generosity is the most fun
you'll ever have with your money; we also believe it's the antidote to
the negative effects of wealth. Living generously helps us take our
minds off our money and put our eyes on our mission. No one em-
bodies that quite like St. Katharine Drexel.

You'll remember the Drexels from earlier in the book. Francis
Drexel was a *very* successful banker in nineteenth-century Philadelphia, and after his passing, left his estate (worth over $350 million
in modern dollars) to his three daughters. All three were very generous with their inheritance, but one of them, Katharine, used her
fortune to establish a new religious order of sisters. In 1913, with the
introduction of federal income tax, over one third of the money she
used to educate and serve the poor was no longer available as it went
to the government instead. But shockingly, in 1921, a federal tax law
was amended so that those who gave over 90 percent of their annual income to charity would be exempt from taxation. For all intents
and purposes this could've been called the Mother Katharine law
because she (and her charitable work) was known to be likely the
only beneficiary of its passing.

Saint Katharine was clear about her relationship with money
even before she became a religious sister. She had firm boundaries in
place about when enough was enough and that whatever remained
should be given away. Her story is incredibly inspiring and very re-
latable. But don't assume that she didn't like nice things — in her
twenties, before entering religious life, she spent a month at a European spa recharging and resting after a bout of ill health. She enjoyed the opportunities wealth brought! But when it came time to
take a vow of poverty, renounce her claim to her inheritance, and
instead pass it to her religious order, she did so without hesitation

because she was clear about the role money played in her life.

Staircase Giving

How beautiful (and radical!) would it be to emulate Mother Katharine and live a reverse tithe in your lifetime: living on ten and giving ninety! Practically speaking, this involves a lot of discernment and discussion as your income, goals, family, and mission change with time. Don't mishear me and say this is what you're called to — in fact, most people will never reach an income level that would allow them to give away 90 percent of their income. But for those who do? What a heroic act of generosity and blessing it can be. For most of us, giving at least 10 percent will be the norm. Through prudently investing money and setting aside funds for retirement, we will likely be in a position where we can give even more during our golden years. Not 90 percent but as generous as can reasonably be — both equally pleasing to God.

In either situation, you don't (normally) wake up one day and begin living a reverse tithe. A staircase giving approach is a more appropriate path for how the antidote, generosity, will practically look as your wealth grows. For example: any money earned, up to $100,000 take home pay, give a tenth. Anything over that amount up to $150,000, give twenty percent. Anything above that amount, up to $200,000, give thirty percent. So on and so forth, all the way up to 90 percent of income being given. Eventually, if your needs (and many wants) are taken care of, you will not need more money even if you earn more, and thus, everything is given away beyond that number.

What a treasure we have in Saint Katharine's story. May we be so blessed to humbly manage our money as generously as she did! Living generosity is a deeply personal calling. However this looks for you practically, as long as your end goal is to be as generous as you prudently can be, you won't be steered wrong.

This is again where we use a financial examination of conscience to guide our decisions. There are certain purchases we can easily afford today that we would've naively declared "excessive" eight years ago without knowing the context of our life now. We can also deceive ourselves that we're giving generously just because it's "more than that person gives," even though we're certainly capable of giving more ourselves. The act of giving, while critical to keeping money healthy, doesn't automatically baptize or justify all other spending or purchases. Constant discernment is the name of the game.

3. Reviewing Our Role

Earlier we discussed the idea that all our money belongs to God and we are mere managers of that money while we're on earth. When we truly understand that all our money is entrusted to us by God, it invokes humility. What an honor to steward any gift for another, let alone one as impactful as money, and for not just anyone — but God of the entire universe!

As your wealth grows, you will inevitably come to a fork in the road where you have a big financial decision to make. The temptation is to grab for control and to impulsively pick whatever route feels good in the moment. By pausing and reflecting on your role as a humble manager and inviting God to show you how to honor him in your finances, the path becomes clearer. Sometimes the answer aligns with what you initially wanted, sometimes not. But knowing we managed our money in alignment with the owner's (God's) will brings far more peace.

4. Building a Life of Virtue

 *Jonathan*

The key to navigating wealth, really money of any amount, is knowing who you are and who you are meant to be.

More money doesn't make people mean, or picky, or snotty, or jerks. More money doesn't make people generous, or kind, or happy. More money, like super-soldier serum in the Marvel universe, simply *reveals who you already are.*

If you're a stingy, covetous jerk when you're making $30,000/ year, you'll likely be a stingier, more covetous jerk when you're making $300,000. And if you're generous and kind even when the paychecks are small, it follows you'll be more generous and even kinder when the paycheck is bigger.

So much of the burden of wealth either comes by encouraging us to turn inward, and become overly preoccupied with our own comfort, or by tempting us to imagine we are above the fray, in a sense. Thus, the cure is to do the opposite and live in truth. The remedy for any vice or temptation is the opposing virtue.

The Catholic Church explains, "A virtue is an habitual and firm disposition to do the good. It allows the person not only to perform good acts, but to give the best of himself. The virtuous person tends toward the good with all his sensory and spiritual powers; he pursues the good and chooses it in concrete actions." (*Catechism of the Catholic Church*, 1803; hereafter CCC)

What are these virtues? While there are seven virtues, three theological and four cardinal, I'd like to highlight the latter, also known as the human virtues, to assist in your financial journey.

Prudence

First up, let's chat prudence. According to the CCC, "*Prudence* is the virtue that disposes practical reason to discern our true good in every circumstance and to choose the right means of achieving it" (1806, emphasis original). What a powerful virtue when it comes to handling your personal finances! Prudence offers you the wisdom to see the ultimate good for your money — whether it's budgeting for that family vacation to make memories, taking care of a single parent's mortgage, or setting aside funds for future emergencies. Prudence can guide you *away* from impulsively Amazon-ing or Target-ing your paycheck to death, and instead help you wisely use your money to protect the truest goods.

Justice

"*Justice* is the moral virtue that consists in the constant and firm will to give their due to God and neighbor" (CCC, 1807, emphasis in original). When it comes to money, the temptation might be to think of Robin Hood — take the money from the (supposedly greedy) rich and give it to the poor — that's justice, right? Not necessarily. Financial or economic justice can be complex, but *all* parties must be treated with justice, never one at the expense of another.

Cultivating the virtue of justice "disposes one to respect the rights of each and to establish in human relationships the harmony that promotes equity with regard to persons and to the common good" (CCC 1807).

Fortitude

"*Fortitude* is the moral virtue that ensures firmness in difficulties and constancy in the pursuit of the good" (CCC 1808, emphasis in original). In our social-media-consumed world, it's easier than ever to grow exhausted with the challenges of our culture. Fortitude provides the strength to keep fighting battles despite the weariness of life. When it comes to money, strong fortitude can come in handy when tackling a mountain of debt or saving for emergencies. It's understandable to get discouraged when it feels like you're treading financial water and not making progress — and in those moments, the virtue of fortitude can keep you persevering toward the goal.

Temperance

"*Temperance* is the moral virtue that moderates the attraction of pleasures and provides balance in the use of created goods" (CCC 1809, emphasis in original). Financially speaking, temperance is the virtue that allows you to *enjoy* money and the opportunities it brings without *being consumed* by money and the opportunities it brings. Think of a new lotto winner who's grown up without a lot of money. Without temperance, the fortune could be gone in a matter of months, as the pursuit of indulging all whims and fancies takes the driver's seat and drains the money until it's gone. Temperance offers freedom: the ability to draw a line in the sand on how far indulgence will go, lest the endless pursuit of it takes over. It brings balance to the table.

If you work to cultivate virtues in your heart, mind, and actions now, you will be ready to do the good thing at all times and in all circumstances. You will know how to identify and choose the good now as you build wealth, and later once it's under your care, you will be prepared to undertake the great responsibility that has come your way.

Be Not Afraid

 Amanda

We were married on October 22, 2011, the first ever feast day of our hero, Pope St. John Paul II. Thirty-three years prior, on October 22, 1978, he was inaugurated and preached passionately in St. Peter's Square. He issued many challenges to the crowds, each one ending with the now famous, "Be not afraid!" It resonated deeply and wound up becoming a rallying cry during his pontificate.

As we wrap up this intense but necessary chapter, we issue you the same charge: Be not afraid.

When you handle money using the WalletWin Method, you will inevitably start seeing incredible results. Sure, you'll be kicking debt to the curb and watching your emergency savings grow. Or you'll have cash saved up for that next new-to-you vehicle purchase or family vacation. More importantly, you'll have less stress, worry, and exhaustion in your life. Instead, you'll have space for more peace and joy, and time for what matters most to you.

Yes, we have to warn you about obstacles wealth can bring with it. But when you build healthy boundaries and have smart financial habits as your guide, you have nothing to fear.

Conclusion

Where to Go from Here

▶ *Amanda*

That fateful early summer evening back in 2008, when I first encountered Jonathan with his long hair, laptop boombox, and embarrassing dance moves, I did what you're never supposed to do. I judged the book by its cover.

Thankfully, I had many more chances to see the book in the right light and understand how far off my initial estimations truly were. My life would be severely lacking without fully knowing Jonathan and having the gift of his presence each day.

A lot of people fall into the same trap with money based on their personal histories and experiences. Many of us were not taught from a young age the right way to look at money. We're judging the book with the wrong cover — or in the wrong setting. But not you anymore. You've done the work to understand money in a new way. You know how to spot unhealthy attitudes and beliefs around finances, and what healthy habits you can replace them with instead. You're ready to overhaul your relationship with money and make living generously your life (and wallet's) aim.

We don't take lightly that you invested your time and mental energy to read this book. We're humbled and honored to walk the journey with you.

Now it's time to invest your time and energy into applying the WalletWin Method to your life. Start with the Financial Phases, working the Money Milestones one-by-one. You'll see the financial wins unfold before your very eyes. We want to celebrate that journey with you! Feel free to tag or message us @WalletWin on social media so we can cheer you on from the bleachers.

Let's get to it. Time to get out of debt, build wealth, and change the world through generosity. We can't wait to see how God will use your "yes" to managing your money wisely. The impact it will have in your own life and in the world will be a remarkable one. We're grateful to play even the tiniest of roles in helping you kick off the shackles of money stress and step more firmly into who you were created to be.

Grab a phone, hit play on that O'Jays song, and let's sway together down the sidewalk toward financial freedom.

Acknowledgments

As we wrap this book up, we'd like to take a few words to acknowledge those who helped make this happen.

First up, we'd like to thank(?) COVID-19. Not for the havoc it wreaked on the world, *obviously*, but for moving up the timeline of this book. You see, we didn't think this book would be written for a few more years, because we had many other projects on our plates. But then, one by one, several projects we had lined up completely fell apart. With the world around us financially hurting, and while locked down at home with three children under five, we pivoted and moved the book timeline way up. Our goal was to get it into the hands of those carrying money stress, and reeling from this ultimate financial wakeup call, ASAP.

In order to make it happen, we did a lot of juggling in 2020. Trading off who was working, who was wrangling the children, and who was making sure dinner wound up on the table … it was one heck of a dance. A massive shout out to my mom, who took six weeks off work to watch our girls several days a week so we could double down and write without someone interrupting. A big thanks to my dad too, who spent many afternoons crawling around on the floor playing "lion" with his granddaughters to give my mom a break. Without both of your help, this project wouldn't have been finished! We owe you two a *really* nice steak dinner!

Huge shoutout to our FinCon family who helped make this book possible. Over the years, you've helped us launch our business, inspired us, expanded our understanding and knowledge of personal finance, and encouraged us when life and business got hard. Some of you walked with us as you wrote your own books, and others lent their expertise on nuanced tax law. We appreciate you!

To our small band of early test readers: Thank you for working through our early draft of this book. Your comments both validated the path we were on and helped us improve. One of our early readers who deserves an extra special thanks is WalletWin's very own "guy in the chair," a.k.a. Hannah Crites. She's the Ned to our Peter, the Chloe to our Jack. Hannah is one of our earliest WalletWinners who's been kickin' tush ever since she began. Along the way we roped her into freelancing a few hours a week with us. What began as a friendly working relationship evolved into a genuine lifelong friendship *and* a fantastic combo of skillsets to run WalletWin. We love you, Hannah!

To our girls — Josephine, Charlotte, and Eleanor. Thank you for being the inspiration behind our entire financial journey. We didn't know you when we started out, tackling our mountain of debt and clawing to build savings, but we fought to break free and create a strong foundation for the day we'd meet you. Thanks for being understanding for the many hours we had to put into writing this book. This last year was hard on everyone, but you all were real troopers. We always appreciated receiving the cards, notes, and cookies you'd bring us after our writing sessions. Special shoutout for always keeping us humble too — nobody was quicker to remind us that "we aren't cool" just because we're writing a book. We're blessed to be your parents!

⚐ *Jonathan*

This book would not exist without you, Amanda. Not only would we be down an author and the book would be nothing but food metaphors, but you've been the driving force moving this book, our business, and our lives forward. You see opportunities I do not and encourage us to take action even when I may be more comfortable staying back or taking more time. You are a wonderful mother and fantastic business partner — there's no one else I'd rather work with shoulder-to-shoulder in raising a family or building a business. Thank you for all you do, especially putting up with my lame jokes.

➤ Amanda

To the love of my life, Jonathan, without whom my life would be far less adventurous and entertaining. Thank you for always bringing my harebrained schemes and ideas to life — whether it's making a COVID Dough music video, fixing up a vintage RV, getting out of debt in less than a year, or adding another member to the Tex Fam (furry or human). You're always up for the challenge and throw your entire self into making our dreams a reality. All your little ladies (including me) think you are hilarious, even if we claim to not know you when you're embarrassing us. Thank you for keeping our eyes fixed heavenward, on the ultimate prize.

•••

Big shout out to Panera Bread for launching their unlimited coffee membership right as we started writing this book and providing us with a $10/month co-working space! A *lot* of this book was typed out over a hot cuppa at our local West Omaha Panera. To all the employees who saw us all the time and came to recognize our names on the order screens, thank you for the hot coffee, a comfortable place to work, and your welcoming smiles.

To the team at OSV, without whom this book wouldn't be possible. From our earliest conversations with Joe Wikert and Jason Shanks on how WalletWin and OSV could partner together, to Mary Beth Giltner answering all our questions about writing a book, to Rebecca Martin, whose editing has helped make this book so much better than what we started with. We are so grateful to have worked with the best in the biz to bring this book to life.

Last and certainly not least, to our WalletWin Community! It's not easy to talk about money, let alone change your habits around it. You all have invited us, vulnerably, into that sacred space. We're humbled, honored, and grateful to walk with you in your journeys to creating lasting financial peace for yourselves and your families. Thank you for putting in the work, for trusting us to provide the plan, and for sharing your stories to offer hope to others. Special shoutout to all the WalletWinners who wrote their stories down for this book — we know many people will see themselves in your words and find the courage to begin their own journey.

Free Resources

Here's a handy list of all the checklists, guides, and other free resources we've mentioned throughout this book. Visit WalletWin.com/book and grab your copies today!

Banking
Best Bank Accounts — WalletWin.com/banking

Budgeting
BudgetJamz Playlist — WalletWin.com/jamz
BudgetJoggers — WalletWin.com/budgetjoggers
Budgeting Sheet PDF — WalletWin.com/budgetsheet
YNAB How-To Videos — WalletWin.com/howtoYNAB
Free 34-Day Trial to YNAB — WalletWin.com/YNAB
Example Budget Party for Couples — WalletWin.com/budgetparty

Buying a Home
Real Estate Agent Interview Questions — WalletWin.com/realestate
Credit Score Overview — WalletWin.com/fico

Debt
No New Debt Pledge — WalletWin.com/pledge

Insurance

Insurance Checkup Tool — WalletWin.com/insurance
Blessing Box Checklist — WalletWin.com/blessingbox

Investing/Retirement

Recommended Financial Advisors — WalletWin.com/advisors

Money Mindset

Personal History Inventory — WalletWin.com/mindset
Financial Personality Quiz — WalletWin.com/quiz
Financial Examination of Conscience — WalletWin.com/examination

Notes

Chapter 1

1. Quoted in Alan D. Wolfelt, Ph.D, *The Mourner's Book of Faith: 30 Days of Enlightenment* (Fort Collins, Colorado: Companion Press, 2013), 158.

Chapter 2

1. "Why Arbonne?," 30 Day Live Well, Arbonne, https://www.30daylivewell.com/become-a-consultant.

2. Popular Arbonne phrase. See "Independent Consultant," Arbonne, https://www.arbonne.com/au/en/join-us/independent-consultant.

3. The promise of a life made easy in an MLM is often broken. The typical annual earnings of a salesperson for this particular MLM? $120–$502 in 2019. (See "Independent Consultant" web page.) Money doesn't let you "live the life of your dreams" or "own your life," but if it did, I'd imagine it'd take more than five hundred bucks and annoying all your friends.

4. See David Marchese, "Paul McCartney Is Still Trying to Figure Out Love," *The New York Times Magazine*, December 5, 2020, https://www.nytimes.com/interactive/2020/11/30/magazine/paul-mccartney-interview.html.

5. A good indication that Jesus was talking about a real camel going through a real needle, not some gate in the city walls that

only required someone to take the saddlebags off their camel before going through, a common interpretation (or even misinterpretation) of this passage.

6. See St. Ignatius of Loyola, "The Fourth Day: Meditation on Two Standards," *Spiritual Exercises*, Christian Classics Ethereal Library, https://www.ccel.org/ccel/ignatius/exercises.xiii.v.html.

7. Sarah McVeigh, "What It's Like to Grow Up With More Money Than You'll Ever Spend," The Cut, March 28, 2019, https://www.thecut.com/2019/03/abigail-disney-has-more-money-than-shell-ever-spend.html.

8. See Shelby B. Scott et al., "Reasons for Divorce and Recollections of Premarital Intervention: Implications for Improving Relationship Education," *Couple and Family Psychology: Research and Practice* 2, no. 2 (2013): 131–145, https://doi.org/10.1037/a0032025.

9. See "PwC's 8th annual Employee Financial Wellness Survey," PwC US, 2019, https://www.pwc.com/us/en/industries/private-company-services/images/pwc-8th-annual-employee-financial-wellness-survey-2019-results.pdf.

Chapter 4

1. See Howard V Hayghe, "Family Members in the Workforce," *Monthly Labor Review* (March 1990): 14–19, https://www.bls.gov/opub/mlr/1990/03/art2full.pdf.

Chapter 5

1. As evidenced by the collection of songs you'll find on our Budget Jams playlist at Walletwin.com/jamz.

Chapter 6

1. See "People: May 14, 1928," *Time*, May 14, 1928, http://content.time.com/time/subscriber/article/0,33009,787256,00.html.

2. See Associated Press, "Troy Polamalu has hair insured," *ESPN*, https://www.espn.com/nfl/news/story?id=5513644.

3. Insurance riders extend or change the coverage in the

associated policy in some way. Think of it as an amendment or "P.S." stapled onto your existing insurance policy. We don't recommend life insurance policies for children, but if funeral costs ($8,000–$10,000 on average) would financially ruin you, adding a child rider to your term life insurance policy is the most affordable way to add that coverage.

Chapter 9

1. See "Planning & Progress Study 2020," Northwestern Mutual, https://news.northwesternmutual.com/planning-and-progress-2020.

2. See "Planning & Progress Study 2020."

3. See "Sick of Student Loan Debt and Fed Up with the Shame: How Millennials Really Feel," SoFi, https://www.sofi.com/blog/millennial-student-debt-survey/.

4. See Matt Shulz, "2021 Credit Card Debt Statistics," LendingTree, https://www.lendingtree.com/credit-cards/credit-card-debt-statistics/.

5. See "Planning & Progress Study 2020."

6. David Gal and Blakeley B. McShane, "Can Small Victories Help Win the War? Evidence from Consumer Debt Management," *Journal of Marketing Research* 49, no. 4 (2012): 487–501, https://doi.org/10.1509/jmr.11.0272.

7. Moty Amar et al., "Winning the Battle but Losing the War: The Psychology of Debt Management," *Journal of Marketing Research* 48, no. SPL (2011): S38–S50, abstract, https://doi.org/10.1509/jmkr.48.spl.s38.

8. See Keri L. Kettle et al., "Repayment Concentration and Consumer Motivation to Get Out of Debt," *Journal of Consumer Research* 43, no. 3 (October 2016): 460–477, https://doi.org/10.1093/jcr/ucw037.

9. Not only did Teddy hunt them, but *Gazella Granti Roosevelti*, a subspecies of the Grant's Gazelle, is named after the 26th US President.

10. See Drazen Prelec and Duncan Simester, "Always Leave Home Without It: A Further Investigation of the Credit-Card

Effect on Willingness to Pay," *Marketing Letters* 12 (2001): 5–12, https://doi.org/10.1023/A:1008196717017.

11. See Kelly Dilworth, "Average Credit Card Interest Rates: Week of May 5, 2021," CreditCards.com, http://www.cpiscooter .com/average-credit-card-interest-rates-week-of-may-5-2021/.

Chapter 10

1. See "The Role of Emergency Savings in Family Financial Security: How Do Families Cope with Financial Shocks?," The Pew Charitable Trusts, https://www.pewtrusts.org/~/media /assets/2015/10/emergency-savings-report-1_artfinal.pdf.

Chapter 11

1. USCCB, *Catholic Household Blessings and Prayers*, quoted in "Blessing of a New Home," Catholic News Agency, https://www .catholicnewsagency.com/resource/242595/blessing-of-a-new -home.

2. See Sean Becketti, "Why America's Homebuyers & Communities Rely on the 30-Year Fixed-Rate Mortgage," FreddieMac, https://www.linkedin.com/pulse/why-americas-homebuyers -communities-rely-30-year-sean-becketti/.

3. See "U.S. Home Sellers Realized Average Price Gain of $57,500 in First Quarter of 2019, Down Slightly from Last Quarter," ATTOM, https://www.attomdata.com/news/market-trends /q1-2019-u-s-home-sales-report/.

Chapter 12

1. An index is a collection of financial holdings that represent a particular segment of the financial market. Some more famous ones include the S&P 500, made up of the 500 largest US companies; the Dow Jones Industrial Average made up of thirty large, well-known companies; or the Nasdaq Composite Index, which is made up of the 2,500+ securities (stocks and other investments) that trade on the Nasdaq Exchange. The calculations for how these indexes are created and valued vary, but all are designed to give investors an easy-to-digest indicator for how a particular part of

the market is doing.

2. See Berlinda Liu and Gaurav Sinha, "SPIVA U.S. Year-End 2020 Scorecard," S&P Dow Jones Indices, S&P Global, https://www.spglobal.com/spdji/en/documents/spiva/spiva-us-year-end-2020.pdf.

3. See Alicia H. Munnell, Anthony Webb, and Wenliang Hou, "How Much Should People Save?," *Issues in Brief* 2014, no. 11 (2014).

4. Roth accounts are so named because Senator William Roth introduced the bill that added them to US tax law.

5. IRA stands for Individual Retirement Account, a designation outlined in the US tax code that confers on qualifying accounts certain tax benefits to encourage people to save and invest for their retirement. They also have some accompanying regulations, like a minimum age when you can withdraw without penalties.

6. While there are limits on how much you can put in those tax-favored retirement accounts, there's no limit to how much you can invest. So, if you haven't hit 15 percent with a combination of your employer-sponsored plan (401(k), etc.) and an IRA, then move on to regular (non-tax-favored) investment accounts.

Chapter 13

1. Quoted in *Moments of Peace in the Presence of God* (Grand Rapids: Baker Publishing Group, 2004), 358.

2. See Gary R. Pike, George D. Kuh, and Ryan C. Massa-McKinley, "First-Year Students' Employment, Engagement, and Academic Achievement: Untangling the Relationship between Work and Grades," *NASPA Journal* 45, no. 4 (2008): 560–582, https://eric.ed.gov/?id=EJ826786.

3. See Andrew DePietro, "Average Cost of College Has Jumped an Incredible 3,009 percent in 50 Years," Yahoo! Finance, https://finance.yahoo.com/news/average-cost-college-jumped-incredible-122000732.html.

4. See Liz Knueven, "The Average College Tuition Keeps Rising, and It's Just the Start of College Costs," Insider, Business

Insider, https://www.businessinsider.com/personal-finance/average-college-tuition.

5. Contribution limits, income restrictions, and other information offered in this chapter is current as of writing. Laws and regulations can change, so always be sure to kccp up-to-date with current limits, exclusions, and the like.

6. See Annie Nova, "To Get a Bigger Paycheck after College, Start Working Now," CNBC, https://www.cnbc.com/2019/05/31/college-students-who-hold-a-job-end-up-with-higher-paychecks-later-on.html.

7. See Pike, Kuh, and Massa-McKinley, "First-Year Students' Employment, Engagement, and Academic Achievement."

8. Kevin O'Leary (@kevinolearytv), "There's a saying that goes: 'If you want something done, give it to a busy mom.' I'm a firm believer that's true," Twitter, July 5, 2015, 1:31pm, https://twitter.com/kevinolearytv/status/617762767823482880.

Chapter 14

1. Dave Ramsey, "We did some in-depth research to get this stat," Facebook, July 19, 2020. https://www.facebook.com/daveramsey/photos/we-did-some-in-depth-research-to-get-this-stat-people-like-to-argue-about-invest/10157532813510886/.

Chapter 15

1. "Overview of Overall Giving: Based on Data Collected in 2017 About Giving in 2016," The Indiana University Lilly Family School of Philanthropy at IUPUI, https://generosityforlife.org/wp-content/uploads/2019/12/Overall-Giving-2017-PPS-JB-Comment-CJC.pdf.

2.Paul VI, *Populorum Progressio*, par. 3.

3. Thomas Aquinas, *Summa Theologiae*, II-II, q.66, a.2.

4. Leo XIII, *Rerum Novarum*, vatican.va, par. 22.

Chapter 16

1. John XXIII, Opening Address to the Second Vatican Council, October 11, 1962.

2. See Dan Souza, "Why Nacho Cheese Doritos Taste Like Heaven," Serious Eats, https://www.seriouseats.com/science-of-chips-ingredients-msg-why-nacho-cheese-doritos-taste-like-heaven. Check this article out — it's incredible. Need an easier to type link? Try WalletWin.com/doritos.

About the Authors

In January 2012, Jonathan and Amanda Teixeira had $25,000 in debt and a deep desire to break free. A short — and zealous — seven and a half months later they wrote their last check to Sallie Mae and closed the doors on debt forever. Since kicking debt to the curb, they've focused on saving, investing, and giving in a way that set them up for total financial peace for a lifetime.

Upon hearing their story, a few people asked them money questions — and they answered. That snowballed into hundreds of answers, speaking at events, and providing financial coaching.

They launched WalletWin in 2017 to help as many people as possible get out of debt, save money, and transform the world through generosity through their online course, membership, and podcast.

While not traveling the United States in their Class A WalletWinnebago, Jonathan and Amanda live in Omaha, Nebraska, with their three daughters Josie, Charlotte, Ellie, and crazy but lovable Labrador Retriever, Wrigley.